'Scènes de Gynécées'

'Scènes de Gynécées'

Figured Ostraca from New Kingdom Egypt: iconography and intent

Joanne Backhouse

Archaeopress Egyptology 26

Archaeopress Publishing Ltd
Summertown Pavilion
18-24 Middle Way
Summertown
Oxford OX2 7LG

www.archaeopress.com

ISBN 978-1-78969-345-4
ISBN 978-1-78969-346-1 (e-Pdf)

Cover image: Drawing on limestone. WoB.36: Louvre E 14337 (photograph by Joanne Backhouse).

Printed in England by Severn, Gloucester

This book is available direct from Archaeopress or from our website www.archaeopress.com

Contents

Chapter 5

'*Scènes de Gynécées*': Repeat Motifs

Chapter 6
Conclusions

List of Figures

Chapter 1

Deir el-Medina: The History of Excavation and the Nature of the Site

Chapter 2

Catalogue of Painted Wall Decoration Found in the Village

Chapter 3

Catalogue of '*Scènes de Gynécées*' Figured Ostraca and Comparative Evidence

Chapter 4

'*Scènes de Gynécées*': The Corpus

Chapter 5

'*Scènes de Gynécées*': Repeat Motifs

General Abbreviations

Berlin Museum: Ägyptisches Museum Berlin

BM: British Museum, London

Brussels Museum: Musées Royaux d'Art et d'Histoire, Brussels

Cairo: The Egyptian Museum Cairo

CE: Comparative Evidence

EAS: Egyptian Antiquities Service

EB: Elaborate Beds

F: Fragments

IFAO: Institut Français d'Archéologie Orientale, Cairo

K: Kiosks

KV: Valley of the Kings

Leiden Museum: Rijksmuseum van Oudheden

Louvre: Musée du Louvre

Manchester Museum: The Manchester Museum

Munich Museum: Staatliches Museum Ägyptische Kunst, Munich

Petrie UC: University College London – The Petrie Museum

SCA: Supreme Council of Antiquities

Stockholm: Medelhavsmuseet

TT: Theban Tomb

Turin Museum: Museo Egizio di Torino

VA: Vandier d'Abbadie (numbering commonly used for the figured ostraca as published by Vandier d'Abbadie)

WoB: Women on Beds

WP: Wall Painting

Acknowledgements

This monograph is based upon research undertaken for my PhD at the University of Liverpool. There are many people to whom I owe thanks for the completion of this work. Firstly, I must express my gratitude to my supervisor, Steven Snape for his support and encouragement throughout all of my research. I would also like to acknowledge the University of Liverpool for awarding me a studentship, which paid my tuition fees. With regard to the task of transforming the research into a publication, I must again thank Steven Snape; also, my PhD examiners, Chris Eyre, University of Liverpool and Kasia Szpakowska, Swansea University, for their insightful comments. I would particularly like to thank Chris Eyre for the detailed notes he provided regarding updating and improving the text.

The goodwill of museum curators worldwide made this work possible. Many allowed me to visit and photograph objects; this long list of thanks includes Guillette Andreu-Lanoë from the Louvre, Nadine Cherpion when at IFAO, Sofia Häggman from the Medelshavmuseet, Anna Garnett at the Petrie Museum, University College London, John Taylor at the British Museum and Paolo Del Vesco at Museo Egizio.

Other curators and excavators kindly photographed objects and sent me the digital images. For their assistance I am deeply indebted as often distance prevented me from visiting in person. This long list of thanks includes Sara Carmello, Andreas Dorn, Toivari-Viitala, Carolyn Graves-Brown, Campbell Price and Maarten Raven. An additional thanks should also go to Sonia Focke from Munich Museum and Klaus Finneiser from Berlin Museum who assisted me repeatedly with my enquiries into both figured ostraca and female figurines.

Further gratitude must be expressed to the Director of IFAO, Laurent Bavay, for granting me permission to publish photographs taken at IFAO for study purposes. This publication would not be possible without their cooperation. Furthermore, authorisation was also granted to include images from key texts from the work of IFAO scholars, including Bruyère, Vandier d'Abbadie and Cherpion; all of which are essential to this publication.

I must also thank my long-suffering friends for their patience and understanding for my preoccupied nature and lack of time to share with them, during my studies and again when preparing the text for publication. I am also extremely grateful to Cheryl Hanson for her expert assistance with proof-reading the final draft. My last and largest thanks go to my Mother who has supported me throughout this relentlessly.

Introduction

The aim of the study is to examine a particular set of images found only on ostraca from New Kingdom Egypt. These scenes show women, often with a child, sitting on a bed in a domestic environment; alternatively, they depict women with a child in a kiosk, in an outdoor setting. The purpose of this research is to examine why these images were drawn and to explore what these representations meant to their creators and viewers. The functionality of the ostraca will also be analysed, considering if they were objects in their own right or merely practice pieces for larger scale compositions.

This monograph has developed from research I undertook for my doctorate studies at the University of Liverpool. This examined '*Scènes de Gynécées*' Figured Ostraca: Their Relationship to the Material Culture of New Kingdom Egypt. Consequently, it had a wider remit than this publication. This consisted of two volumes. Firstly, the catalogue of the ostraca and associated discussion; secondly, a catalogue of so called 'ladies on beds' figurines from New Kingdom Egypt and discussion. Volume I, considering the ostraca, has been edited to form this publication. It is hoped Volume II, focusing on the 'ladies on beds' figurines, will be published at a later date.

Deir el-Medina has yielded over five thousand ostraca, most are fragments of limestone with a limited number of potsherds (Bruyère 1952a: 60). It is likely the fragments of limestone were collected from the foothills of the cliffs on the West Bank of Thebes, where they had accumulated from natural erosion, or they were collected from the debris of the tombs by the craftsmen. One ostracon, in the Fitzwilliam Museum (EGA 4324.1943: Brunner-Traut 1979: 40-41, Plate XII), depicts a stonemason at work in a tomb with a chisel and mallet, hacking out the tomb shaft, demonstrating vividly their access to the material. Therefore, they represent a resource readily available to the workmen. The ostraca were predominantly inscribed with hieratic text for administrative purposes, denoting lists of workers, materials, accounts and letters, with a small proportion containing hymns to the gods, cult rituals and love songs (Bruyère 1952a: 61). Thus, they provide valuable insights into daily life in ancient Egypt. The ostraca containing hieratic text were published extensively by Černý (1935), Posener (1938) and more recently by Gasse (2005) and Grandet (2011). In addition, a valuable bibliography of research on the hieratic ostraca is now maintained by the University of Leiden (https://dmd.wepwawet.nl/bibliography.htm).

A significant number of ostraca contain an image; these have been referred to as figured ostraca. Satirical scenes, depictions of animals and human figures are the most common subject matter. Images of kings and gods are to a lesser degree also part of the repertoire. Examples were published initially by Schäfer (1916), Davies (1917a) and Werbrouck (1953). They were later published and catalogued in detail by Vandier d'Abbadie (1937, 1959).

A number of figured ostraca display images of women sitting on beds, often with a child, while a smaller number depict women in kiosks, also with a child. They were identified as a coherent group and classified as '*Scènes de Gynécées*' by Vandier d'Abbadie (1937: 80). She suggested these scenes, taking place in what she described as the female part of the house, depicted the family life of 'women of quality' in Egyptian society (Vandier d'Abbadie 1937: 81). Fifty-nine such scenes are considered in this study. These images do not appear in the formal repertoire of Egyptian art; they are not represented in tombs, temples or on stelae. The scenes are noteworthy because it is the women who are the focus of the narrative. They are the main protagonists; they are not subsidiary figures, as is common in more formal Egyptian art, which often depicts women as wives, mothers or daughters of the primary male figure. By comparison, in the '*Scènes de Gynécées*' the only men who appear are servants. This makes the images a unique source of data from ancient Egypt.

The aim of this study is to understand the purpose and intent of these objects, why the images were drawn and what functions the ostraca served. To facilitate this, the '*Scènes de Gynécées*' figured ostraca have been catalogued in a series of related groups. The primary one being 'women on beds'; this includes images which show any part of a woman and a bed. Fifty-three 'women on beds' scenes are analysed in this study, referred to throughout as 'WoB'. The scenes may illustrate a woman sitting or lying on a bed; alternatively, it may show a female attendant approaching a bed. A complete image is defined as one in which both ends of the bed are visible. The 'women on beds' dataset includes a small sub-group of ostraca, referred to as 'elaborate beds' due to the highly decorative nature of the beds, which were possibly decked with floral garlands as suggested by Schäfer (1916: 30). Three 'elaborate beds' scenes are considered in this study; referred to throughout as 'EB'. This sub-group provides a link between the 'women on beds' and kiosk scenes. The latter is a small but significant group of images which show women with a child in a kiosk; three examples are examined in this study, referred to throughout as 'K'. The kiosk scenes provide the strongest link to wall paintings found at Deir el-Medina. Fifteen figured ostraca referred to specifically as 'fragments' are also included in the study; they are denoted as 'F' throughout the work. Although all ostraca are fragments by definition; the objects drawn are now only partially visible. Scenes on the 'fragments' are incomplete and piecemeal. However, the remnants suggest that they were part of 'women on beds', 'elaborate beds' or kiosks scenes; although it is not always possible to determine which dataset the fragment would have belonged to.

Fourteen scenes of comparative evidence are also examined, in order to aid our understanding of the main corpus. These are referred to throughout the study as 'CE'. These include images of goddesses suckling a child, scenes of offering and presentation and servant girls. Uniquely, the comparative evidence includes two images of female figurines drawn on ostraca, graphically illustrating the link between figured ostraca and three-dimensional representations. This has been noted by previous scholars, for example Pinch (1983: 406-10).

In order to place the ostraca in the context of the society in which they were created, a brief overview of the nature and excavation history of Deir el-Medina is outlined. This will aid our understanding of the context of the ostraca and the material culture found at the site. In addition, a catalogue of the surviving wall paintings in the village allows for comparison between the figured ostraca and domestic decoration. This is essential for the progression of research, as much previous scholarship believed there to be a link between the wall paintings and the ostraca (Brunner-Traut 1956:64-5; Vandier d'Abbadie 1937:5). These are referred to as 'WP' throughout the study. With regard to the figured ostraca, the methods of representation, materials used, and nature of the scenes are analysed to provide an overview of the corpus. To gain an understanding of what the '*Scènes de Gynécées*' figured ostraca meant to their creators and viewers, the imagery will be deconstructed into individual components. Repeat motifs are identified and examined; furthermore, links between those themes are considered. Where relevant, contemporaneous material culture will be analysed, in order to understand the meanings attached to the images on the ostraca.

Chapter 1

Deir el-Medina: The History of Excavation and the Nature of the Site

1.1: History of Excavation

Early in the 19th Century objects from Deir el-Medina began to appear in Europe, primarily due to the work of European collectors such as Drovetti and Salt. This was a time of unsanctioned 'excavations' and exploration of the site; no scientific methods were employed, and no recording of the 'excavations' were carried out. Maspero described Deir el-Medina in 1886 as being strewn with the debris of statues, stelae, pottery and mummies shredded amongst open tombs, many of which had been partially demolished and burnt (Bruyère 1959: 1). This was the result of many years of uninhibited exploitation of the site.

The first organised excavations took place between 1905 and 1909 by Schiaparelli, working for the Museo Egizio (Turin). Although he did not publish full reports on his work, from an examination of artefacts in Museo Egizio, it is likely that he excavated tombs, votive chapels, and the rock-cut sanctuary of Meretseger and Ptah. Furthermore, before he left the site in 1909, he exposed some houses buried beneath the sand; this was the first discovery of the walled village. It is difficult to assign a context to the objects discovered by Schiaparelli as he was excavating the village and tombs concurrently (Weiss 2015: 227). Subsequently, Baraise was employed by the Egypt Antiquites Service to reconstruct the Ptolemaic temple; his short report included a list of Ramesside finds (Baraise 1914). The next scholar to excavate at the site was Möller, working for Berlin Museum, between 1911 and 1913. This included a small section of the village close to the Ptolemaic temple. Anthes (1943) later published a brief report based on Möller's notes. Due to the First World War, the concession for Deir el-Medina was transferred to the Institut Français d'Archéologie Orientale (IFAO) in 1914 and they began working at the site in 1915.

From 1922 until 1951 excavations were directed by Bruyère and reports were regularly published. The most significant publication, for this research, is the report on the 1934-35 season, which records the clearing of the village (Bruyère 1939). Due to the prevalent number of lootings taking place in Luxor at this time, the excavation was carried out in one season with a large number of local workers. There are a number of problems with the text, for example it is difficult to identify find spots as many artefacts were grouped together and listed according to a particular house or area (Weiss 2015: 24). Moreover, as Weiss notes, some objects published in the 1939 text were not found in the village. This can be confirmed when Bruyère's notebooks are consulted. Despite these qualifications Bruyère's (1939) text remains a key work in the history of settlement archaeology in Egypt. Also, of great value to this study are the reports on the Western Cemetery (Bruyère 1937a), the Eastern Cemetery (Bruyère 1937b) and the worship of Meretseger (Bruyère 1929, 1930). Bruyère ceased working at Deir el-Medina in 1951, but the site was re-opened by IFAO in 1969.

Bonnet and Valbelle had two short seasons at the site in 1975 and 1976. They wished to investigate the development of the village over time, particularly the pre-Ramesside occupation of the site (Bonnet and Valbelle 1975, 1976). This work formed the basis of the most substantial report on the village in recent times (Valbelle 1985). IFAO has continued working at the site and numerous reports have been published in recent years. An excellent overview of the work of IFAO at Deir el Medina, including conservation work, is provided by Gobeil (2015:16-19).

1.2: Nature of the Site

1.2a: Location and Development

Deir el-Medina is situated on the West Bank of Thebes, currently half a mile from the cultivated land of the Nile flood-plain. Located close to the necropoli of the Valley of the Kings and the Valley of the Queens, it was created to house the workers who constructed the royal tombs. The nexus of the site is a walled village, divided by a road with houses on either side. The earliest archaeological evidence is dated to Tuthmosis I, which consists of mud bricks stamped with his cartouche (Bonnet and Valbelle 1975: 436-440, Plate LXVI; Bruyère 1936: 329). However, the village was probably established by Amenhotep I, who along with his mother Ahmose Nefertari was venerated at the site (Černý 1927). Bonnet and Valbelle (1975: 442) identified at least 12 phases of construction. There was a period of expansion under Tuthmosis III, while during the Amarna period it is likely most, if not all, residents left the site to follow the royal court to Amarna. The village was reorganised and expanded under Horemheb, with a reconstruction of the village to the north and south (Bonnet and Valbelle 1975: 440). There was a further expansion under Rameses III and Rameses IV to the south of the village. The excavated evidence dates predominantly to the 19th and 20th Dynasty, little remains of the earlier Eighteenth Dynasty settlement. Therefore, most objects recorded by Bruyère in the village are likely to be from the Ramesside period but can only be given a general date of the New Kingdom.

1.2b: The Walled Village

Sixty-eight compact houses were excavated by Bruyère, which vary in size between 40 and 120 sq. m. (Valbelle 1985:117). Constructed in a standard linear fashion, the houses are similar in terms of layout and spatial distribution, see Figure 1.1. The first room was entered directly from the road and the floor was below street level; this room often contained a structure Bruyère (1939: 57) referred to as a '*lit clos*', the significance of which is discussed in Section 1.4. Although no fragments of roof were found by Bruyère, he proposed the first room of the house was covered by trunks of palm trees, with the roof partially open to aid ventilation and lighting (Bruyère 1939: 54-55). However, Koltisa (2007: 22-24) has subsequently suggested that this room was unroofed, based on similar evidence from Amarna. Irrespective of the roofing, this was the most public part of the house. It opened directly into the second room of the house, which was at ground level, larger and more elevated than the first. It almost always contained a single column or two, to support the ceiling and was often decorated with small altars, false doors, niches and a divan, which was a low sofa without arms or a back; this room often had a cellar below. The second room led to a single room or two small rooms, with no decoration; these were most likely used as storerooms. From here a kitchen was situated which also included niches in the walls. From the kitchen, staircases were located, one towards the upper terrace and the other leading to the cellar.

The most noteworthy feature is the juxtaposition of secular and cultic elements of architecture. Bruyère (1939: 50) referred to the first two rooms as '*une salle d'apparat*'. The first room contained the '*lit clos*', significant for this study as it is upon this structure that all surviving painted decoration in the village was found. In the second room of the house niches, altars and false doors were common. In addition, the kitchen often contained a small shrine referred to as '*un laraire*', of which an almost complete example survives in the British Museum (EA 597; Bierbrier 1982b: Plate 66-67). There has been much discussion regarding 'sexed space' at Deir el-Medina. Meskell (1998: 219) suggested the first room of the house was female orientated and centred on married, fertile women of the household, due to the architectural features, objects and wall paintings found in the room. Meskell proposed the second room of the house was the sphere of high-status males and subsequent rooms were used for domestic chores. This echoes Bruyère's original assessment of the domestic space at Deir el-Medina (Bruyère 1939: 71).

However, the concept of 'sexed space' has been criticised. Both Harrington (2005: 80) and Kleinke 2007 (as cited in Weiss 2015: 30) question the separation of male and female zones as both rooms contain cultic features. Furthermore, no Egyptian terminology describes the purposes of the various rooms (Weiss 2015: 29). Given the limited space in the village it is likely the rooms were multi-functional to a degree. Nonetheless, the first room of the house was clearly

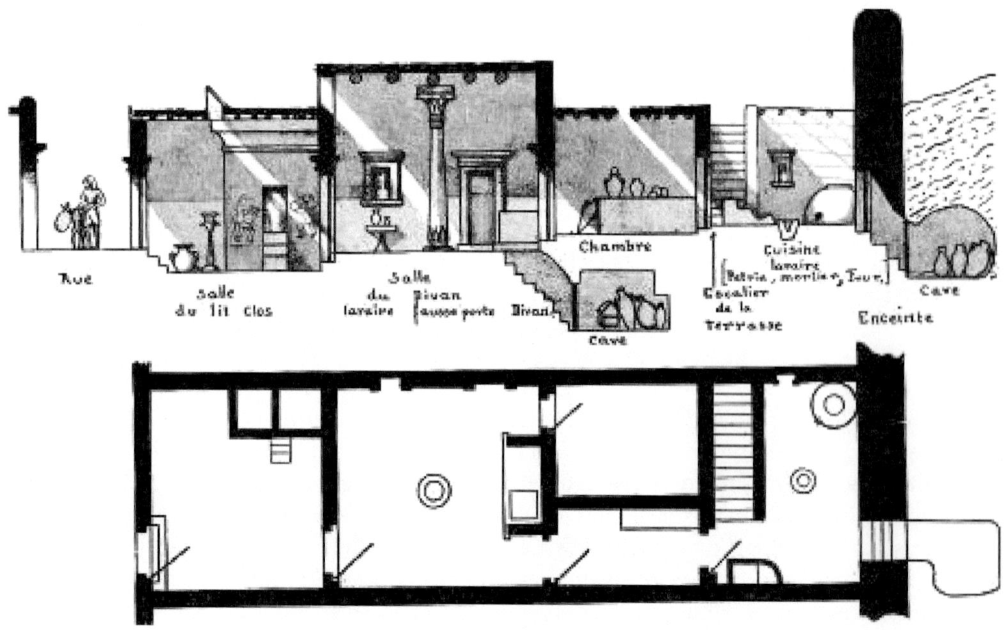

Figure 1.1: Linear design of houses at Deir el-Medina (Bruyère 1939: 50, Figure 15) © IFAO.

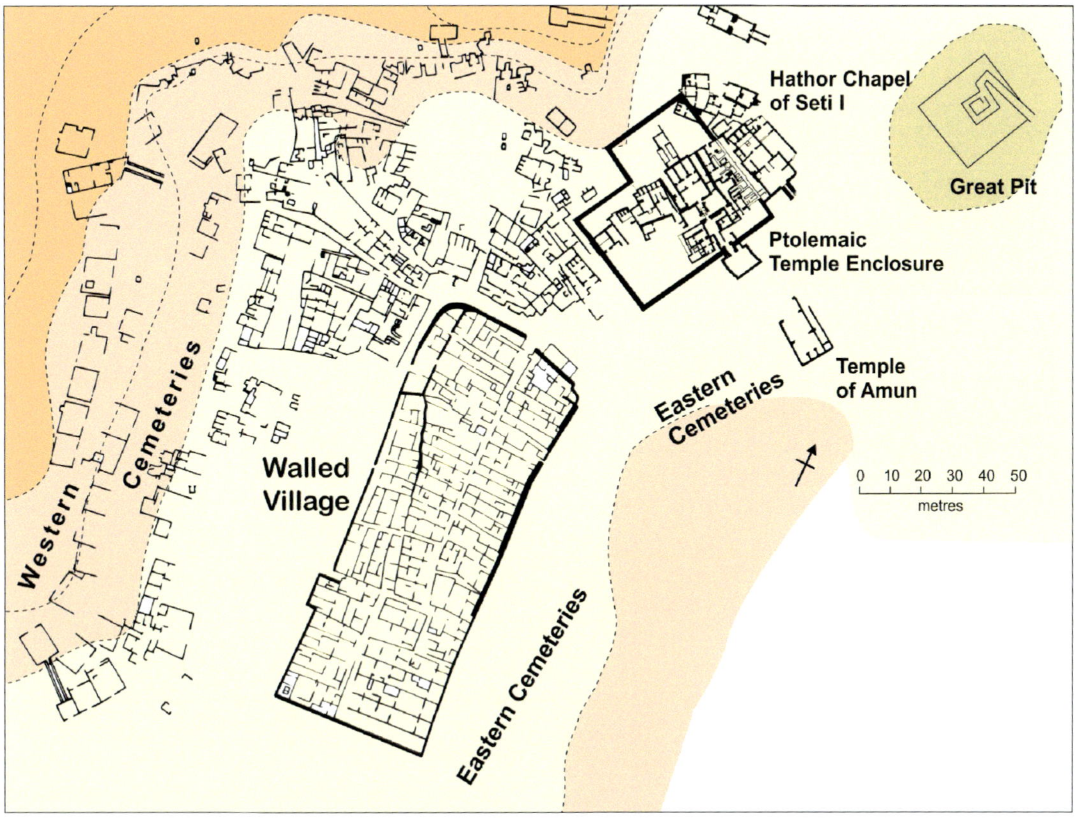

Figure 1.2: The site of Deir el-Medina (Image produced by Peter Robinson based on Bierbrier 1982a: 66-67).

the most public space, opening to the road and the most decorated; this accords with Kemp's (1979: 52-53) suggestion that the first room of the house was used to celebrate childbirth.

1.2c: The Eastern Cemetery

The walled village is flanked by rising ground to the east and west of the village, see Figure 1.2. The Eastern Cemetery is dated to the 18th Dynasty (Andreu 2002: 22). This contains simple burials with no superstructures; the cemetery here is stratified by age with neonates and the young at the bottom and adults at the top (Bruyère 1937b: 11). These burials were mainly simple shaft tombs with single vaults used for an individual or a small family.

1.2d: The Western Cemetery

The majority of tombs date to the 19th and 20th Dynasty and are more elaborate, with many consisting of full tomb complexes (Andreu 2002: 30). These are comprised of two elements: the chapel and burial chamber. The former was the visible superstructure, often topped with a brick pyramidion. Here family members could leave offerings and worship the cult of their dead ancestors. The subterranean burial chamber often contained multiple vaults which housed several generations; therefore, burials would have entailed repeat visits by the living to bury their dead relatives. It could be suggested these features created or perhaps reflected a strong sense of lineage and ancestry.

1.2e: Places of Worship

Bruyère identified at least 32 cult buildings at Deir el-Medina (Bomann 1991: 39). In addition to the temple of Hathor built by Seti I, which was probably the focal point of worship in the village. These buildings have been re-examined by Bomann (1991: 39-55) and are dispersed to the south, the southwest, the north and northeast of the later Ptolemaic temple. Due to their diversity Bruyère used a variety of terminology to describe these structures including *Chapelle Votive, Chapelles des Confrèries, Chapelle, Chapelle Religieuse* and *Temple*. Bomann's (1991: 73) re-analysis of the evidence found votive chapels focused principally on royal and private ancestor cults.

1.2f: Rock Cut Shrine

A shrine consisting of seven natural and manmade grottos was cut into a ravine on a path that lay between the Valley of the Queens and the village of Deir el-Medina. Bruyère (1929: 5) believed the shrine was sacred to Meretseger and Ptah and that many stelae dedicated to those deities once embedded in the rock had been taken to Museo Egizio by Schiaparelli. Possible manifestations of the cult of Meretseger are discussed in Section 5.2c.

1.2h: Workmen's Huts and 'Le Chapelle du Col'

Also, on the outskirts of the settlement, on the path between the walled village and the Valley of the Kings, Bruyère excavated a group of 78 huts which he referred to as *'les huttes de la station de repos'* (Bruyère 1939: 347-348). He believed the huts provided a temporary settlement and he assumed, as they contained no kitchens, meals must have been brought up to the site by those residing in the village. However, more recent work has found evidence of fireplaces, both inside and outside of the huts, suggesting cooking could have been carried out in situ (Toivari-Viitala *et al.* 2010: 1). Pottery from the huts has been dated primarily to the late 19th Dynasty with a small amount from the mid-18th Dynasty and the later New Kingdom (Toivari-Viitala *et al.* 2012: 11).

1.3: The Working Week at Deir el-Medina

Although the huts are not a great distance from the walled village it is likely the workmen resided there during their workdays, possibly to alleviate the need to carry equipment to the site on a daily basis. The Egyptian calendar was divided into 12 months, each of 30 days, which were comprised of three, ten-day weeks. As demonstrated by Janssen (1980: 132) the last two days of a week were always free and, in most instances, the first day of the next week was also free. The weekend provided an opportunity for social and communal activities; as noted by Eyre (1987: 176) the workers had considerable free time, rarely working more than two-thirds of the available days and often working much less. However, for periods of the working week women and children may have been the primary residents of the village; this may account for the abundance of female orientated imagery and objects found at the site. However, it is difficult to determine if this is due to the exceptional levels of preservation at Deir el-Medina or the unique nature of the site.

1.4: *'Lit clos'*

The only surviving painted wall decoration in the village was found on the *'lit clos'*. Bruyère (1939: 57) so named these rectangular, mud brick structures as they reminded him of a type of boxed bed in Brittany. Contemporary scholars, for example Weiss (2009: 196), have suggested using a more neutral term, but for the sake of continuity with earlier scholarship this research will use the term *'lit clos'*. On average they were 1.70 m in length, 0.80 m wide and 0.75 m in height. They were fully or partially enclosed and had a small staircase of bricks, between three and five steps, situated on the most exterior wall (Bruyère 1939: 56-57). As Cherpion (2006: 12) notes the staircases are narrow, fragile and completely impractical. Bruyère identified three main types, see Figure 1.3. They were often constructed in the corner of the room, incorporating the exterior walls of the house. They were commonly plastered, white-washed and some had evidence of painted decoration still surviving. This is catalogued in Chapter 2, WP.1-10.

Bruyère (1939: 61) counted 28 *'lit clos'* but in Weiss' (2009: 197) re-analysis of the data, she records 29. They were most often found in the first room of the house but four were also discovered in the second room of the house and one in the third room of a house (Weiss 2009: 196, n. 4). There has been much debate regarding the function of these structures since Bruyère's publication (Cherpion 2006; Koltsida 2006; Weiss 2009). Bruyère (1939: 64) referred to these as *'lit-autel'* and he proposed a multi-functional use for them, as have many subsequent scholars. He suggested they may have been used as a subsidiary conjugal bed or a bed where the sleeper received prophecies and revelations from the divine. In conclusion, Bruyère (1939: 64) viewed *'la salle du lit clos'* as *'une sort de gynécées, de chambre de la naissance, analogue au sanctuaire de la déese dans un temple de triade.'* Most scholars now believe the *'lit clos'* functioned as altars; similar evidence of mud brick domestic altars has been found at Amarna (Stevens 2006: 234) and Lacovara (1997: 64) has suggested

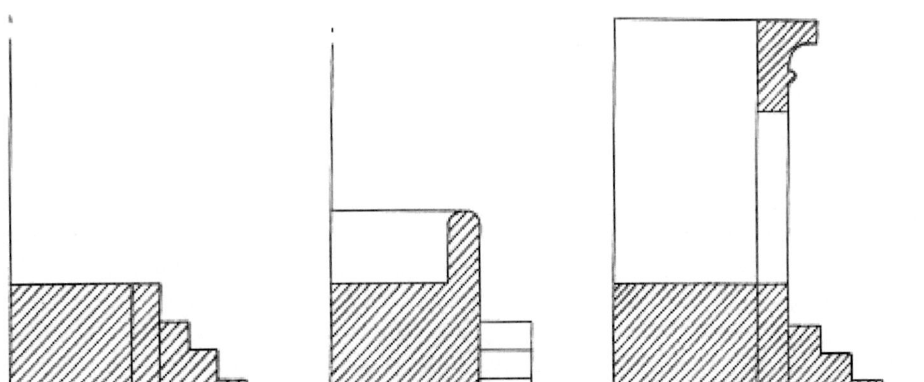

Figure 1.3: Types of *'lit clos'* found at Deir el-Medina, as identified by Bruyère (Bruyère 1939: 57, Figure 18) © IFAO.

comparable features were found in the houses in the north village at Malkata.

Weiss' (2009: 203) analysis of the limited number of artefacts found on the '*lit clos*' also suggests the structures were used as altars. For example, fragments of statues, most likely of Amenhotep I and his mother Ahmose Nefertari, who were worshipped in the village, were found on the '*lit clos*' in house N.E. XI. A damaged offering table was also found next to the '*lit clos*' (Bruyère 1939: 256-7). In addition, Weiss (2009: 205) cites two examples of figured ostraca which may depict a '*lit clos*'. One example, published by Keimer (1940-45: Plate XVIII, 59) shows the workman Hay before a table of offerings, behind which the god Thoth sits on an enclosed structure. This has five steps, a cavetto cornice and a small opening; it resembles the '*lit clos*' found at Deir el-Medina. The structure is depicted both in profile, for the staircase, and frontal view for the main edifice, a common practise in Egyptian art. The current location of this ostracon is unknown. The other example, in the Louvre, Figure 1.4, shows Meretseger on a baseline below which an enclosed structure is depicted. Keimer (1940-45:18) believed this to be a tomb or sanctuary. However, it is possible this is a '*lit clos*', given the similarity to the structure depicted on the example published by Keimer (1940-45: Plate XVIII, 59) as cited above.

Figure 1.4: Figured ostracon from Deir el-Medina showing Meretseger on a raised platform, before a table of offerings, Louvre E 25301 (Photograph Author's own).

Chapter 2

Catalogue of Painted Wall Decoration Found in the Village

2.1: Academic Context

Many scholars have noted the links between the figured ostraca and the wall paintings which survive at Deir el-Medina. Vandier d'Abbadie (1937: 5) observed both were created using similar techniques and materials, while Brunner-Traut (1956: 64-65) suggested the '*Scènes de Gynécées*' were trial sketches for the domestic wall paintings in the village. However, Brunner-Traut's theory was questioned by Peterson (1973). Peterson examined the ostraca from the Gayer-Anderson Collection, now in the Medelshavmuseet, Stockholm; he compared the find spots and the subject matter. Peterson (1973) noted more varied themes were depicted on the ostraca found at Deir el-Medina in comparison to those recovered from the Valley of the Kings, which he argued included many representations of the king. Furthermore, Peterson suggested that the ostraca from the Valley of the Kings were drawn with a higher degree of skill than those found in the village.

Earlier scholarship had also proposed that the figured ostraca were preparatory sketches for paintings on royal and private tombs (Borchardt 1910; Maspero 1912: 168-169). Dorn's (2011) work at the Valley of the Kings, between 1998-2005, disputes this; Dorn notes the ostraca rarely contained images depicted in the royal tombs. Furthermore, Dorn (2011: 221) states 'the notion that ostraca may have served as templates or something similar must be abandoned.' More recent scholarship has considered the use of repeat motives and the varied skill levels displayed on the ostraca (Cooney 2012). Cooney (2012: 147) suggests the figured ostraca were part of a 'knowledge transfer' whereby successive generations of artists increased their proficiency by drawing well known themes using the methods of representation commonly practised by ancient artists. For the purposes of this study it is the choice of subject matter that is significant and the context within which it was found. This suggests the ostraca were objects in their own right, depicting images which were meaningful to the community, not simply part of a learning curve.

A catalogue of painted wall decoration found at Deir el-Medina is produced here to allow a comparison between the '*Scènes de Gynécées*' figured ostraca and the surviving wall paintings from the village. While there is no evidence to suggest the ostraca considered in this study were practice pieces for the wall paintings there are some common iconographic motifs, for example the depiction of the god Bes, the inclusion of convolvulus leaves and the illustration of a kiosk scene. The repeat motifs found on the ostraca are discussed in Chapter five.

WP.1

House	S.E. VIII, Deir el Medina
Published	Bruyère 1939: 60, 273, Figure 145, Plate X Vandier d'Abbadie 1938: Figure 1 Cherpion 2006: Figures 8 and 9

Figure 2.1: Wall decoration when excavated by Bruyère, House S.E. VIII, Deir el-Medina (Vandier d'Abbadie 1938: 28, Figure 1) © IFAO.

Figure 2.2: Wall decoration of House S.E. VIII, Deir el-Medina as published by IFAO 2006 (Cherpion 2006: 17, Figure 8) © IFAO.

Found in the first room of the house, this is the most substantial example of painted wall decoration remaining in the village. Painted on the narrow foot-end of the '*lit clos*', the scene is framed in a multi-linear tri-coloured border. Only the lower portion remains; it shows a young woman turning towards the viewer's left. Her upper legs are placed together until her knees and her feet are hip distance apart; she pivots on the tips of her toes, filling the pictorial surface diagonally. In her right hand she holds a flute; her left hand is missing. She appears naked but is heavily adorned; she wears bracelets, anklets and in the original watercolour copy made by Vandier d'Abbadie (1938: Figure 1), the remains of a floral collar can be seen around her neck. In addition, a cape or a shawl is draped around her left shoulder; the exact nature of this garment is difficult to ascertain. Furthermore, she is embellished with a tattoo of the god Bes, in schematic form, on each thigh.

The painting is vibrantly coloured. The female figure has been sketched with an ochre outline and a pale, delicate, beige flesh tone. She is lithe and sensuously drawn; the original watercolour shows her navel and rolls of flesh were indicated to suggest a softly curved abdomen and her pubic triangle was marked darkly. The subtlety of her skin tone is contrasted by the rich yellow background; the same colour as the bracelets, anklets and flute. Around the scene several vines are woven from which trail heart-shaped leaves, commonly referred to as convolvulus leaves. The vines are a dark, rich, ochre but the leaves are a deep, almost Prussian blue; they overlap the figure and suggest an overhanging canopy or trellis, or trailing vines held by the female figure.

There are several points of comparison to the '*Scènes de Gynécées*' figured ostraca. Most notable is the inclusion of the convolvulus leaves, seen in both the 'women on beds' and the kiosk scenes. However, it must be noted this stylised foliage is commonly included in New Kingdom tomb scenes; convolvulus is discussed in Section 5.6. The depiction of the god Bes is the most prolific motif in the 'women on beds' dataset, incorporated into the feet of the beds. In this wall painting his image is used as a tattoo. An image of a tattooed dancer is found on one ostracon from Deir el-Medina, Figure 2.3, but the tattoo is a pattern of dots, as seen on figurines from the Middle Kingdom (Winlock 1942: 72, Plate 35). However, Bes tattoos are often found on images of musicians and dancers depicted in New Kingdom tomb scenes, as discussed in Section 5.1f. Therefore, the motif of the Bes tattoo is used selectively in Egyptian representations in the New Kingdom, but no examples have been found on figured ostraca.

Figure 2.3: Figured ostracon of a dancer from Deir el-Medina, IFAO VA 2868 (Photograph Author's own) © IFAO.

The cape or shawl around the shoulder of the 'dancer' in WP.1 is similar to that worn by women in the kiosk scenes K.1-3 and also on EB.2. There are no images of dancers in the '*Scènes de Gynécées*' figured ostraca although scenes of dance appear in the tomb of Ay at Amarna, see Figure 5.12, which shows the harem or women's quarters (Davies 1908: 20, Plate XXVIII). However, none of these women wear the idiosyncratic cape or shawl. The most comparable image to WP.I is found on an ostracon from Deir el-Medina, Figure 2.4. This shows a woman who is naked with exception of a cape or shawl around her shoulders and who plays the double flute.

There are, however, many images of female musicians and dancers found on figured ostraca from Deir

Figure 2.4: Figured ostracon depicting a musician from Deir el-Medina, IFAO VA 2399 (Photograph Author's own) © IFAO.

el-Medina, most of which are depicted naked but heavily adorned with jewellery and elaborate wigs (Vandier d'Abbadie 1937: Plates LXIII, LV-LVII). They are shown in a variety of poses, often acrobatic or in striking postures. This suggests there was a lack of standardisation for the depiction of dancers and musicians; a degree of freedom was possible. This is also seen in tomb scenes in general, for example the tomb of Nebamun (Parkinson 2008: 72-73, Figure 83).

There are furthermore, two tomb scenes which contain a similar image to WP.I. The first is found in the Nineteenth Dynasty tomb of Harmose at Hierakonpolis, Figure 2.5; Vandier d'Abbadie (1938: 28) noted the similarities. Although the image is much damaged the dancer appears to hold vines of convolvulus leaves and pivots on the tips of her toes. Musicians and dancers are also depicted with convolvulus leaves in the Twentieth Dynasty tomb of Kynebu (TT 113) as illustrated in Baines and Malek (2000: 106-7).

WP. 2

House S.E. I, Deir el-Medina
Published Bruyère 1923: Plate I
Bruyère 1939: 60, Plate X
Brunner-Traut: 1955, 15, Figure 15

Found in the first room of the house, this scene was painted on a partition wall. Bruyère (1939: 60) classified this as a '*lit clos*' but Weiss (2009: 197) has subsequently raised doubts about the nature of the structure. The painted decoration runs along one side of the wall; the wall is broken by a staircase which is not central to the wall, see Figures 2.6 and 2.8. It is 1.22 m in length; only the lower portion of the wall survives which now stands at 75 cm in height. The painted decoration starts at 50 cm from ground level and runs for 28 cm. The entire room was whitewashed. The composition is placed on a multi-linear border which is likely to have framed the image. The scene shows four pairs of feet enclosed by two column bases; the column to the viewer's left is better preserved and suggests they were papyri form. One pair of feet is slightly raised and resting on a plump cushion, which lies against a palm trunk. It is likely these belonged to a woman sitting on a stool. The feet behind the seated figure are darker in colour; Bruyère (1923: 122) noted those in front of the seated figure consisted of one pair of saffron coloured feet and another of pale pink. Bruyère suggested this represented the three nations controlled by Egypt. Entwined between the feet are vines with large heart-shaped leaves, most likely convolvulus.

Bruyère reconstructed the scene, Figure 2.9, by comparing it to an ostracon in the British Museum, K.2 (Bruyère 1923: 132, Figure 5). This was before he excavated the numerous examples of figured ostraca from Deir el-Medina, found between 1930-1950. He

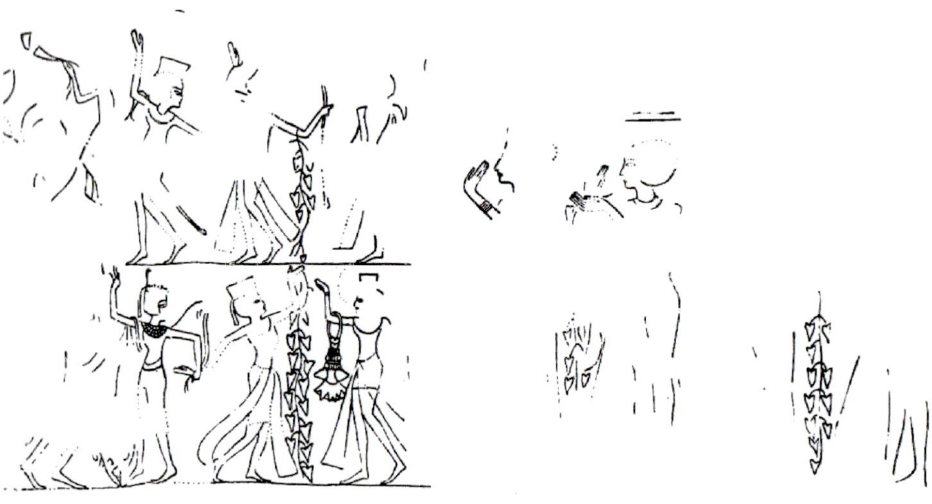

Figure 2.5: Scene of dancing from the Nineteenth Dynasty tomb of Harmose at Hierakonpolis (Wreszinski 1927: Plate 44).

Figure 2.6: Remains of the *'lit clos'* House S.E. I at Deir el-Medina when excavated by Bruyère (Bruyère 1939: 60, Plate X) © IFAO.

Figure 2.7: Remains of the painted wall decoration of House S.E. I at Deir el-Medina as published by Bruyère (Bruyère 1923: Plate I) © IFAO.

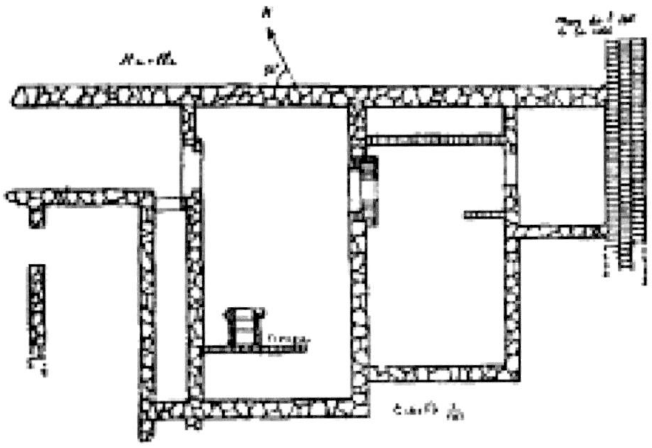

Figure 2.8: Location of the painted wall decoration in House S.E. I at Deir el-Medina (Bruyère 1923: 122, Figure 1) © IFAO.

believed the seated figure to be Hathor nourishing Horus; it is noteworthy that Bruyère (1923: 133) believed the imagery to be related to rebirth with the goddess giving her son, who symbolised all the dead, divine milk for a second life. Bruyère (1923: 124) also considered if the goddess was Isis in her role as divine mother suckling Horus; in doing so he made the significant suggestion that the image was a symbol and did not represent the earthly domain. At a later date Bruyère (1926: 86) also speculated that the nursing female was perhaps Meretseger, due to similarity with a scene in the Deir el-Medina tomb of Neferrenpet (TT 336), see Figure 5.9. The wall painting has been subsequently reconstructed by Brunner-Traut, Figure 2.10. This is a more likely rendition given the comparative evidence from Deir el-Medina.

While the upper portion of WP.2 cannot be reconstructed with certainty this image provides the strongest link between wall paintings and the '*Scènes de Gynécées*' figured ostraca, particularly the kiosk scenes. Both contain a seated figure resting on a palm trunk, surrounded by attendants, enclosed by papyri form columns, with convolvulus leaves threaded through the scene. Kiosk scenes, however, are only represented three times in the '*Scènes de Gynécées*' dataset, with possibly three further examples in the 'Fragments' dataset. This suggests the iconography had a restricted use, although it does appear to be standardised.

Figure 2.9: Reconstruction of the painted wall decoration of House S.E. I, Deir el-Medina by Bruyère (Bruyère 1923: 132, Figure 5) © IFAO.

Figure 2.10: Reconstruction of the painted wall decoration of House S.E. I, Deir el-Medina by Brunner-Traut (After Brunner-Traut 1955: 15, Figure 5).

WP. 3

House N.O. XII, Deir el-Medina
Published Bruyère 1939: 59, 286, Figure 157, Plate IX
Weiss 2009: 198-199

Found in the first room of the house, the painted decoration on the narrow or foot-end of the '*lit clos*' shows a papyrus skiff in the marshes, which contains papyrus rods and flowers. Most scholars, for example Koltsida (2007: 23), follow Bruyère in suggesting this is a male sailor. However, it is more likely to be a female skipper due to similar images found on figured ostraca from Deir el-Medina, for example, Figure 2.14. There are numerous examples of this motif on figured ostraca found at Deir el-Medina (Vandier d'Abbadie 1937: 138-139, Plates LX, XXVII; Vandier d'Abbadie 1959: 224-226, Plates CXVI, CLIV – CV). Furthermore, the motif of a woman in a papyrus skiff is found on votive beds, common in the Theban region during the Third Intermediate Period (Teeter 2010: 159).

The image of papyrus boats in the marshes is a standard scene in Egyptian tombs. This is particularly popular in New Kingdom tombs when the male tomb owner is depicted fishing and fowling, for example the tomb of Nakht (TT 52) (Davies 1917b: Plate XXIII). Much has been written on the symbolism attached to the

Figure 2.11: '*Lit clos*' with painted decoration in House N.O. XII, Deir el-Medina (Bruyère 1939: Plate IX) © IFAO.

Figure 2.12: Line drawing by Bruyère of the surviving decoration of House N.O. XII, Deir el-Medina (Bruyère 1939: 286, Figure 157) © IFAO.

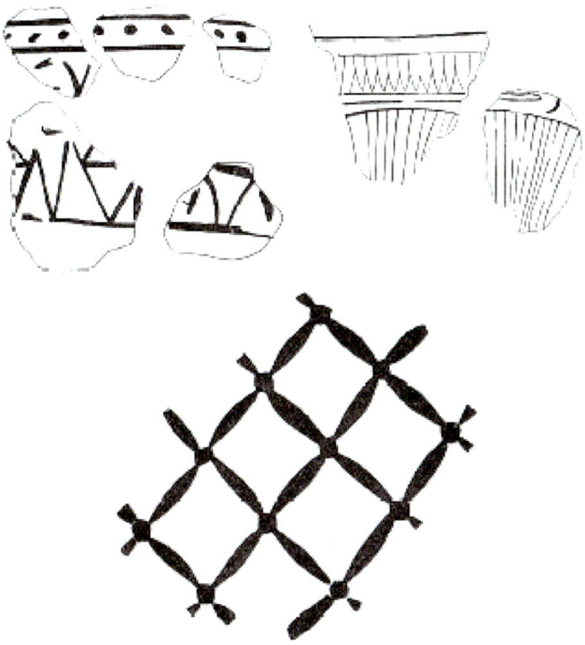

Figure 2.13: Remains of additional decoration from the '*lit clos*' at House N.O. XII, Deir el-Medina (Bruyère 1939: 287, Figure 158) © IFAO.

imagery, for example Germond (2008). The image of a female skipper on board a papyrus skiff can be traced back to the depiction of Queen Hetepheres II and her daughter Meresankh III in their Old Kingdom tomb at Giza (Dunham *et al.* 1974: 4, 10, Figure 4). This relates to the pulling or shaking of papyrus for Hathor ritual.

Figure 2.14: Figured ostracon from Deir el-Medina, showing a woman in a papyrus skiff, IFAO VA 3019 (Photograph Author's own) © IFAO.

A similar image is found in a small number of Old Kingdom tombs dating to the 5th and 6th Dynasty at Saqqara. Teeter (2010: 161-166) discusses the evolution of the imagery.

WP. 4

House	C.VII
Published	Bruyère 1939: 311, Figure 182, Plate IX
	Weiss 2009: 198-199

Figure 2.15: '*Lit clos*' with painted decoration in House C.VII, Deir el-Medina (Bruyère 1939: Plate IX) © IFAO.

Figure 2.16: Line drawing by Bruyère of surviving painted decoration in House C.VII, Deir el Medina (Bruyère 1939: 311, Figure 182) © IFAO.

Found on a front panel of a '*lit clos*', discovered in the first room of the house, the painted decoration was white on a grey background and measured 69 x 53 cm. Bruyère (1939: 59) describes this as a scene of toilette with a woman kneeling, who is assisted by her slave or helper. This interpretation has been questioned by subsequent scholarship (Weiss 2009: 199). The scene is difficult to interpret as only the lower portion remains. Furthermore, there are no scenes which are immediately comparable; scenes of toilette focus on women sitting on beds or in kiosks. There is no indication of the relationship between the kneeling and standing figure with the exception of size differentiation, which suggests a disparity in status or age. It is possible that convolvulus leaves are depicted behind the kneeling figure, but this is not certain.

WP. 5

House N.E.XIII
Published Bruyère 1939: 259, Figure 136, Plate IX

This image is white on a grey panel, found on the front of a '*lit clos*'. The structure was found in the front room of the house and had a central staircase. Only the lower portion remains; it is likely this

Figure 2.17: '*Lit clos*' with painted decoration in House N.E. XIII, Deir el-Medina (Bruyère 1939: Plate IX) © IFAO.

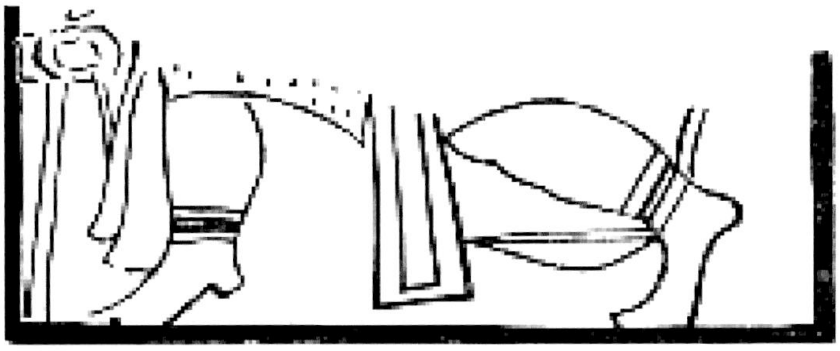

Figure 2.18: Line drawing by Bruyère of surviving painted decoration in House N.E. III, Deir el-Medina (Bruyère 1939: 259, Figure 136) © IFAO.

Figure 2.19: Wooden panels depicted the god Bes, from a bed from the tomb of Yuya and Tuya, Cairo 51110 (Davis 1907: 36).

depicted the god Bes. Pivoting on up-raised heels he turns towards the viewer's left. He wears a spotted kilt with a long sash to the front. He holds a knife in his left hand in a protective capacity and a *sa* symbol in his right hand. Although Bes is the most prevalent motif in the '*Scènes de Gynécées*' figured ostraca he is not depicted in this pose in this dataset. However, similar imagery is found on New Kingdom furniture, for example panels from a bed found in the tomb of Yuya and Tuya (KV 46), which show Bes holding a *sa* symbol and a knife, Figure 2.19. The tomb contained three beds (Cairo 51110, 51112, 51109) and three chairs (Cairo 55113, 55112, 55111), most of which were elaborately carved featuring the gods Bes and Taweret (Quibell 1908: 50-53). The concept of using panels to decorate a wooden bed is also similar to the decorative scheme used to embellish the '*lit clos*'.

WP. 6

House S.O. VI
Published Bruyère 1939: 330, Figure 202, Plate IX

In the first room of the house of Sennedjem Bruyère found the remains of a design on the bottom of the '*lit clos*'. This was a white drawing on a grey background, most likely of the god Bes dancing. This is similar in design to WP.5. He also noted finding three bricks with drawings on the ground near the '*lit clos*'; he believed they belong to a canopy which enclosed the structure.

Figure 2.20: '*Lit clos*' with painted decoration in House S.O. VI, Deir el-Medina (Bruyère 1939: Plate IX) © IFAO.

Figure 2.21: Line drawing by Bruyère of surviving painted decoration in House S.O. VI, Deir el-Medina (Bruyère 1939: 330, Figure 202) © IFAO.

WP. 7

House N.E.X
Published Bruyère 1939: 255, Figure 131

Bruyère recorded that while only traces of the '*lit clos*' survived in the first room of the house many fragments of decoration were recovered. These suggest that the panels on either side of the staircase were decorated with images of the god Bes making music and dancing, while a longer panel ran the length of the bed forming a canopy which enclosed the space, as seen in Figure 2.22. Bruyère (1939: 58) noted this panel was 70 cm in height and the canopy rose to the ceiling, with an elevation above the ground of c.2.50 m. The canopy depicted the god frontally with wings outstretched, holding lotus flowers in his hands. He is shown with a short kilt, with a long sash to the front, a thick mane and a beard, with

Figure 2.22: Line drawing by Bruyère of surviving painted decoration in House N.E.X, Deir el-Medina (Bruyère 1939: 255, Figure 131) © IFAO.

the remains of feather plumes on his head. While Bes is the most prevalent motif in the '*Scènes de Gynécées*' figured ostraca, he is only depicted winged once (EB.1) in this dataset.

WP. 8

House N.E.XII
Published Bruyère 1939: 257, Figure 133
Weiss 2009: 198, Figure 3

Bruyère (1939: 257) noted the '*lit clos*' in the first room of the house was decorated with grey panels and possibly white outline. In the debris of the room he also found fragments of decoration, Figure 2.23. As noted by Weiss (2009: 198) it is unlikely they form one single Bes figure; it is more probable they are part of an image containing several representations of the god, as found in Amarna, see Figures 2.24 and 2.25.

Figure 2.23: Line drawing by Bruyère of surviving painted decoration in House N.E. XII, Deir el-Medina (Bruyère 1939: 257, Figure 133) © IFAO.

Figure 2.24: Wall painting found in House 3, Main St, Amarna, when excavated by Kemp (Kemp 1979: Plate VIII) Image courtesy of the Egypt Exploration Society.

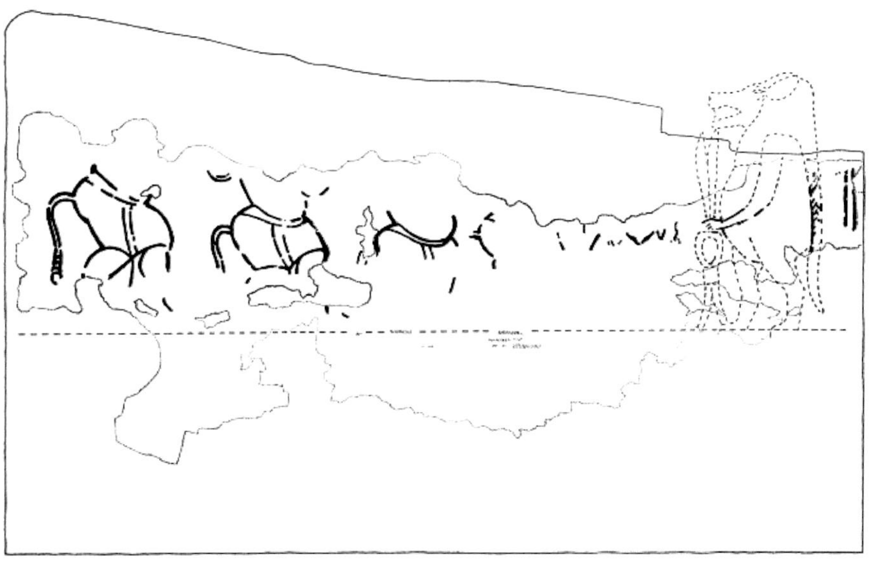

Figure 2.25: Reconstruction of wall painting, found in House 3, Main St, Amarna, by Kemp (Kemp 1979: 48, Figure 1) Image courtesy of the Egypt Exploration Society.

WP. 9

House S.E. IX
Published Bruyère 1939: 276, Figure 148

Bruyère (1939: 276) reported that while house S.E.IX was almost completely destroyed, the first room of the house contained remnants of a '*lit clos*'. This included a mask of the god Bes in high relief, made of moulded clay with painted decoration. The fragments show he wore a tall feather headdress, a full beard and his tongue protruded in a mischievous manner. He is depicted frontally; this combination of ferocious and comic elements is seen commonly in the figured ostraca 'women on beds' dataset.

Figure 2.26: Fragments of moulded clay representing the god Bes, from House S.E. XI, Deir el-Medina, as found by Bruyère (Bruyère 1939: 276, Figure 148) © IFAO.

WP. 10

House C.V
Published Bruyère 1939: 305, Figure 136

This image found on a '*lit clos*' in the first room of the house was identified by Bruyère (1939: 305) as the god Bes dancing. As other scholars have noted the depiction is ambiguous and it is not possible to determine the exact nature of the scene (Weiss 2009: 197). This image, drawn on a grey background with white outline, is framed in a multi-linear border, drawn on a base line.

Figure 2.27: Line drawing by Bruyère of surviving painted wall decoration in House C.V, Deir el-Medina (Bruyère 1939: 305, Figure 136) © IFAO.

Chapter 3

Catalogue of '*Scènes de Gynécées*' Figured Ostraca and Comparative Evidence

3.1: Methodology and Terminology

This chapter consists of a series of catalogues of figured ostraca, primarily those which form the '*Scènes de Gynécées*'. These include the 'women on beds' scenes, 'elaborate bed' scenes, kiosk scenes and the fragments dataset. The latter is comprised of highly fragmentary examples whose remnants suggest they contained a '*Scènes de Gynécées*' image; however, due to their piecemeal nature it is not always possible to determine which dataset they would have belonged to. Scenes of a comparative nature are also considered, including images of mother goddesses, servant girls, and gift giving. It is hoped by their inclusion they will aid our understanding of the '*Scènes de Gynécées*' and enable us to place the corpus into the context of contemporaneous society.

Many of the ostraca in this study were personally inspected and photographed by the author, including those at IFAO, the Louvre, the Medelshavmuseet, UCL Petrie Museum, Museo Egizio and the British Museum. In addition, many curators and researchers worldwide kindly sent me digital images of the ostraca in their collections or which they had personally excavated. There are a limited number of ostraca in private collections or lost during the war, for which no digital images are available. In these cases, the line drawings from the original publications have been utilised.

The find spots of the ostraca are noted in the catalogue if known, for example the '*Kom du Sud*', '*Le Grand Puits*' and the '*Kom du Grand Puits*'. The descriptors refer to locations on the site, as designated by Bruyère during his work at the village; they refer to two primary locations. Firstly, a heap of rubbish which accumulated during the life of the village, found at the foot of the south wall of the enclosure, referred to as the '*Kom du Sud*' by Bruyère. Secondly, a man-made pit, dug in antiquity, to the north of the village, which had become filled with debris, referred to as '*Le Grand Puits*' by Bruyère. These loci are discussed in Section 4.1.

The current location of the ostraca is also recorded, if known. In addition, for those ostraca published by Vandier d'Abbadie, the number she assigned ostraca for publication purposes is also given. This is referred to as the VA number.

3.2: 'Women on Beds' dataset

WoB.1

Present location	Cairo JE 63806 (entered museum 1934)
Find spot	Deir el-Medina, '*Kom du Sud*', excavated 1930 (marked 24.1.30)
Published	Vandier d'Abbadie 1937: 69, Plate L VA number 2337 Backhouse 2012: 28, Figure 1
Dimensions	-
Material	Limestone
Colour	Black and ochre/red

WoB.1: Cairo JE 63806 (Vandier d'Abbadie 1937: 69, Plate L) © IFAO.

This ostracon shows a woman sitting on a bed facing the viewer's right. She wears a long enveloping wig with a fillet, surmounted by a cone; her facial features are erased. She is attired in a complex wrap-around dress. Her right arm reaches behind her, while her left arm stretches forward. Her feet are resting on a footstool. A child, long in body, lies against the footboard. One arm reaches upwards while the other lies along the bed, no hands are indicated. The child appears to gaze upwards. An upraised line drawn from the child's genital area could indicate a penis. Vandier d'Abbadie (1937: 82) referred to this image as a scene of the nursery, a subset of the '*Scènes de Gynécées*'.

The bed is highly decorated. It has a footboard to the viewer's left and a deep mattress; the frame has wavy lines drawn upon it, suggesting serpent imagery. The god Bes is incorporated into three legs of the bed, in a cursory manner. Beneath the bed a large, deep vase is shown next to a kohl tube possibly with an applicator, which is adjacent to a mirror. A floral collar is shown hanging from the wall behind the seated woman or this may represent painted wall decoration.

The scene was drawn on a baseline, in outline, with a limited use of colour fill. Several lines score the image, suggesting scratches on the original ostracon.

WoB.2

Present location	French Institute of Oriental Archaeology
Find spot	Deir el-Medina
Published	Vandier d'Abbadie 1937: 70, Plate L VA number 2338
Dimensions	–
Material	Limestone
Colour	Black

Drawn in black outline on a baseline, this ostracon depicts a woman sitting on a bed facing the viewer's right. Her facial features are destroyed but the ends of her enveloping wig are still visible on her shoulder. Her right arm reaches behind her; it is likely she held an object in her outstretched left hand, possibly a mirror. She wears a complex wrap-around dress. A child lies in-front of the seated woman, turning towards the viewer's left. It has upraised arms and bent legs; a penis is suggested by a black line in the genital region and the child appears to wear an elongated head cone. Vandier d'Abbadie (1937: 82) referred to this as a scene of the nursery, a subset of the '*Scènes de Gynécées*'.

The bed has a thin frame supported by legs in the shape of a series of open papyrus umbels, suggesting a floral bouquet, only two are visible. The mattress is rendered with a series of dots giving the impression of depth; to the viewer's right a footboard is shown. A mirror is stowed under the bed, with a dot in the centre of the disc.

WoB.3

Present location	French Institute of Oriental Archaeology
Find spot	Deir el-Medina
Published	Vandier d'Abbadie 1937: 691, Plate L VA number 2343
Dimensions	–
Material	–
Colour	Black, ochre, yellow and white

This faded but still vibrantly coloured ostracon shows a woman sitting on a bed facing the viewer's right. She wears a long enveloping wig; the original line drawing shows this was tied with a fillet, with a lotus flower to the front. She is attired in a complex wrap-around dress. She raises her left hand, while her right arm reaches behind her. A companion approaches facing the viewer's left; her facial features are destroyed. She holds a shallow yellow dish in one hand, possibly containing a cone, while the other hand appears to hold a dish with a foot. Both women are dressed in a similar manner, suggesting they are social equals. The seated

WoB.2: IFAO VA 2338, © IFAO.

WoB.3: IFAO VA 2343 (Photograph Author's own) © IFAO.

woman raises her left hand, possibly in a gesture of thanks to her companion.

The bed has a curved footboard to the viewer's left; the god Bes is incorporated into the two legs of the bed. Beneath the bed is a mirror disc, vividly coloured red; next to this is a kohl tube, with an applicator and stopper. To the viewer's left there appears to be another figure standing behind the bed, the exact nature of which is not apparent. Vandier d'Abbadie (1937: 82) suggested this was a scene of hairdressing, a subset of the '*Scènes de Gynécées*'. This is a rare image, a complete scene, that depicts both ends of the bed, but it does not appear to include a child. The scene was drawn on a baseline, with outline and a considerable amount of colour fill.

WoB.4

Present location	Private Collection
Find spot	Deir el-Medina
Published	Vandier d'Abbadie 1937: 71, Plate LIII VA number 2345
Dimensions	–
Material	Limestone
Colour	Black and ochre

Recorded only in this line drawing, this ostracon drawn in black outline with ochre fill, shows a woman lying on a bed, facing the viewer's left. Although badly damaged it appears to be drawn on a baseline. The recumbent figure supports her head with her left hand, while leaning on her elbow; her right hand reaches forward. The image is of a relaxed, contemplative pose. Her facial features are indicated with a wide, almond shaped eye with pupil, which appears to be looking upwards. She wears a long wig with a fillet and lotus flower to the front; her head is surmounted with a cone. The red ochre colour of her flesh is clearly visible. She appears naked, but the sleeve of a robe is indicated or that of a cape or shawl; she also wears a hip- girdle and bracelets on both wrists. Her pubic triangle is marked heavily in black; her legs are only cursorily drawn, and no feet are visible.

WoB.4: VA 2345 (Vandier d'Abbadie 1937: 71, Plate LIII) © IFAO.

The bed is shown with a footboard to the viewer's left; the frame is decorated with a wavy line, possibly suggesting serpent imagery. Beneath the bed a mirror and kohl tube with an applicator are depicted and a tray containing two large cones. The scene takes place under a canopy, with a fine line running from the left to right, suggesting something was strung from one side to the other. A similar canopy is seen in a number of tombs at Deir el-Medina, for example the tomb of Nakhtamon (TT 335: Bruyère 1926: 161, Figure 108). Vandier d'Abbadie (1937: 71) referred to the structure as a kiosk. However, she did not believe this ostracon belonged in the '*Scènes de Gynécées*' group; she suggested the woman was perhaps asleep, which is unlikely given her wide-eyed pose. Alternatively, she proposed the scene was drawn for amusement and/or the woman represented a courtesan (Vandier d'Abbadie 1937: 84). The ostracon is included in the 'women on beds' dataset as it meets the criteria of the study and contains many common motifs found in the '*Scènes de Gynécées*'.

WoB.5

Present location	French Institute of Oriental Archaeology
Find spot	Deir el-Medina
Published	Vandier d'Abbadie 1937: 71, Plate LIII VA number 2346
Dimensions	–
Material	Limestone
Colour	Black, ochre and yellow

This ostracon shows a woman sitting on a bed, facing the viewer's right. She wears a long tripartite wig, tied with a fillet, which may be floral. She is attired in a complex wrap-around dress, and she is adorned with large hoop earrings. She rests her feet on a footstool. Opposite her a female figure approaches, facing the viewer's left. Although she wears an enveloping

WoB.5: IFAO VA 2346, © IFAO.

wig, she is attired in a similar manner to her seated companion, suggesting they are social equals. The standing figure holds a dish in her upturned hand and raises the other hand, possibly in a gesture of greeting to the seated figure; the two women appear to touch hands. This suggests companionship, social or family bonds. Vandier d'Abbadie (1937: 82) believed this was a scene of toilette, a subset of the '*Scènes de Gynécées*'.

The bed frame is simple in design. It is outlined in black and ochre with a small amount of yellow added; this may represent serpent imagery. Bes is incorporated into the bed leg depicted to the viewer's right; he is shown possibly with a beard and a mane. He wears a long kilt, with a frontal sash.

Overall, the scene has a great sense of intimacy and balance with the two women making eye and hand contact. This is paralleled by the two large convolvulus leaves in the background; the heart shaped leaves are oversized, possibly indicating their importance. The scene, set on a baseline, has been carefully drawn with outline and limited colour fill.

WoB.6

Present location	French Institute of Oriental Archaeology
Find spot	Deir el-Medina
Published	Vandier d'Abbadie 1937: 72, Plate LIV VA number 2349 Minault-Gout 2002: 32, Figure 20
Dimensions	–
Material	Limestone
Colour	Black, ochre/red and yellow

Vandier d'Abbadie (1937: 72) described this image as comprising of fragments depicting a woman sitting on a bed turning towards the viewer's right. She suggested the head of a small child lay in front of the woman, as seen in Image b. However, at the French Institute of Oriental Archaeology only the upper fragment survives (Image a); it would appear the lower portion of the ostracon has been lost. It is likely further damage has resulted in the loss of a section of foliage, illustrated behind the seated figure, as seen in Image b.

The ostracon, as viewed at the French Institute of Oriental Archaeology, shows a seated woman facing the viewer's right. She wears a long enveloping wig, which is tied with a fillet and surmounted with a cone. She is attired in a complex wrap-around dress. Around her neck she wears a broad collar indicated by black and yellow lines; this is possibly a floral collar. Her facial features are delicately drawn, and she has a light beige skin tone.

The woman is sitting on a mattress, the thickness of which is suggested by the depression where she sits.

WoB.6a: IFAO VA 2349, © IFAO.

WoB.6b: IFAO VA 2349 (Vandier d'Abbadie 1937: 72, Plate LIV) © IFAO.

The evidence of some foliage behind the seated figure is still visible. Vandier d'Abbadie (1937: 72) described these as '*lancéolées*', leaves shaped like a lance taping to a point. However, it is not possible to identify these, and the leaves may be the more commonly depicted convolvulus leaves.

WoB.7

Present location	French Institute of Oriental Archaeology
Find spot	Deir el-Medina
Published	Vandier d'Abbadie 1937: 72, Plate LIV VA number 2350
Dimensions	–
Material	Limestone
Colour	Black, ochre/red and white

This ostracon shows the back and upper thighs of a woman sitting on a bed facing the viewer's left. The ochre shade of her skin is clearly visible beneath her robe, the pleats of which are indicated. Long tresses of her black enveloping wig cascade over her shoulders and back. Her left hand reaches behind her. The bed frame is undecorated, and the mattress gives no indication of texture or depth. Behind the woman, to the viewer's

WoB.7: IFAO VA 2350 (Photograph Author's own) © IFAO.

right, oversized leaves can be seen; these are outlined in both black and ochre. Vandier d'Abbadie (1937: 72) referred to these as convolvulus leaves. Underneath the bed, the top of a mirror disc is visible.

WoB.8

Present location	Private Collection
Find Spot	Deir el-Medina
Published	Vandier d'Abbadie 1937: 73, Plate LVII VA number 2353
Dimensions	-
Material	Limestone
Colour	Black and ochre

This photograph is the only record of this ostracon. It shows a woman sitting on a bed facing the viewer's right. She wears a long enveloping wig, which is tied with a fillet and surmounted with a cone. Attired in a complex wrap-around dress, she leans her right arm backwards and stretches her left arm forward. Behind the seated woman is a faint outline, possibly of convolvulus leaves. The bed frame, with a footboard to the viewer's left, has serpent imagery suggested by a faint wavy line and the god Bes is incorporated into the leg of the bed. Beneath the bed a kohl tube with applicator and stopper is depicted next to a mirror with a circular disc and papyrus shaped handle.

WoB.8: VA 2353 (Vandier d'Abbadie 1937: 73, Plate LVII) © IFAO.

WoB.9

Present location	French Institute of Oriental Archaeology
Find spot	Deir el-Medina
Published	Vandier d'Abbadie 1937: 74 VA number 2355
Dimensions	10 x 10 cm
Material	Limestone
Colour	Black and ochre/red

WoB.9: IFAO VA 2355 (Photograph Author's own) © IFAO.

This badly damaged ostracon shows the feet of a woman resting on a footstool; she is facing the viewer's right. It is likely she was sitting on a bed, the frame of which is outlined in black, possibly with serpent imagery. A child lies on the bed facing towards the viewer's left. Behind the child, a woman stands; the lower portion of her long enveloping wig is still visible, as is her arm reaching towards the viewer's right. She is possibly bringing a gift to the seated figure. Vandier d'Abbadie (1937: 84) believed this to be a scene of the nursery, a subset of the '*Scènes de Gynécées*'. The scene is drawn on a baseline with black outline and limited ochre fill.

WoB.10

Present location	French Institute of Oriental Archaeology

Find spot	Deir el-Medina, *Kom du Sud*, excavated 1930
Published	Vandier d'Abbadie 1937: 74, Plate LIV VA number 2359
Dimensions	–
Material	Limestone
Colour	Black and ochre

WoB.10: IFAO VA 2359 (Photograph Author's own) © IFAO.

This badly faded ostracon shows the god Bes incorporated into the leg of a bed, to the viewer's left. A simple bed frame is depicted above the god. A pair of feet under pleated robes is visible; the figure would have faced towards the viewer's right. It is likely this was a woman approaching a female figure sitting on a bed; images of companions show standing figures behind and in front of the seated figure. The composition was drawn on a baseline, using ochre and black outline, with limited colour fill. This ostracon is marked on the side with K.S., designating this as from the '*Kom du Sud*'.

WoB.11

Present location	French Institute of Oriental Archaeology
Find spot	Deir el-Medina
Published	Vandier d'Abbadie: 1937, 74, Plate LIV VA number 2360
Dimensions	–
Material	Limestone
Colour	Black and red

WoB.11: IFAO VA 2360, © IFAO.

This is a rare image in the '*Scènes de Gynécées*', depicting the god Bes in profile. He has one hand on his hip and the other is raised to his head, possibly in a dancing pose. He has a long red beard and his paunch hangs over the top of his kilt. His legs are bent, giving him the impression of movement and his tail is visible. Most remarkably, he is not incorporated into the legs of the bed but free standing. A large dish, with a deep basin, bevelled rim and a curved foot, sits next to the god; it is likely this contained a cone, the markings of which can still be seen. To the viewer's right stands a bed frame, simple in design. It is probable a woman is sitting on the bed, facing the viewer's right; the edge of her robe is visible.

WoB.12

Present location	French Institute of Oriental Archaeology
Find spot	Deir el-Medina, '*Kom du Sud*', excavated 1930 (marked 19.1.30)
Published	Vandier d'Abbadie 1937: Plate LIV VA number 2362
Dimensions	–
Material	Limestone
Colour	Black, ochre and grey

This fragmentary ostracon features a detailed depiction of the god Bes. It is likely that he was incorporated into the leg of a bed. The tall, feathered headdress of Bes joins the frame, which is visible just above the god's head. Bes is drawn in a mixture of black, grey and ochre, with the white of the ostracon used as a base colour. This is a skilled rendition, using three colours of fill to create a lively image full of humour and movement. The god appears to raise his heels and stand on the tips of his toes, as if in a dancing pose, while his tongue

WoB.12: IFAO VA 2362 (Photograph Author's own) © IFAO.

protrudes from his mouth in a mischievous manner. He is clad in a kilt with spots, giving the impression of an animal skin. This is tied with a long red sash, which matches the colour of his protruding tongue.

Beside Bes, to the viewer's right, are two angular lines; it is possible they show the edge of the bed frame. Next to Bes, the pleats of a long robe fall, under which a pair of feet, facing the viewer's left is visible. It is likely this belonged to a woman, given the similarity to other images in the dataset. The feet appear to rest on a small shallow dish with a triangular foot. This looks similar to drinking cups, seen for example, in the banquet of Nebamun and Ipuky, see Figure 5.30. The scene is set on a base line and drawn with considerable skill, using outline and coloured fill.

WoB.13

Present location	French Institute of Oriental Archaeology
Find spot	Deir el-Medina, '*Kom du Sud*', excavated 1930
Published	Vandier d'Abbadie 1937: 75 VA number 2364
Dimensions	9 x 6 cm
Material	Potsherd
Colour	Black, ochre and white

Drawn on a potsherd this ostracon shows a woman lying horizontally, facing the viewer's right. Vandier d'Abbadie (1937: 75) believed that she is reclining on a bed; this is uncertain although she is clearly lying on a white surface outlined in black, which has a small black square drawn upon it. Her lower face, upper torso and midriff are all that remain. Her flesh is ochre coloured, no details are apparent, but she appears to be naked, or at least no robe is visible. She wears a long wig and is raising her right arm. A creature with white skin and black spots lies before her face. Vandier d'Abbadie (1937:75) suggests this is a lizard; if so, this would be a unique image in the dataset. Similar creatures are depicted on the Twenty-second Dynasty coffin of Horaawesheb (British Museum EA 6666) which shows numerous protective deities; the lizards are held as defensive emblems (Taylor 2010: 202-3). It is possible the lizard was drawn previously on the potsherd, then the image of the woman added. However, it appears the whitewash was added first, as demonstrated on the depiction of the bedframe, then black outline added. This would imply the lizard was intentionally incorporated into the scene if not drawn concurrently. Beneath the possible bed frame the top of an object is visible; this may be the applicator of a kohl tube. The verso of the potsherd is marked with 'K.S.', indicating it was found in the '*Kom du Sud*'.

WoB.14

Present location	French Institute of Oriental Archaeology
Find spot	Deir el-Medina
Published	Vandier d'Abbadie 1937: 76 VA number 2365
Dimensions	6 x 6 cm
Material	Limestone
Colour	Black and ochre

This fragmentary ostracon shows the pleats of a long robe; it is likely they belong to a woman sitting on a bed, facing the viewer's right. This image may include the edge of a bed frame and the foot of a pot, as seen on ostracon WoB.11. Alternatively, the tall vertical object may be a kohl tube next to the foot of a pot. At the top of the ostracon, to the viewer's right, a convolvulus leaf is perhaps depicted. The image, drawn on a baseline, in black and ochre outline, with limited colour fill, has been executed with care and attention to detail.

WoB.13: IFAO VA 2364 (Photograph Author's own) © IFAO.

WoB.14: IFAO VA 2365 (Photograph Author's own) © IFAO.

WoB.15

Present location	French Institute of Oriental Archaeology
Find spot	Deir el-Medina
Published	Vandier d'Abbadie 1937: 76 VA number 2368
Dimensions	6 x 7 cm
Material	Limestone
Colour	Black and ochre

WoB.15: IFAO VA 2368 (Photograph Author's own) © IFAO.

This poorly preserved ostracon shows a bed frame with the god Bes incorporated into the leg of the bed, to the viewer's right. His characteristic angular pose, with bent legs and out turned feet is just discernible. Although badly damaged it is probable this scene shows a woman sitting on the bed facing the viewer's right; her robe is visible to the viewer's left, as is a footstool, upon which she rests her feet. Opposite a companion approaches, facing the viewer's left. Her long robe and feet are visible beneath the bed; it is likely she is standing behind the bed turning towards her companion. Vandier d'Abbadie (1937: 76) believed this represented part of a scene of toilette, a subset of the '*Scènes de Gynécées*'. It is drawn on a baseline with black and ochre outline and limited colour fill.

WoB.16

Present location	French Institute of Oriental Archaeology
Find spot	Deir el-Medina, '*Kom du Sud*', excavated 1930 (marked 26.1.30)
Published	Vandier d'Abbadie 1937: 76 VA number 2369
Dimensions	–
Material	Limestone
Colour	Black and ochre

WoB.16: IFAO VA 2369 (Photograph Author's own) © IFAO.

This fragmentary ostracon shows a bed frame with serpent imagery. It is possible the god Bes, depicted to the viewer's extreme left, was incorporated into the leg of the bed. The edges of his angular shape are just visible. Under the bed frame a range of toiletry items are stowed including a mirror, kohl tube with applicator and a large vase, possibly containing a cone. Shading has been used to suggest the lustrous nature of the vase and indicate the lip. A pair of feet is visible facing the viewer's right. It is likely they belonged to a woman sitting on the bed; the tips of another pair of feet are just evident at the extreme right edge of the ostracon. The two pairs of feet would have formed an arch, as seen on ostracon WoB.36. The composition is drawn on a double baseline, in black outline with limited colour fill; it has been composed with care and attention to detail. The excavators' marks indicate this was found on 26th January 1930 at the '*Kom du Sud*'.

WoB.17

Present location	French Institute of Oriental Archaeology
Find spot	Deir el-Medina, '*Kom du Sud*', excavated 1930
Published	Vandier d'Abbadie 1937: 76 VA number 2373
Dimensions	7 x 6.2 cm
Material	Limestone
Colour	Black and ochre

Although this image has little colour remaining, it contains the use of incision, which is rare in the dataset. The god Bes is depicted to the viewer's right, incorporated into the leg of a bed. The bed frame and thick mattress can be seen above his head. A seated figure is visible to the viewer's left; it is likely this is a woman sitting on the bed. The folds of her long robe are discernible, and she appears to rest her feet on a footstool. A dish with a foot and base is shown above the mattress; although it is possible this is a headrest. The dish was perhaps offered to the seated figure by a companion, now destroyed. The scene was composed on a baseline, in black outline with limited colour fill.

WoB.17: IFAO VA 2373 (Photograph Author's own) © IFAO.

WoB.18

Present location	French Institute of Oriental Archaeology
Find spot	Deir el-Medina
Published	Vandier d'Abbadie 1937: 76 VA number 2374
Dimensions	11 x 9.5 cm
Material	Limestone
Colour	Black, ochre and white

Vandier d'Abbadie (1937:77) suggested this ostracon represented a woman sitting on a bed turning towards the viewer's right, with her feet on a mat. However, it is difficult to distinguish the details. A pair of feet, outlined in black with ochre flesh tone, is visible facing the viewer's right and the long pleats of a robe appear to be inscribed into the surface. The feet rest on a white board which is longer in length than most footstools depicted in these scenes. There is a horizontal band which may depict the bed frame and an undefined shape in ochre, which could represent a child lying on the bed. It is possible the ostracon has been used for multiple images and we are viewing the remains of more than one composition.

WoB.18: IFAO VA 2374 (Photograph Author's own) © IFAO.

WoB.19

Present location	French Institute of Oriental Archaeology
Find spot	Deir el-Medina
Published	Vandier d'Abbadie 1937: 78 VA number 2375
Dimensions	5 x 7 cm
Material	Limestone
Colour	Black and ochre

WoB.19: IFAO VA 2375 (Photograph Author's own) © IFAO.

This fragmentary ostracon shows a bed frame with detailed serpent imagery, drawn in black outline and a thick mattress above. Underneath the bed a large pot is shown with a wide bowl and long foot, it also has a lip or a lid. To the viewer's right, the bottom of a long-pleated robe can be seen; a pair of feet resting on a footstool is visible beneath the hem. It is likely these belonged to a woman sitting on the bed facing the viewer's right. The scene is drawn on a baseline with black and ochre outline and limited use of colour fill. Incision is used in addition to painted decoration.

WoB.20

Present location	French Institute of Oriental Archaeology
Find spot	Deir el-Medina
Published	Vandier d'Abbadie 1937: 78 VA number 2376
Dimensions	7 x 7 cm
Material	Potsherd
Colour	Black

WoB.20: IFAO VA 2376 (Photograph Author's own) © IFAO.

WoB.21: IFAO VA 2380 (Photograph Author's own) © IFAO.

Vandier d'Abbadie (1937:78) suggested this black line drawing on a potsherd depicted a woman sitting on a bed facing the viewer's left. Her feet rest on a footstool and her sandal is clearly visible. It is possible the artist made an earlier attempt at drawing this as there is a faint outline also visible of the lower leg and sandal. The leg of the bed takes the form of a woman with upraised arms; papyrus stems with umbels appear to stand beneath the bedframe. The figure wears a short wig and beads crossing her chest diagonally. Her facial features are only rudimentarily drawn in a cursory and schematic manner although, her breasts and pubic triangle are emphasised. There are the remnants of yellow fill on the standing figure. This is a unique depiction in the dataset, with possible links to the iconography found later on votive beds, as discussed by Teeter (2010). Overall, the scene is carelessly drawn with the arms of the female figure overlapping the legs of the seated woman. Again, it is possible we are viewing multiple images; however, the use of black outline alone gives a unity to the composition. The excavator's number 14708 is marked on the potsherd in heavy black ink.

WoB.21

Present location	French Institute of Oriental Archaeology
Find spot	Deir el-Medina
Published	Vandier d'Abbadie 1937: 79 VA number 2380
Dimensions	4.6 x 4.5 cm
Material	Limestone
Colour	Black, ochre and yellow

This fragmentary ostracon shows the knees of a woman sitting on a bed, facing the viewer's right, the folds of her long robe are outlined in ochre. The bed frame is clearly visible, outlined in black with yellow fill and a black wavy line, suggestive of serpent imagery; the mattress of the bed is outlined in ochre. It is possible a child is shown on the lap of the seated woman or on the bed beside her. In addition, a standing figure may be depicted behind the bed, as indicated by the pleats of a long robe which are visible to the viewer's right, at the bottom edge of the ostracon. Incision was also used on this artefact.

WoB.22

Present location	French Institute of Oriental Archaeology
Find spot	Deir el-Medina, '*Kom du Sud*', excavated 1930
Published	Vandier d'Abbadie 1937: 79 VA number 2381

WoB.22: IFAO VA 2381 (Photograph Author's own) © IFAO.

Dimensions	7 x 7.5 cm
Material	Limestone
Colour	Black and ochre

This badly damaged ostracon has breaks around its edge and an uneven surface. Vandier d'Abbadie (1937: 79) believed that it depicted a woman sitting on a bed facing the viewer's left. However, personal inspection by the author reveals it shows a woman sitting on a bed, facing the viewer's right; her lower robe and feet are distinguishable, as is the black outline of the bed frame. A standing figure approaches the seated figure, turning towards the viewer's left. The ochre flesh of her feet, legs and arms can be identified, as can the long black tresses of her wig. The outline of her robe can be seen, including a translucent sleeve. It is likely she is holding an object, possibly a gift for her seated companion. The excavator's mark, top left, indicates that this artefact was found on 26th January 1930 at the '*Kom du Sud*'.

WoB.23

Present location	French Institute of Oriental Archaeology
Find spot	Deir el-Medina
Published	Vandier d'Abbadie 1937: 79 VA number 2382
Dimensions	10 x 12.5 cm
Material	Limestone
Colour	Black, ochre and white

This ostracon, which may have been blackened by smoke, shows a woman sitting on a bed, facing the viewer's right. Her upper body and facial features are destroyed, but the contours of her lower body can be identified, and her long robe is depicted with ochre pleats and white fill. Her legs are on the far side of the bed and the bed frame is outlined in ochre. A small figure, also outlined in ochre, is visible to the viewer's left. They wear a kilt and their head is depicted in profile, turning towards the viewer's right, although their body is rendered frontally. It is possible that this is the god Bes, incorporated into the leg of the bed. Although a profile facial depiction of the god is rare in this dataset. Behind the seated woman stands a person or an object. This may have been a scene of hairdressing, similar to ostracon WoB.3.

WoB.23: IFAO VA 2382 (Photograph Author's own) © IFAO.

WoB.24

Present location	French Institute of Oriental Archaeology
Find spot	Deir el-Medina, '*Kom du Sud*', excavated 1930 (marked 24.1.30)
Published	Vandier d'Abbadie 1937: 80 VA Number 2385
Dimensions	7 x 7 cm
Material	Limestone
Colour	Black and ochre

WoB.24: IFAO VA 2385 (Photograph Author's own) © IFAO.

This badly damaged ostracon depicts a woman sitting on a bed facing the viewer's right. The surface is uneven, with a break cutting the head from the seated figure; the ends of a long enveloping wig remain, falling onto her shoulders. The woman leans her right arm behind her body. Her flesh is ochre coloured; the pleats of the sleeve of her robe can be seen. The black outline of the bed frame is visible. To the viewer's left, behind the seated figure, a small black outline is depicted; this could be convolvulus leaves. At the bottom of the ostracon, to the viewer's right, a red pot appears beneath the bed. The image was drawn on a baseline. Excavators' marks on the verso reveal this object was found at the '*Kom du Sud*', on the 21st January 1930.

It is possible that the black markings are smoke damage. Furthermore, there is a deep scratch running diagonally across the ostracon and evidence of incision at the top right. Although, the incision may be accidental damage and not a decorative feature.

WoB.25

Present location	French Institute of Oriental Archaeology
Find spot	Deir el-Medina
Published	Vandier d'Abbadie 1937: 80 VA number 2386
Dimensions	5.5 x 5.1 cm
Material	Limestone
Colour	Black, ochre, white and green

WoB.25: IFAO VA 2386 (Photograph Author's own) © IFAO.

This colourful fragment, with breaks around the edges and across the surface, shows a bed frame outlined in black with an ochre stripe. It has a thick footboard, but the leg of the bed is plain in design. To the viewer's right the torso of a woman can be seen. The bottom of her black wig is visible; her hair falls behind her shoulder and lacks definition. It is possible she is wearing a white broad collar. She turns towards the viewer's right and could be sitting on the bed or standing behind the bed. Her arm, which is ochre coloured is also visible. There is a dark ochre shape on the mattress of the bed; it is possible this is a child, but it lacks clarity.

The background of the scene is very colourful with a geometric design of black, white and light ochre. Vandier d'Abbadie (1937: 80) suggested that this could be a garland however; it may represent painted wall decoration. Beneath the bed a pile of objects can be seen, the exact nature of which is difficult to determine.

WoB.26

Present location	French Institute of Oriental Archaeology
Find spot	Deir el-Medina, '*Kom du Grand Puits*', excavated 1949 (marked 13.3.49)
Published	Vandier d'Abbadie 1959: 187, Plates CXX, CXXII VA number 2859
Dimensions	-
Material	Limestone
Colour	Black and ochre

WoB.26: IFAO VA 2859 (Photograph Author's own) © IFAO.

Drawn on an uneven surface in black outline, the scene shows a woman sitting on a bed facing the viewer's left. Her facial features are destroyed and only the ends of her short wig are visible. She wears a complex wrap-around dress and it is possible a child is sitting on her lap. She holds a bouquet of papyrus flowers in her right hand, although only one is clearly visible now. The woman's feet rest on a footstool and the contours of her lower body are evident, as is the edge of her robe.

The god Bes is incorporated into the outer legs of the bed, which has a tall footboard to the viewer's left and a thick mattress to the viewer's right. It is possible the bed had a central leg, which also incorporated the god Bes; however, this is not clear. Various objects are depicted beneath the bed including a kohl tube with stopper and a mirror. The disc of the mirror is ochre coloured, as is the upper body of Bes (to the viewer's right); the addition of colour may be accidental or applied later. To the view's left a tall bouquet of papyrus flowers can be seen, similar in design to those incorporated into the legs of the bed, as seen on ostracon WoB.2.

The uneven surface of the ostracon has been used to create a foreground in which a cat is depicted in the centre of the image. Vandier d'Abbadie (1959:187) suggested this was foreign to the scene and the drawing inferior in style. Given the badly erased nature of the artefact it is difficult to make a judgement, although it is drawn in the same black outline as the body of the sketch, suggesting it was created contemporaneously. Heart shaped convolvulus leaves are also depicted in the foreground.

WoB.27

Present location	French Institute of Oriental Archaeology
Find spot	Deir el-Medina, '*Le Grand Puits*', excavated 1949 (marked 24.3.49)
Published	Vandier d'Abbadie 1959: 158, Plate CXXI VA Number 2860
Dimensions	–
Material	Limestone
Colour	Black and ochre

WoB.27: IFAO VA 2860, © IFAO.

This fragmentary ostracon shows a woman sitting on a bed facing the viewer's right. She wears a long tripartite wig with individual braids differentiated. The ochre tone of her flesh is visible beneath her robe from neck to thigh; this then fades to white, although no pleats of her robe are shown. She wears a floral collar around her neck, which is similar in design to the floral collar hanging on the wall. This may represent a real floral garland or painted wall decoration. Serpent imagery is visible on the bed frame. The excavators' markings indicate this was found in '*Le Grand Puits*' 23rd March 1949.

WoB.28

Present location	Unknown
Find spot	Deir el-Medina, '*Le Grand Puits*', excavated 1949 (marked 20.2.49)
Published	Vandier d'Abbadie 1959: 188, Plate CXXI VA Number 2861
Dimensions	–
Material	Limestone
Colour	Black and ochre

WoB.28: VA 2861 (Vandier d'Abbadie 1959: 188, Plate CXXI) © IFAO.

Vandier d'Abbadie (1959: 188) believed this ostracon was stored at the French Institute of Oriental Archaeology; however, it has not been possible to locate it in their archive. The ostracon, as published by Vandier d'Abbadie, shows a woman sitting on a bed, the frame of which is just visible; she turns to the viewer's right. She wears a voluminous pleated robe and a long enveloping black wig. It is likely a female companion stood behind her; the ends of her wig can be seen to the viewer's left. The excavators' markings indicate this was found in '*Le Grand Puits*' on 20th February 1949.

WoB.29

Present location	French Institute of Oriental Archaeology
Find spot	Deir el-Medina, '*Kom du Grand Puits*', excavated 1950 (marked 28.1.50)
Published	Vandier d'Abbadie 1959: 188, Plate CXXI VA Number 2862
Dimensions	–
Material	Limestone
Colour	Black, ochre, grey and white

WoB.29: IFAO VA 2862 (Photograph Author's own) © IFAO.

Drawn with a high degree of skill, this ostracon shows the frame of a bed, decorated with serpent imagery. Above which, upon the upper edge of the ostracon, the folds of a robe are shown; it is likely a woman sat on the bed facing the viewer's right. Beneath the bed a variety of objects are displayed. From the viewer's left the legs and feet of Bes are shown in a stylised manner. He wears a spotted kilt, suggestive of animal skin; this has a long sash hanging to the front. It is likely he was incorporated into the leg of the bed. Next to this a large pot is drawn; the ochre outline is visible and black has been added in parts to suggest a lustrous surface. The bowl has a rim and deep base, with a small foot; inside the bowl a large elongated cone is depicted. Adjacent to this, a mirror is illustrated; the disc is drawn with an ochre outline and white fill, to suggest a gleaming surface. Next to this a kohl tube, with applicator and stopper, is depicted. All items sit on a black baseline. The excavators' markings indicate this was found in the '*Kom du Grand Puits*' in 1950.

WoB.30

Present location	French Institute of Oriental Archaeology
Find spot	Deir el-Medina, '*Kom du Grand Puits*', excavated 1950 (marked 17.12.50)
Published	Vandier d'Abbadie 1959: 187, Plate CXXI VA Number 2863
Dimensions	–
Material	Limestone
Colour	Black and ochre

This fragmentary ostracon shows a bed frame with serpent imagery. To the viewer's left a footstool can be seen with the tip of a foot resting upon it. It is likely

WoB.30: IFAO VA 2863 (Photograph Author's own) © IFAO.

this belonged to a woman sitting on the bed, facing the viewer's right; the edges of her robe are also visible. A child is depicted on a thick mattress, facing the seated figure. Bes is incorporated into the leg of the bed, to the viewer's right; incision has been used to define his tall, plumed feather headdress. The marks are clear and white limestone is evident beneath; it is possible this was a later addition to the composition, or it could be accidental. The scene has been drawn with a black outline and limited ochre fill; it was composed on a black baseline.

WoB.31

Present location	French Institute of Oriental Archaeology
Find spot	Deir el-Medina, marked (N.E.T.)
Published	Vandier d'Abbadie 1959: 189, Plate CXXI VA Number 2866 Bruyère 1952a: 66, Figure 53
Dimensions	–
Material	Potsherd
Colour	Whitewash and black

Drawn in black outline on a white-washed potsherd, this ostracon depicts a woman lying on a bed facing the viewer's left. The image is crudely drawn and lacks detail. The woman appears to wear a long wig; no robe is depicted. One arm lies flat against the bed; the other is raised. Rolls of flesh are shown on her abdomen and her navel is indicated. The footboard of the bed is seen behind her head. The scene is atypical in many respects, including material, orientation and iconography. The ostracon was found during Bruyère's excavation in 1946 and is marked with

WoB.31: IFAO VA 2866 (Photograph Author's own) © IFAO.

N.E.T. which Toivari-Viitala (2014: 235-6) suggests came from '*au nord de l'enceinte du temple*' found in '*maison J*'. This was an area of votive chapels; Bruyère used a variety of terms to describe places of cult outside the home.

WoB.32

Present location	French Institute of Oriental Archaeology
Find spot	Deir el-Medina, '*Kom du Sud*', excavated 1930
Published	Vandier d'Abbadie 1937: 77, Plate LIV VA Number 2363
Dimensions	–
Material	Limestone
Colour	Black and ochre

WoB.32: IFAO VA 2363 (Photograph Author's own) © IFAO.

This ostracon shows the god Bes incorporated into the leg of a bed. It is drawn in black outline with ochre details. A large dish stands next to the god, which contains a tall cone. It is likely a woman is sitting on the bed; her robes are just visible to the viewer's left. There is evidence of incision, possibly used to suggest the footboard of the bed or the robes of a standing companion; although this may have been natural damage which incurred through use and disposal.

WoB.33

Present location	Louvre E 14295
Find spot	Deir el-Medina, Theban Tomb 210, Tomb of Raweben
Published	Bruyère 1928: 22-23 Vandier d'Abbadie 1937: Plate XLIX VA Number 2335
Dimensions	–
Material	Limestone
Colour	Black and ochre

WoB.33: Louvre E 14295 (Vandier d'Abbadie 1937: Plate XLIX) © IFAO.

This ostracon was found in the tomb of Raweben (TT 210) by Bruyère (1928: 22-23), who referred to it as an 'ex voto'. An inscription on the lintel above the entrance to the tomb indicates Raweben was the son the sculptor Piay, who lived during the reigns of Horemheb, Rameses I and Seti I. Many monuments of Piay have been recovered from Deir el-Medina, although Raweben's tomb is poorly preserved (Davies 1999: 178-179). Raweben appears only fleetingly in the archaeological record of the village. He is mentioned on an ostracon which names him as the father of Ramose; the ostracon is dated to the reign of Rameses II (Davies 1999: 180).

As the only '*Scènes de Gynécées*' ostracon with a firm context from a tomb, this is a unique find. However, the imagery is consistent with others in the dataset. It shows a woman sitting on a bed facing the viewer's right; she rests her feet on a foot stool and is attended by two companions. One stands in front of her and offers a large ornate dish, with a sculptured foot and detailed rim; it is likely this contained a cone. While the other attendant stands to the rear, possibly arranging her hair. Vandier d'Abbadie (1937:82) suggested this was a '*Scènes de Gynécées*', accompanied by a scene of hairdressing. There is a circular, ochre shape close to the chest of the seated figure; this may be a child.

All women are attired in a similar manner, suggesting they are social equals. All wear long black wigs, the style of the seated figure's wig is not apparent, but her companions wear enveloping wigs. All wigs are tied with a fillet and surmounted with a lotus flower; head cones are visible on two of the women, but it is likely they were worn by all three. The women are attired in complex wrap-around dresses; most detail is preserved on the companion to the viewer's right. The women are dressed in their finery with earrings visible on two and the remains of a floral collar seen on the seated central figure.

The narrative is composed around the bed. This has a large footboard to the viewer's left and the frame has remnants of serpent imagery. The scene is drawn on a black baseline and is well balanced.

WoB.34

Present location	Louvre E 143375
Find spot	Deir el Medina
Published	Vandier d'Abbadie 1937: 72, Plate LIII
	VA Number 2352
Dimensions	–
Material	Limestone
Colour	Black and ochre

This fragmentary ostracon depicts a woman turning towards the viewer's right. Her head and upper torso are all that remain. She wears a dark wig, tied with a fillet, possibly floral, with a lotus flower to the front. She raises her right hand in a gesture of thanks or greeting. The translucent folds of her gown are visible on her arm. There appears to be a child lying in front of her, only a foot and lower leg are visible now. Given the similarity to other scenes in the dataset it is likely the woman is sitting on a bed, upon which the child lies.

To the viewer's right, the head and hands of a figure can be seen pouring water from a tall vase into a bowl. They wear a lotus flower, fillet and cone upon their head. It is likely this was a companion to the figure opposite. Vandier d'Abbadie (1937: 69, 82) believed this ostracon to be a scene of toilette, a subset of the '*Scènes de Gynécées*'.

The scene takes place under a decorative border. This may have been a horizontal floral garland hung on the walls or it may represent painted wall decoration, either of which would indicate a room bedecked.

WoB.34: Louvre E 14375 (Photograph Author's own).

WoB.35

Present location	Louvre E 14336
Find spot	Deir el-Medina
Published	Vandier d'Abbadie 1937: 72, Plate LII
	VA Number 2347
	Andreu 2002: 115, Number 55
Dimensions	10 x 6.2 x 0.7 cm
Material	Limestone
Colour	Black, ochre, white and yellow

This small ostracon shows the lower body of a woman, facing the viewer's right. There is a child upon her

WoB.35: Louvre E 14336 (Photograph Author's own).

knee, which raises a hand in a playful gesture towards the seated figure. The woman wears a pleated robe with the fringed edge visible and rests her feet upon a foot stool. Her feet are rudimentarily drawn. Given the integration of the god Bes into the furniture leg, it is likely this was a bed upon which the woman sat. The god has his hands on his hips. He wears a tall, plumed feather headdress and kilt, with a sash to the front. Serpent imagery is also seen on the bed frame. The ostracon is very smooth and was possibly chosen due to its suitability as a drawing surface.

WoB.36

Present location	Louvre E 14337
Find spot	Deir el-Medina
Published	Vandier d'Abbadie 1937: 70-71, Plate LIII VA Number 2341 Andreu 2002: 112-113, Number 52 Backhouse 2012: 29, Figure 3
Dimensions	11.5 x 7.6 x. 2.2 cm
Material	Limestone
Colour	Black, ochre and grey

In this incomplete scene a woman approaches from the viewer's right, turning towards the viewer's left. She carries a vase and bowl in her hands. Smoke appears to be rising from the bowl, although it has been suggested that this is water (Andreu 2002: 113). The woman is attired in a complex wrap-around dress. She wears an enveloping wig tied with a fillet, surmounted with a cone, with a lotus flower to the front. Opposite her the feet and lower robe are all that remain of a companion; it is likely this was a woman sitting on a bed, the frame of which is visible behind both women. It is probable that she was attired in a similar manner to the standing figure.

The scene takes place beneath a decorative border, which may represent a horizontal floral garland or painted wall decoration. Convolvulus leaves are delicately drawn and threaded through the scene. The bed frame has serpent imagery and a thick mattress. The image has a natural symmetry with the two pairs of feet touching to form an arch. Andreu (2002: 113) suggests the standing figure is either a woman of the household or the mistress of the house herself. It is more likely the mistress of the house is seated receiving offerings and gifts, presented by a member of her family or a close friend. The intimate nature of the scene and similarity in style of dress suggests the two women were social equals.

At over two centimetres in thickness this is a substantial piece of limestone. Composed on a black baseline with considerable coloured fill, it has been drawn with care and attention to detail. This suggests this ostracon was created to be displayed, possibly in the home.

WoB.36: Louvre E 14337 (Photograph Author's own).

WoB.37

Present location	Louvre E 25302
Find spot	-
Published	Keimer 1940-1945, Plate IV - 13
Dimensions	12.3 x 11.4 x 1.9 cm
Material	Limestone
Colour	Black and ochre

WoB.37: Louvre E 25302 (Photograph Author's own).

Keimer (1940-1945: 4) believed this ostracon showed a woman sitting on a bed, turning towards the viewer's left, with a child behind her. However, it is more likely to depict a woman sitting on the bed reaching towards a child in front of her; which lies on a thick mattress. All that remains of this figure is her arm, stretching towards the child. Brunner-Traut (1956: 70) also believed Keimer's interpretation to be incorrect.

The main figure is depicted wearing a waist length enveloping wig. Individual braids are indicated, including one thick plait at the back; the wig is tied with a fillet, possibly floral, the string of which is visible at the top of her head which is surmounted with a cone. She is attired in a complex wrap-around dress; a large-bat wing sleeve is visible as she reaches towards her seated companion. Ochre diagonal lines may represent serpent imagery on the bed frame. A faint ochre line encompasses the figures suggesting a canopy. The ostracon has no firm provenance although Keimer (1940-1945: 1) believed it came from the Theban necropolis.

WoB.38

Present location	Louvre E 23518
Find spot	Deir el-Medina
Published	Vandier d'Abbadie 1937: 84, 77, Plate LIII VA Number 2344
Dimensions	8.5 x 12 x 2.2 cm
Material	Limestone
Colour	Black and ochre

This unique scene shows a woman sitting on a bed facing the viewer's right; she cradles a child in her arms. She wears a long headdress or headscarf, similar to a figurine found in a tomb at Deir el-Medina (Bruyère 1937a: Figure 41). This is tied with a fillet, with a lotus flower to the front and surmounted with a cone. The sleeve on her dress is visible but no pleats are indicated; she wears a broad collar, delineated with four black lines. Her legs and feet are perhaps behind the bed frame; two legs of the bed can be seen, which take the form of the god Bes, rudimentarily drawn. The bed also has a footboard to the viewer's left; it is plain and defined with a double line. Vandier d'Abbadie (1937: 82) referred to this as an image of the nursery, a subset of the '*Scènes de Gynécées*'.

WoB.38: Louvre E 23518 (Photograph Author's own).

The most idiosyncratic feature of the scene is the small black figure with an upraised arm which appears above the child. Vandier d'Abbadie (1937: 84) suggested this was the *ka* of the infant, the shadow of the new-born. She believed the image depicted celebrations following a royal birth, as only living monarchs were depicted with their *ka*. However, there are no indications to suggest the seated woman is royalty. It is possible a mirror is depicted to the viewer's right, next to the black figure, with a circular disc outlined.

Behind the seated figure, to the viewer's left, four women raise their arms in a gesture of adoration, celebration or of offering. One, if not two of them, hold something in their hands but the exact nature remains unclear. Vandier d'Abbadie (1937: 84) believed they were clapping and singing in praise of the birth of the child. They are all dressed in long translucent robes which reveal their slender figures. Their pubic triangles are indicated, and it is possible one or two of them are wearing a hip-girdle. They are all decorated with ochre coloured cones upon their heads. Convolvulus leaves encircle the bed, suggesting a floral canopy.

The scene is drawn in black outline with ochre fill added for cones, flesh and the bed frame only; the scene is set on a black baseline. The composition is well balanced and carefully drawn; although the seated figure appears much larger than her companions, suggesting her superior status.

WoB.39

Present location	Louvre E 25324
Find spot	Deir el-Medina
Published	Vandier d'Abbadie 1937: 70, Plate L VA number 2340
Dimensions	2.1 x 11.7 x 2.1 cm
Material	Limestone
Colour	Black and ochre/red

This fragmentary ostracon shows the corner of a bed frame. Two legs of the bed remain, which take the form of the god Bes; he wears a tall, feather plumed headdress and a kilt, with a long sash to the front. The bed frame is decorated with a wavy line suggesting serpent imagery. The feet of a woman, facing the viewer's right, can be seen behind the bed, with the pleats of her robe

WoB.39: Louvre E 25324 (Photograph Author's own).

outlined in ochre. She appears to be standing behind a woman sitting on the bed, seen at the extreme right of the scene. Only the lower back and a portion of the wig remain of the seated figure. A child is lying on the bed with its head against the footboard to the viewer's left; the child appears to have an outstretched arm. Vandier d'Abbadie (1937: 82) referred to this as a scene of the nursery, accompanied by a scene of hairdressing, both of which she suggested were subsets of the '*Scènes de Gynécées*'.

The composition has been drawn with an ochre outline first, with black added later, both outline and fill.

WoB.40

Present location	Berlin ÄM 21461
Find spot	Deir el-Medina, excavated 1913, near the '*Kom du Sud*'
Published	Schäfer 1916: 30 Brunner-Traut 1956: 70/71, Plate XXV Andreu-Lanoë 2013: 318, Figure 167b
Dimensions	11.5 x 10 x 1 cm
Material	Limestone
Colour	Black, ochre and yellow

This incomplete scene shows a woman sitting on a bed facing the viewer's right. She wears a long tripartite wig tied with a fillet; this may be floral, with a lotus flower to the front and surmounted with a cone. She is attired in a complex wrap-around dress, of which great attention to detail has been paid. The transparent nature reveals the contours of her body and the fringed edge of the central cloth is defined. She also wears a broad collar. Her right hand reaches behind her and her left hand stretches in front, holding a bowl which is yellow in colour. She rests her feet on a footstool. It is likely the full scene contained a standing woman to the viewer's right, approaching the seated figure. She may have been offering a vase; vases and bowls were commonly seen together.

WoB.40: Berlin ÄM 21461, © Staatliche Museen zu Berlin – PK, Ägyptisches Museum und Papyrussammlung, photograph: Sandra Steiß.

The bed is richly decorated with a high footboard to the viewer's left; the bed frame has serpent imagery and an ornate frill hangs from it. This may be a floral garland, as suggested by Schäfer (1916: 30) in relation to ostracon EB.1. The god Bes is incorporated into the central leg of the bed. Behind and above the seated figure two large floral collars are depicted; these may represent hanging floral collars or painted wall decoration. Convolvulus leaves are threaded throughout the scene; they are delicately drawn with heart shaped leaves on a twisting vine. The image has been drawn on a baseline and carefully executed, demonstrating a high degree of artistry.

WoB.41

Present location	Berlin ÄM 21773
Find spot	Deir el-Medina, excavated 1913, near the '*Kom du Sud*'
Published	Schäfer 1916: 30 Brunner-Traut 1956: 70, Plate XXV
Dimensions	8 x.10.8 cm
Material	Limestone
Colour	Black and ochre/red

This badly erased ostracon shows a woman sitting on a bed facing the viewer's right. She wears a long tripartite wig with a lotus flower to the front, surmounted with a cone. Her facial features are destroyed but an ochre colour skin tone can be determined. She stretches her right arm behind her; the rest of her features are now lost. It is likely she sits with her legs on the rear side of the bed, with a companion approaching, facing the viewer's left. A mirror disc with a black outline, ochre fill and a black handle can be seen in the centre of the scene; it is probable the seated figure held the mirror

WoB.41a: Berlin ÄM 21773, © Staatliche Museen zu Berlin – PK, Ägyptisches Museum und Papyrussammlung, photograph: Sandra Steiß.

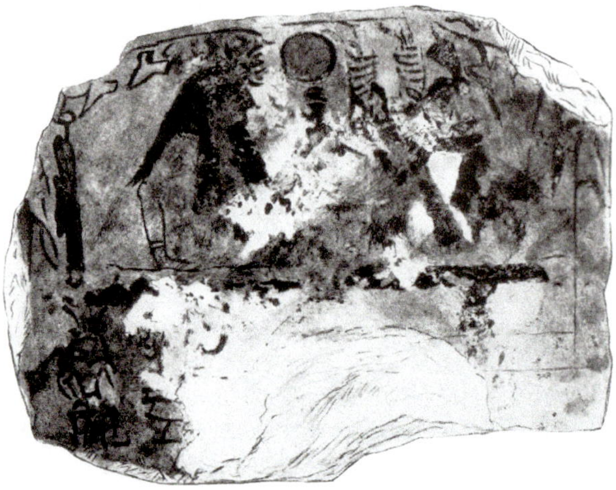

WoB.41b: Berlin ÄM 21773 (Brunner-Traut 1956: 70, Plate XXV).

to admire her appearance. The attendant could be presenting a floral collar, or this could be hung in the background.

The scene takes place under a canopy which has convolvulus leaves wrapped around it. Much of the definition of this has been lost but the original photograph from Brunner-Traut's publication shows the canopy distinctly, see WoB.41b. To the viewer's left the god Bes is visible incorporated into the leg of the bed. Next to Bes part of a deep bowl with a rim and foot can be seen, the right side of which is erased. It is likely another figure of the god Bes, incorporated into a bed leg, was depicted to the viewer's right, although now badly damaged. The bed has a tall footboard to the viewer's left.

WoB.42

Present location	Turin S.06305
Find spot	Deir el-Medina, excavated 1905
Published	Turin Museum Online Catalogue

WoB.42: Turin S.06305 (Photograph Author's own).

Dimensions	10.4 x 8 x 1 cm
Material	Limestone
Colour	Black, ochre and white

Found by Schiaparelli, the incomplete scene shows the lower back of a woman sitting on a bed, facing the viewer's right. To her rear, also facing the viewer's right, stands another woman. Both women are similarly attired, suggesting they are social equals; more details survive of the standing figure. She wears a long black enveloping wig tied with a fillet, surmounted with a cone. She is clad in a complex wrap-around dress. In her outstretched hands she holds a floral collar; the tie ending is visible. It is likely she is offering the collar to her seated companion.

The bed frame contains serpent imagery. Beneath which a mirror is depicted; it is outlined in black, with white fill for the disc, suggesting a luminous surface. Next to this a kohl tube and applicator stand, also outlined in black with white fill. The scene has been carefully drawn on a black baseline with outline and fill. The intimate and touching nature of this moment in time has been captured by the ancient artist. The tonal palette is subtle but may have faded over time.

WoB.43

Present location	Turin S.07403
Find spot	Deir el-Medina, excavated 1905
Published	Turin Museum Online Catalogue
Dimensions	4.5 x 4 x 0.5 cm
Material	Limestone
Colour	Black, ochre and grey

WoB.43: Turin S.07403, © Museo Egizio, photograph by Franco Lovera.

Found by Schiaparelli, this ostracon shows a woman sitting on a bed facing the viewer's right. In her outstretched hand she holds a bowl. It is likely she wears a complex wrap-around dress, demonstrated by the folds of pleated fabric falling over the bed frame. The bed is shown with a deep cushion; the frame is decorated with a serpent motif. Before the seated figure a companion approaches; it is likely this is a female dressed in a similar manner. In her extended hand she holds a lotus flower; the petals are individually drawn and sharply pointed, suggesting a blue lotus. This is a rare example of reciprocal gift giving; it implies social intimacy and possibly kinship.

WoB.44

Present location	Turin S.06289
Find spot	Deir el-Medina, excavated 1905
Published	Trapani 2012: 539, Figure 6 Turin Museum Online Catalogue
Dimensions	20.5 x 15 cm
Material	Limestone
Colour	Black, grey and ochre

WoB.44: Turin S. 06289 (Photograph Author's own).

This large ostracon shows a woman sitting on a bed facing the viewer's left. She wears an enveloping wig, which falls heavily over her shoulders and back; individual plaits can be differentiated. She is clad in a voluminous robe, most likely a complex wrap-around dress; the pleats of which are outlined in ochre and hang over the edge of the bed. A child lies in front of her, turning towards the viewer's right. The child has a long body, which suggests it is not newly born. The limbs are delineated in black outline with ochre fill. The child's head is turned upwards, and it appears to wear a necklace of black beads. Although the scene is badly damaged, it is possible a female attendant stands behind the child, suggested by the lower tresses of a long black wig, and the child is in effect turning towards her.

The bed upon which the woman and child sit is drawn with an ochre outline, with black outline added to some sections. It has a thick cushion; upon which the presence of the woman and child causes a slight indentation. Ochre shading is used to suggest the plumpness of the material. The bedframe has two sections outlined in black. The upper portion is decorated with a serpent, drawn with a black upper outline and ochre lower outline. Grey marks are used to indicate the pattern of the skin. Beneath the bed two large bowls stand; they have a rim, a deep base and small foot. Bowls of this type are depicted on many of the '*Scènes de Gynécées*' for example WoB.29. As is common in other depictions, the two bowls contain cones. One is ochre coloured; the other has markings suggesting an uneven surface. In addition, a mirror is stowed under the bed. The handle appears off centre; it is possible it takes the form of a standard. If so, this would be a unique depiction in the dataset. Next to the mirror is a kohl tube and applicator. The god Bes is incorporated into the two visible legs of the bed, both are damaged. He is shown with a tall, feather plumed headdress and wearing a kilt, most likely with a sash to the front.

To the rear of the woman, to the viewer's right a mass of dark foliage curves around the scene. These may be convolvulus leaves; it is possible they form a canopy over the woman and child. The scene is drawn on a base line, with attention to detail, utilising much colour fill.

WoB.45

Present location	Stockholm MM 14045
Find spot	Unknown (From the Gayer-Anderson Collection)
Published	Peterson 1973: 104, Plate 136
Dimensions	15.5 x 7.1 cm
Material	Limestone
Colour	Black, ochre and yellow

This ostracon shows a standing woman turning towards the viewer's left. She wears a long enveloping wig, tied

WoB.45: Stockholm MM 14045
(Photograph Author's own).

with a fillet from which a lotus flower blossoms. The pointed petals and small flower suggest it was a blue lotus; it has been drawn with great attention to detail. The woman wears a complex wrap-around dress and large hoop earrings. She holds, in outstretched hands, a bowl and vase, both of which are yellow in colour. It is likely these were a gift to a female companion sitting opposite her; the edge of the bed frame and possibly the bottom of her robe and toe are just visible. A creeping plant tendril, with flowers in bloom, runs behind the standing figure; this may have formed a canopy over the bed. The scene has been drawn with skill on a black baseline; the palette is subtle and suggests a skilled artist.

WoB.46

Present location	Stockholm MM 14061
Find spot	Unknown (From the Gayer-Anderson Collection)
Published	Peterson 1973: 104, Plate135
Dimensions	11.1 x 9.2 cm
Material	Limestone
Colour	Black and ochre

The scene depicts a woman sitting on a bed facing the viewer's right; all that remains is the bottom of her pleated robe. The bed frame is outlined in black with serpent imagery. Lying on the bed is a child, facing the seated figure. It is depicted in detail with black outline and ochre fill for the flesh; facial features are indicated,

WoB.46: Stockholm MM 14061
(Photograph Author's own).

and tuffs of hair cover the head. The child raises a hand towards a standing figure in a playful gesture of affection.

Approaching the seated woman is a female companion, facing the viewer's left. She is clad in a complex wrap-around dress. She wears a long enveloping wig with a fillet, which may be floral; a large discus earring is also depicted. The facial features of the standing figure are crudely drawn in a cursory manner. She raises her hands in a gesture of offering towards the seated figure. She holds a yellow shallow dish in one hand, the other hand is destroyed; it is likely she carried a tall vase in this. Her feet are rudimentarily drawn and are disproportionately large. Sketched on a black baseline, the scene is crudely executed and lacks refinement.

WoB.47

Present location	Stockholm MM 14070
Find spot	Unknown (From the Gayer-Anderson Collection)
Published	Peterson 1973: 103, Plate 133
Dimensions	11.6 x 18.1 cm
Material	Limestone
Colour	Black, ochre, pink and grey

This badly faded ostracon incorporates some unique motifs into a standard genre. A woman sits in the middle of a bed facing the viewer's right. Although her facial features are destroyed the tresses of her wig are still visible, as is her lower body. She wears a complex wrap-around dress. Her feet are draw at an angle, which gives a sense of movement, as if she is swinging her legs. She reaches an arm forward towards the woman approaching from the viewer's right. The standing female figure is naked, except for a hip-girdle which is visible on her left thigh only; it does

WoB.47: Stockholm MM 14070
(Photograph Author's own).

not continue around her torso. Her pubic triangle is clearly indicated. She also wears a long wig, probably originally enveloping in style, tied with a small fillet; her facial features are delicately drawn.

Behind the standing figure a disproportionately large monkey approaches the scene. It is outlined in black and has been coloured a blue/green shade with particular attention being given to the facial features. This has been carefully drawn with the texture of fur indicated by small black lines. There is a band or ribbon tied around the waist suggesting the animal was domesticated but it could also be mimicking the girdle worn by the female attendant. The monkey appears to be holding something, possibly a bolt of cloth or ivory tusks. This could be a parody of tribute scenes found in New Kingdom tombs, for example the tomb of Rekhmire (TT 100) (Davies 1935: Plate VI).

To the viewer's left a naked figure stands. Peterson (1973: 103) notes the difficulty of identifying the sex of the attendant but suggests it is most likely to be a woman due to the nature of the scene. However, the shaved head is unusual for female figures in this dataset. A similar figure was published by Keimer (1940-45: 9, Plate VII 18), which he believed to be female. The figure is badly proportioned with elongated legs and a steatopygous body. The naked figure appears to hold two objects, both of which are difficult to identify but one could be a fan. The nudity of the subsidiary figures suggests they are servants not social equals.

Bes is incorporated into the legs of the bed; serpent imagery is also seen on the bed frame. A tray with a large cone is stowed under the bed; the cone has markings suggesting an undulating substance or form. Artistically and iconographically the scene is complex, there is a lack of unified baseline with the servant figures and the monkey in the foreground. All human figures are drawn with a black outline and ochre fill for the flesh. However, there is tonal variety with the inclusion of the monkey.

WoB.48

Present location	Stockholm MM 14 137
Find spot	Unknown (From the Gayer-Anderson Collection)
Published	Peterson 1973: 103, Plate 134
Dimensions	5.2 x 7.7 cm
Material	Limestone
Colour	Black, ochre and white

WoB.48: Stockholm MM 14137
(Photograph Author's own).

This is a rare scene, which shows a figure sitting on the bed facing the viewer's left. No robe is evident; the ochre tone of the flesh is clearly visible. Given the similarity to other scenes in this dataset it is likely to be a woman. She wears a black, ill-defined wig, tied with a fillet, surmounted with a cone and with a lotus flower to the front. She stretches out her right arm and holds a dish containing an elongated cone; alternatively, this could be bread as suggested by Peterson (1973: 103). Beneath the bed two more elongated cones are outlined in ochre; it is possible these are on a ledge which is part of the bed. A child lies behind the seated woman, raising an arm in a gesture of affection. The woman rests her feet on a footstool.

Next to the seated woman, to the viewer's left, three large flowers bloom; their stems and petals are clearly defined. It is towards these the seated figure turns. The bed is surrounded by an abundance of foliage, which suggests a canopy. It could be convolvulus leaves, but it is depicted in a haphazard style which makes identification difficult. The bed is crudely drawn, with a footboard to the viewer's right and two legs which take the form of papyri columns.

The scene may have been composed on a baseline which is now largely destroyed. It was drawn with a black outline with ochre and white fill. Overall, the image lacks refinement and skill but contains some unusual and noteworthy features of iconography.

WoB.49

Present location	Previously Munich Ä11 (Destroyed in World War II)
Find spot	–
Published	Brunner-Traut 1956: 71, Figure III
Dimensions	18 x 16 cm
Material	Limestone
Colour	Black, ochre, yellow and white

WoB.49: Previously Munich Ä11, destroyed in WWII (Brunner-Traut 1956: 71, Figure III).

This artist's impression is the only record of this ostracon which was destroyed in World War II. It shows a woman sitting on a bed facing the viewer's right. Her right arm stretches behind her; only her upper body remains. In front of her face is an ill-defined object. Behind her a companion approaches carrying a bowl containing a cone, which is marked to suggest an uneven surface. It is likely both women were dressed in a similar manner; most probably clad in complex wrap-around dresses. Both wear a long enveloping wig tied with a three-quarter fillet, which is surmounted with a cone. The seated figure may also wear a broad collar and a lotus flower attached to her fillet. There is a black mark on the faces of both women, the meaning of which is unknown. It must be remembered this is an artist's impression, of which the accuracy is unknown.

The bed is depicted with a footboard to the viewer's left. It is likely that the god Bes was incorporated into the leg of the bed, as suggested by the angular shape drawn to the viewer's left, beneath the bed frame. Convolvulus leaves thread through the scene, possibly attached to a canopy of vines, now mostly destroyed.

WoB.50

Present location	Munich ÄS 1543
Find spot	–
Published	Brunner-Traut 1956: 71, Plate XXVI
Dimensions	14 x 12.5 cm
Material	Limestone
Colour	Black, ochre and beige

While Brunner-Traut (1956: 71) stated this ostracon was destroyed in the war it has been located in Munich

WoB.50a: Munich ÄS 1543, © State Museum of Egyptian Art, photograph by Marianne Franke.

WoB.50b: Munich ÄS 1543 (Brunner-Traut 1956: 71, Plate XXVI).

Museum. Although the colour has faded considerably since the copy was made, it is evident that there are a number of inaccuracies between the original and the artist's impression. The ostracon shows a woman sitting on a bed facing the viewer's right. She raises a hand in a gesture of greeting or thanks to a female figure standing before her. Her companion approaches from the viewer's right and presents a bowl and vase to the seated figure; their hands touch suggesting bonds of kin or friendship. Both are clad in similar attire, confirming their status as social equals. The standing figure is best preserved. She wears a long enveloping wig, tied with a fillet; it is likely this was surmounted with a cone and lotus flower to the front. These details were not shown in the original copy (Image b). An earring is also visible beneath her wig and her facial features are delicately drawn. Both women wear a complex wrap-around dress and their feet are visible beneath their robes; their toes touch forming an arch. This parallels the gesture of greeting above; it also creates a sense of intimacy.

The bed frame has serpent imagery and a thick mattress. The original copy (Image b) suggests there was a vine with convolvulus leaves forming a canopy over the bed; this has not survived. Similarly, the original copy suggests convolvulus leaves also trailed from a vine held by the standing figure; the vine has survived but not the leaves.

Although badly erased, the subtle palette suggests this is the work of a skilled artist; the flesh is light beige not a heavy ochre colour. The scene was composed on a black baseline; drawn with outline and colour fill.

WoB.51

Present location	Brussels E 6777
Find spot	–
Published	Werbrouck 1953: 98 Brunner-Traut 1955: 12 Backhouse 2016: 156
Dimensions	12.5 x 12 cm
Material	Limestone
Colour	Black, ochre/red and yellow

Image not available due to copyright restrictions

This badly damaged ostracon was bought in Cairo or Luxor but was believed to be from Deir el-Medina by Werbrouck (1953: 98). He describes this as a scene of the harem. A digital image of this ostracon was examined for my PhD research but due to copyright restrictions it cannot be reproduced here. After a close examination of the image it was not possible to clarify the exact nature of the scene. However, a woman could be identified in the centre of the ostracon, facing the viewer's right. Only the top of her wig remains, surmounted with a cone. She is shown with her feet resting on a footstool, which is outlined in yellow and black. Given the similarity with other images in this dataset it is likely she is sitting on a bed. This was also the belief of Werbrouck (1953: 98); it is likely the angular shape to the viewer's right is the god Bes incorporated into the leg of the bed. A faint yellow line suggests a bed frame. Werbrouck (1953: 98) also proposed there was a child included in the scene; though, it is not possible to confirm this given the current state of preservation of the ostracon.

Behind the seated figure, to the viewer's left, a female companion stands with raised arms. This could be a scene of hairdressing. The companion, wearing a head cone and fillet, is shown with ochre coloured flesh. At least one more attendant is included in the scene, shown with raised arms before the seated figure, to the viewer's right. A floral collar is depicted at the top of the ostracon to the viewer's right; this may have been hung on the wall or may have indicated painted wall decoration. It is possible convolvulus leaves are shown to the viewer's right also.

The badly faded nature of the ostracon makes precise analysis difficult, but it appears the scene was drawn on a baseline and it includes a number of key motifs in the 'women on beds' dataset.

WoB.52

Present location	Brussels E 6779
Find spot	–
Published	Werbrouck 1953: 98 Backhouse 2016: 156
Dimensions	7 x 8.5 cm
Material	Limestone
Colour	Black and ochre/red

Image not available due to copyright restrictions

This fragmentary ostracon was believed to have come from Deir el-Medina by Werbrouck (1953: 98). A digital image of this ostracon was examined for my PhD research but due to copyright restrictions it cannot be reproduced here. Although badly faded it was possible to identify a woman standing to the viewer's right, turning to the viewer's left. She is wearing a long enveloping wig and is attired in a complex wrap-around dress. Her arms are raised in a gesture of offering; the goods she carries cannot be recognised but it is likely to be a tall vase and shallow dish.

The scene to the viewer's left is badly damaged; the outline of a bed frame is still visible, it includes a serpent motif, drawn in black outline. It is likely a woman sat on the bed facing the viewer's right, to receive the gifts from her standing companion. A large black convolvulus leaf is still visible in the centre of the ostracon. Although only a small portion of the scene remains, the iconography is consistent with the 'women on beds' dataset. It is possible the black markings to the viewer's right represent smoke damage.

WoB.53

Present location	SCA Magazine near Carter House, Qurna, O.WHTM 543
Find spot	Workmen's huts, '*Le Col*' (area between Deir el-Medina and Valley of the Kings)
Published	Toivari-Viitala 2014: 234, Figure 1
Dimensions	9.9 x 10.9 x 2.2 cm
Material	Limestone
Colour	Black and ochre/red

WoB.53: O.WHTM 543, SCA Magazine near Carter House, Qurna, © Toivari-Viitala.

This ostracon was found in a heap of rubble in one of the workmen's huts at Deir el-Medina (Toivari-Viitala 2014: 233). It was probably in the debris from the earlier excavation by the French Institute of Oriental Archaeology in 1935 when the huts were first cleared. It was drawn predominantly in black outline with ochre/red additions and limited fill. The scene shows a woman sitting on a bed facing the viewer's right. She wears a long black enveloping wig, with traces of ochre/red added. The wig is carelessly drawn but still the focal point of the scene. A fillet is tied around the wig, which is surmounted with a cone and a lotus flower to the front. The details paid to the coiffure are lacking in the facial features, which are rudimentary with only faint indications of an eye and mouth. The woman wears a complex wrap-around dress; this is schematically drawn and lacks the voluminous pleats seen in other examples in the dataset. Her right arm is slightly bent and reaches behind her, her left arm stretches forward. It is likely there is a child lying in front of the seated woman, towards whom she reaches.

The scene takes place under an arch of convolvulus leaves. Those to the viewer's left are drawn in black, while those to the viewer's right are drawn in ochre; all are sketched in a loose and free style. The bed has a footboard to the viewer's right; this is plain in design. The god Bes is incorporated into three legs of the bed, although much faded.

There appears to be a white mottled layer on the lower portion of the scene. This may be damage which occurred in antiquity or the result of weathering in modernity, most likely the latter.

3.3: 'Elaborate Beds' dataset

EB.1

Present Location	Berlin ÄM 21451
Find Spot	Deir el-Medina, excavated 1913, near the '*Kom du Sud*'
Published	Schäfer 1916: 30 Brunner-Traut 1956: 69, Plate XXV
Dimensions	12 x 15 cm
Material	Limestone
Colour	Black

This ostracon was found by Möller in 1913, when he was excavating Deir el-Medina for Berlin Museum, although it was not recorded in Anthes' (1943) later publication of Möller's work. It has been broken into two and subsequently joined together, although two large sections to the top left and bottom centre are missing. The image is drawn in black outline only; it shows a woman sitting on an 'elaborate bed', facing the viewer's right. She appears naked, except for a broad collar; her legs hang over the bed and no dress is depicted. She holds a child in her left arm, balanced in the bend of her

EB.1: Berlin ÄM 21451, © Staatliche Museen zu Berlin – PK, Ägyptisches Museum und Papyrussammlung, photograph: Sandra Steiß.

elbow. The child is also rudimentarily drawn, without care and attention.

An attendant sits or stands on the far side of the bed, turning towards the viewer's left. They too appear naked, but it is possible they also wear a broad collar. They raise a mirror and kohl tube in a gesture of offering to the seated figure. Their headdress is conical in shape with one long lock falling from the crown; these are discussed in Section 5.3d. Schäfer (1916: 30) believed the scene depicted the birth of a king and suggested the officiant was in fact the king wearing the white crown of Upper Egypt.

The bed is highly elaborate. It has a tall footboard and deep mattress; beneath the frame a series of thrills hang. Schäfer (1916: 30) suggested the bed was decorated with garlands. Three figures of the god Bes are incorporated into the legs of the bed. The figure to the viewer's left shows Bes playing a lute and standing on the drum of the bed leg; this is floral in design. Given the baseline, seen to the viewer's left, it is likely all three figures stood upon drums forming the feet of the bed legs. The central depiction of Bes shows the god winged and holding papyrus flowers. To the viewer's right Bes is also shown winged. No indications of a beard or plumed headdress are seen on these images of the god, which is unusual in this dataset.

EB.2

Present Location	Stockholm MM 14 005
Find spot	Unknown (From the Gayer-Anderson Collection)
Published	Peterson 1973: 103, Plate 132 Backhouse 2012: 30, Figure 4 Andreu-Lanöe 2013: 318, Figure 167a
Dimensions	18 x 18.9 cm
Material	Limestone
Colour	Black

This badly damaged ostracon has been broken into three and subsequently joined together. Originally from the Gayer-Anderson Collection it has no firm provenance but 'Der el Bahri' is written in pencil on one of the broken edges. Some figured ostraca were found during the Metropolitan Museum's excavations at Deir el-Bahri. A limited number have been published, for example by Winlock (1942: Figure 41) but this ostracon is not included in any of these publications.

Drawn in black outline only, the scene depicts a woman sitting on a bed facing the viewer's right. Her facial features are delicately rendered. She wears a long tripartite wig, with the tresses reaching to her hip region; this is tied with a fillet and surmounted with a large cone decorated with vertical lines to give a sense of texture. Peterson (1973: 103) noted she is clad in a large semi-transparent robe. However, although the sleeves are visible the lower edge of the robe is not indicated. It is possible she is wearing a cape or shawl around her shoulders, as seen in kiosk scenes K.1-2. She is also adorned in a broad collar decorated with a series of semi circles and a large disc shaped earring. Her legs hang over the bed and she is long in body.

EB.2: Stockholm MM 14005 (Photograph Author's own).

A child sits on her lap and is facing the viewer's left. The seated woman gives him her left breast. The child has carefully drawn facial features; he is naked except for a broad collar and possibly an earring. He has a long body and similar adornments to the seated woman; he does not look new-born.

The bed is highly decorated with a thick mattress raised at the left side, beneath which four rows of decorative thrills can be seen. It is possible these are garlands as suggested by Schäfer (1916: 30), in relation to ostracon EB.1. The god Bes is incorporated into the legs of the bed; he is shown in a squat position with hands on his hips and knees slightly bent with legs turned outwards. He has bulging eyes and pendulous breasts, with rolls of fat below a large, round navel. He wears a double layered spotted kilt, giving the suggestion of animal skin, with a long loin cloth, which reaches to the ground.

To the viewer's right, behind the seated woman, the remnants of a floral collar are visible; this is intricately woven. This may have been hung on the wall or represent painted wall decoration. To the viewer's left a mirror is visible and most likely the lower portion of a kohl tube. Encircling the bed are arrow shaped convolvulus leaves. Drawn on a black baseline with a confident and assured line, this was the work of a skilled artist.

EB.3

Present location	Petrie UC 45679
Find spot	-
Published	University College London Petrie Collection Online Catalogue

EB.3: Petrie UC 45679 (Photograph Author's own). Courtesy of Petrie Museum of Egyptian Archaeology.

Dimensions	c.8 x 9 x 2 cm
Material	Limestone
Colour	Black and ochre/red

This poorly preserved ostracon depicts the frame and one leg of an elaborate bed. Drawn in black and ochre/red outline, the god Bes is incorporated into the leg of the bed, to the viewer's left. Wearing a broad collar, one ear appears raised while the other slightly droops, giving him a comic, inquisitive appearance. Behind him several rows of thrills hang from the bed frame, perhaps garlands, as suggested by Schäfer (1916: 30) in relation to ostracon EB.1. Although badly damaged, it is possible to identify the arm and facial profile of a figure to the viewer's top right. This is likely to be a woman sitting on the bed or her companion.

3.4: Kiosk dataset

K.1

Present location	Louvre E 2533
Find spot	Deir el-Medina
Published	Vandier d'Abbadie 1937: 70, 83, Plate LII VA Number 2339 Vandier d'Abbadie 1957: 22-23, Plate 2 Andreu 2002: 113, Figure 53 Backhouse 2012: 31, Figure 5 Andreu-Lanoë 2013: 320, Figure 168
Dimensions	15.1 x 11.5 x 2.5 cm
Material	Limestone
Colour	Black, ochre, yellow and blue

This ostracon was originally conserved at the Museum of Agriculture in Cairo and donated to the Louvre in

K.1: Louvre E 2533 (Photograph Author's own).

1952. It shows a woman sitting on a stool, of which only the plump cushion remains. She holds a child in her lap, which is supported in the bend of her left arm. She cups her breast to give it to the child, whose arm reaches towards her in a gesture of affection. The child has a long body and is angular in form with its legs stretching vertically towards the seated figure. It is possible a penis is suggested by an upraised line in the midriff and genital region; this is uniform in the kiosk dataset. The child wears a side lock of youth and also possibly a broad collar; suggesting it is not a new-born child. The seated woman wears a broad collar and cape round her shoulders; the folds of the translucent fabric are visible on the extreme left of the scene. She is portrayed wearing a striking, heavy tripartite hairstyle, the significance of which is discussed in Section 5.3c. A female attendant offers the seated figure a mirror and kohl tube. She is naked except for a hip-girdle and also has a distinctive coiffure; the significance of which is discussed in Section 5.3d. The scene takes place under a kiosk or a temporary structure with heart shaped convolvulus leaves wrapped around a papyri shaped column and support.

Scholars disagree on the artistic worth of this ostracon. Vandier d'Abbadie (1937: 83) believed it appeared foreign, strange and morbid. While Andreu (2002:113) suggested it was not without elegance. The scene has an unusual colour palette, the features of the protagonists are outlined in light ochre then parts are emphasised in darker ochre. The flesh tone is yellow with facial features only rudimentarily inscribed; similarly, digits are only cursorily drawn. The use of shades of blue is also rare in this dataset, being the most expensive colour in the ancient artists' palette, yet traces are seen on the convolvulus leaves and broad collar. There is also a high degree of detail with colour used for the mirror handle and kohl tube stopper, which contrast each other and are the focal point of the scene; the mirror is depicted frontally, looking directly towards the viewer. The composition is well balanced with the two women making eye contact; their hair line is almost at the same level, despite one sitting and one standing, suggesting the superior status of the former. The extensive use of colour, harmony of the composition and substantial size of the ostracon suggest it was created for display.

K.2

Present location	British Museum EA 8506
Find spot	–
Published	Bruyère 1923: 124, Figure 2 Vandier d'Abbadie 1957: 22, Figure 3 Peck and Ross 1978: 889, Plate 14 Russman 2001: 67 Demarée 2002: 9 Backhouse 2012: 28, Figure 2
Dimensions	16.5 x 8.5 cm
Material	Limestone
Colour	Black

K.2: British Museum EA E8506, © Trustees of the British Museum.

Drawn in black outline in a confident manner, this ostracon has a jagged edge and has been broken in two but subsequently joined together. Bought by the British Museum in 1843, it has no firm provenance, but it has been suggested it came from Deir el-Medina (Demarée 2002: 9). In terms of composition, it is similar to other examples in the kiosk dataset, both of which were found at Deir el-Medina. Furthermore, the facial features of the female figure are so similar to those seen on ostracon F.11 they could be drawn by the same artist. As ostracon F.11 was found at Deir el-Medina, it is likely this ostracon was created there also.

The composition is split over two registers. In the uppermost a kiosk or temporary structure is depicted, comprised of papyri form columns and a support, around which heart shaped convolvulus leaves are wrapped. Under this a woman sits on a stool, facing the viewer's right; the stool is striped like the trunk of a palm tree, with a thick cushion. The woman appears naked but is heavily adorned in a broad collar, ankle bracelets, earrings and a hip-girdle. She also wears a heavy tripartite wig, discussed in Section 5.3c. Two additional side locks of hair fall from her temples to her shoulders; these curl upwards at the ends. The wig is tied with a thick white fillet. Around her shoulders she wears a cape or shawl. She is also attired in sandals with up turned ends. These are similar in design to palm leaf sandals dated from the Ramesside period, for example British Museum EA 4464. As ancient Egyptians are often shown bare foot these elaborately designed sandals indicate high status (Freed 1981: 34). Her prestige is further elevated as she rests her feet on a cushion. The woman cups her left breast, possibly indicated by three curved lines, in her right hand, and offers it to the child she cradles in her left arm. The infant raises an arm towards its mother in a gesture of affection. The child is not a new-born baby; it has a long body and wears a broad collar. Its facial features are carefully drawn, and a penis maybe indicated by an upraised line in the genital region. The child wears a side lock of youth and tuffs of hair are possibly drawn.

The convolvulus leaves run into the lower register, suggesting compositional unity. This depicts a servant offering a mirror and kohl tube. Although Lilyquist (1979: 97) notes that it is very unusual for a man to be shown holding a mirror, the servant is likely to be male due to his distinctive hairstyle. A similar coiffure, of a shaved head and long locks, is also seen on ostracon K.3 and on an ostracon in Brussels (E 6370: Werbrouck 1953: 99, Figure 11). The servant here has well defined facial features with an upturned nose, eye with pupil indicated and eyebrow. He also wears a large earring.

K.3

Present location	French Institute of Oriental Archaeology
Find spot	Deir el-Medina, '*Grand Puits*', excavated 1949 (marked 21.2.49)
Published	Vandier d'Abbadie 1957: 21: Plate 1.1 VA Number 2858 Vandier d'Abbadie 1959: 187, Plates CXX, CXXII Minault-Gout 2002: 40, Plate 25 Backhouse 2012: 31, Figure 6
Dimensions	6 x 10 cm
Material	Limestone
Colour	Black

This ostracon is drawn with care and attention in black outline with limited black fill. It depicts a woman sitting on a stool with a deep cushion; the base of the stool has been compared to a palm trunk by Vandier d'Abbadie (1957: 25). The woman turns to the viewer's right; her facial features are badly damaged, but she appears to wear a distinctive heavy tripartite wig, as seen on ostraca K.1 and K. 2. She is attired in a broad collar and wears bracelets on her right arm. She is dressed in a translucent robe, the bottom edge of which is visible. It is possible she is also wearing a cape or shawl around her shoulders or these could be the sleeves of a robe. She holds a male child in the bend of her left arm and offers him her breast, indicated by three lines. Her naval is also conspicuously marked.

She rests one foot on a footstool, the other is held by a small black figure, over a large bowl. Vandier d'Abbadie (1957: 21, 26) assumed this to be a Nubian female attendant washing the feet of her mistress; however, there is no indication of the sex of the servant from the depiction. Although the size of the figure and the pose does suggest they are assisting with the ablutions of their mistress. The significance of scenes of toilette and grooming are discussed in Section 5.3e. In front of the seated woman an attendant stands. Although the image is badly erased, a tall conical headdress can be seen; the meaning of these hairstyles is discussed in Section 5.3d, and the lower part of a pair of legs are also visible. Between the seated and standing figure, a hieroglyphic inscription was written; it is now barely legible. Vandier d'Abbadie (1957: 28) noted it once said, 'to give beautiful plants and fruits, offerings of the gardens and fields alike'. This is the only example of text in the '*Scènes de Gynécées*' dataset. Although, stylistically it is more probable the standing figure held a mirror and kohl tube.

Around the scene convolvulus leaves are threaded; it is likely they were entwined around a kiosk or temporary structure as seen on ostraca K.1 and K.2. To the viewer's right a young man is depicted; he has a shaved head and long locks as seen on ostracon K.2. He lifts his left hand to his head and the soles of his feet are raised; Vandier d'Abbadie (1957: 21) suggested he is in a dancing pose. He wears a long double kilt and broad collar; his navel is also shown. Behind the seated figure a tame monkey sits, which eats fruit and appears to hold one paw out in a gesture of offering to the seated figure. The scene was set on a baseline and includes several elements of narrative; the most dominant of which is the seated nursing mother who is larger than her standing attendants, demonstrating her superior status.

K.3: IFAO VA 2858 (Photograph Author's own) © IFAO.

3.5: Fragments dataset

F.1

Present location	French Institute of Oriental Archaeology
Find spot	Deir el-Medina
Published	Vandier d'Abbadie 1937: 72, Plate LII VA Number 2348
Dimensions	–

F.1: IFAO VA 2348 (Photograph Author's own) © IFAO.

Material	Limestone
Colour	Black and ochre

The upper torso of a child lying on a bed is seen on this small fragment. The body of which is outlined in black and the flesh is ochre coloured. It wears a broad collar and it turns towards the viewer's left. The facial features are defined but partially erased. It lies on a thick cushion or mattress of a bed; the bed frame is just visible and has serpent imagery depicted. Vandier d'Abbadie (1937: 72) believed this fragment belonged to the '*Scènes de Gynécées*' dataset. It is likely this was part of an image of a woman sitting on a bed.

F.2

Present location	French Institute of Oriental Archaeology
Find spot	Deir el-Medina
Published	Vandier d'Abbadie 1937: 73, Plate LIV VA Number 2351
Dimensions	–
Material	Limestone
Colour	Black, ochre and white

F.2: IFAO VA 2351 (Photograph Author's own) © IFAO.

This small fragment with a crack down the centre shows a dish held in an upturned hand. This is received by an upraised hand; it is likely this belonged to a woman sitting on a bed facing the viewer's right. The lotus flower, which may have adorned her head, is still visible to the viewer's left. Her companion, offering the dish, may have also held a tall vase from which water was poured. It is possible she also carried vines of convolvulus leaves, trailing from her hand, as seen on ostracon WoB.50. The scene takes place under a decorative border; this may represent horizontal garlands hung on the walls or painted wall decoration. Vandier d'Abbadie (1937: 73) classified this as a scene of toilette, part of the '*Scènes de Gynécées*' dataset.

F.3

Present location	French Institute of Oriental Archaeology
Find spot	Deir el-Medina
Published	Vandier d'Abbadie 1937: 74 VA Number 2356
Dimensions	7 x 5 cm
Material	Limestone
Colour	Black and ochre/red

F.3: IFAO VA 2356 (Photograph Author's own) © IFAO.

This fragment shows a mirror and kohl tube, with an applicator, held by a figure, probably a woman, turning towards the viewer's left. The objects are delicately drawn; the mirror disc is outlined in red, with a black handle and the kohl tube is delineated in red with a black stopper. They are asymmetrically balanced. The officiant is wearing a large black wig, tied with a fillet, surmounted with a cone, with a lotus flower to the front. The sleeve of a long flowing robe is visible on the arm holding the mirror. It is likely this was part of a kiosk or an 'elaborate bed' scene, given that mirrors and kohl tubes are presented in these two datasets. There is also a faint outline of convolvulus leaves at the top and bottom left of the scene.

F.4

Present location	French Institute of Oriental Archaeology
Find spot	Deir el-Medina
Published	Vandier d'Abbadie 1937: 75, Plate LIV VA Number 2361
Dimensions	–
Material	Limestone
Colour	Black and ochre

Using only black and ochre, with the white of the ostracon as a base colour, this fragment shows the god

F.4: IFAO VA 2361 (Photograph Author's own) © IFAO.

Bes in great detail. He is depicted with his knees slightly bent, with bow shaped legs; he rests his hands on his hips. His body is illustrated in black with white relief used to differentiate his breast plate. He wears a short white kilt with a long sash to the front; he is adorned in a black and white striped collar. His upper body is shown ochre red. Given his frontal pose it is likely he was incorporated into the leg of a bed. Next to him is a large bowl with a rim; this has been drawn with an ochre outline and black fill added in parts to suggest a lustrous surface. This contains an oversized cone outlined in ochre, with markings to suggest an uneven substance.

It is likely this fragment belonged to the 'women on beds' dataset. The scene was composed on a baseline; it has been drawn with skill and suggests an artisan familiar with the genre and technical expertise.

F.5: IFAO VA 2370 (Photograph Author's own) © IFAO.

F.5

Present location	French Institute of Oriental Archaeology
Find spot	Deir el-Medina
Published	Vandier d'Abbadie 1937: 77 VA Number 2370
Dimensions	7 x 3 cm
Material	Limestone
Colour	Black, ochre and yellow

All that remains of this fragment is an image of the god Bes incorporated into the leg of a bed. He is outlined in black with yellow fill added for his mane; his upper body has been coloured with ochre fill. He is in characteristic squat pose, wearing a kilt with a long sash to the front. The bed frame is outlined in black with red and yellow fill, possibly suggestive of serpent imagery. It is likely this was part of a larger scene showing a woman sitting on a bed.

F.6

Present location	French Institute of Oriental Archaeology
Find spot	Deir el-Medina
Published	Vandier d'Abbadie 1937: 77 VA Number 2371
Dimensions	4 x 3.5 cm
Material	Limestone
Colour	Black, grey and ochre

This fragment shows the god Bes incorporated into the leg of a bed. He wears a tall, feather plumed headdress, above a lion-like mane. He is outlined in black with ochre used for fill on his upper body. The bed frame is

F.6: IFAO VA 2371 (Photograph Author's own) © IFAO.

outlined in black and ochre; it has grey and ochre detail suggesting serpent imagery. It is likely this was part of a larger scene showing a woman sitting on a bed.

F.7

Present location	French Institute of Oriental Archaeology
Find spot	Deir el-Medina, '*Kom du Sud*', excavated 1930 (marked 19.1.30)
Published	Vandier d'Abbadie 1937: 77 VA Number 2372
Dimensions	5.3 x 4 cm
Material	Limestone
Colour	Black, ochre/red and grey

F.7: IFAO VA 2372 (Photograph Author's own) © IFAO.

This fragment, drawn on a baseline, shows the god Bes incorporated into the leg of a bed. He is shown schematically, outlined in black with ochre/red details added to emphasize his upper body, the frontal sash of his kilt and his tall, feather plumed headdress. The bed frame is depicted with a black outline, with the addition of serpent imagery. Next to the god Bes is a large dish with a rim, a deep bowl and a curved foot; it is likely it contained a cone. It is probable that this fragment belonged to the 'women on beds' dataset.

F.8

Present location	French Institute of Oriental Archaeology
Find spot	Deir el-Medina
Published	Vandier d'Abbadie 1937: 80 VA Number 2387

F.8: IFAO VA 2387 (Photograph Author's own) © IFAO.

Dimensions	5.3 x 2.1 cm
Material	Limestone
Colour	Black, green, light ochre and white

This fragmentary ostracon has an unusual tonal palette and is drawn in a careless manner. It shows the god Bes; it is likely he was incorporated into the leg of the bed, with the cushion or mattress just visible above his head. At the top of the ostracon, to the viewer's left, a pair of arms can be seen; they hold a vase and bowl. They also carry a vine of leaves; possibly convolvulus. It is likely these belonged to a female companion approaching a woman (now destroyed) sitting on the bed. Although the scene lacks artistic skill it conforms to the iconography of the 'women on beds' dataset, particularly the offering of a bowl and vase, the inclusion of the god Bes and convolvulus leaves.

F.9

Present Location	French Institute of Oriental Archaeology
Find Spot	Deir el-Medina, '*Grand Puits*', excavated 1950 (marked 7.1.50)
Published	Vandier d'Abbadie 1959: 189, Plate CXXI VA Number 2864
Dimensions	–

F.9: IFAO VA 2864 (Photograph Author's own) © IFAO.

Material	Limestone
Colour	Black and ochre

This fragment depicts a figure facing the viewer's right. All that remains is a wig, around which a three-quarter fillet is tied with an ochre string; it is possible earrings are seen beneath the wig. There is a black object or decoration to the top of the head which cannot be identified. In what is now the centre of the scene, a large floral collar hangs from the wall or represents painted wall decoration. To the viewer's left an ochre object can be seen; it is probable that this is the footboard of a bed. It is likely the scene shows a woman sitting on a bed, part of the '*Scènes de Gynécées*' dataset.

F.10

Present location	French Institute of Oriental Archaeology
Find spot	Deir el-Medina, '*Kom du Puits*', excavated 1949-1950
Published	Vandier d'Abbadie 1959: 189, Plate CXXI VA Number 2865
Dimensions	-
Material	Limestone
Colour	Ochre and blue/black

This fragmentary ostracon shows a bed frame with the god Bes incorporated into the leg of the bed. Drawn with a heavy ochre outline, smudges of cobalt blue are visible on Bes' head, upper body and on the bed frame. On top of the bed stands a headrest, outlined in ochre; this is a unique depiction in the dataset. Although it is possible that a headrest is depicted on ostracon WoB.17; but they are more commonly seen in tomb scenes. Above the bed runs a broad ochre line, suggesting painted wall decoration. Given the inclusion of the god Bes into the foot of the bed it is probable this fragment belonged to the 'women on beds' dataset.

F.10: IFAO VA 2865 (Photograph Author's own) © IFAO.

F.11

Present location	Berlin ÄS 21453
Find spot	Deir el-Medina, excavated 1913, near the '*Kom du Sud*'
Published	Schäfer 1916: 30 (Number 39) Brunner-Traut 1956: 69, Plate XXV
Dimensions	2.6 x 4.3 cm
Material	Limestone
Colour	Black

Drawn in black outline and fill this fragment shows the head of a woman facing the viewer's right. She wears a heavy tripartite wig with a thick white fillet. She is also adorned with earrings and a broad collar indicated by three circular bands. Two long locks of hair fall on

F.11: Berlin ÄS 21453, © Staatliche Museen zu Berlin – PK, Ägyptisches Museum und Papyrussammlung, photograph: Sandra Steiß.

either side of her face. Stylistically the ostracon is so similar to K.2 that they are likely to have been drawn by the same artist. As this hairstyle is shown only in the kiosk scenes, this fragment is almost certainly from a larger kiosk scene. Brunner-Traut (1956: 69) believed the fragment was part of a breast-feeding mother scene, while Schäfer (1916: 30) suggested it was the head of a dancer.

F.12

Present location	Berlin ÄS 21477
Find spot	Deir el-Medina, excavated 1913, near the '*Kom du Sud*'
Published	Schäfer 1916: 30 (Number 35) Brunner-Traut 1956: 70, Plate III
Dimensions	6.5 x 6.5 cm
Material	Limestone
Colour	Black, ochre, yellow and blue/ green

F.12: Berlin ÄS 21477, © Staatliche Museen zu Berlin – PK, Ägyptisches Museum und Papyrussammlung, photograph: Sandra Steiß.

This fragment shows a woman turning to the viewer's right; she holds in the bend of her left elbow a child, possibly with a penis indicated. She wears a long tripartite wig and broad collar, with blue segments; Brunner-Traut (1956: 70) suggested this represented faience. Her body and that of the child are an unusual yellow tone, similar to that seen on ostracon K.1. Her facial features are drawn heavily and without delicacy. Although the woman wears a tripartite wig it is not of the heavy style depicted in K.1-3; therefore, this ostracon is unlikely to be part of the kiosk dataset. It is more probable that it was part of an 'elaborate bed' scene. The ochre shading under the woman's left arm and over her right arm could be a cape or shawl as seen on ostracon EB.2. Indications of foliage are visible, with green and red markings in the background.

F.13

Present location	Brussels E 6382
Find spot	-
Published	Werbrouck 1953: 98, Figure 9 Vandier d'Abbadie 1957: 24, Figure 4
Dimensions	-
Material	Limestone
Colour	Black

F.13: Brussels E 6382 (Vandier d'Abbadie 1957, 24, Figure 4) © IFAO.

This fragment depicts a figure with a tall conical headdress, with two long locks of hair, one falling from the crown and the other from the temple. This is very similar to hairstyles seen on ostraca EB.1, K.1, K.3, CE.8 and CE 10-12. These are discussed in Section 5.3d. The facial features and body of the figure are well defined; the navel is drawn and a roll of fat beneath it is suggested. The attendant stands in-between a large papyrus stem to the rear and a large arrow headed leaf, most likely an over-sized convolvulus, to the front. The figure holds a mirror and kohl tube in a gesture of offering. Given the similarity with K.1 and K.3 it is likely this was part of a kiosk scene.

F.14

Present location	Brussels E 6778
Find spot	-
Published	Werbrouck 1953: 98 Brunner-Traut 1955: 12 Backhouse 2016: 186
Dimensions	10 x 16. 5 cm
Material	Limestone
Colour	Black and ochre

Image not available due to copyright restrictions

Bought in Cairo or Luxor, this ostracon was believed to come from Deir el-Medina by Werbrouck (1953: 98). A digital image of this ostracon was examined for my PhD research but due to copyright restrictions it cannot be reproduced here. While only the upper portion of the scene remains Werbrouck suggested it was an image of the 'harem' depicting a woman on a bed. However, the exact nature of the scene is difficult to determine. It shows a woman facing the viewer's left, reaching her right arm forward. There is a deep cushion in front of her which may be the mattress of a bed; she may sit on this or stand behind it. There is a triangular object to the viewer's left, in front of the woman, this is undefined. She wears a long enveloping wig, tied with a three-quarter fillet, possibly floral, and her head is surmounted with a cone. She is attired in a complex wrap-around dress. Behind the seated figure are two undefined objects. A large vine or tendril arches over the scene, entwined in this are flowers and bunches of grapes.

The ostracon has been delicately and skilfully drawn, primarily in black outline with ochre used as a fill. The tendril or vine is a strong ochre colour, serving to frame the scene.

F.15

Present location	Petrie UC 33251
Find spot	-
Published	University College London UCL Petrie Collection Online Catalogue
Dimensions	9.8 x 8 cm
Material	Limestone
Colour	Ochre

In the centre of this ostracon a bed is depicted with a tall footboard and the god Bes is incorporated into the leg of the bed. To the viewer's right a papyri form column on a base is shown. This could form part of a kiosk, as seen on ostraca K.1 and K.2, or more likely an indoor temporary structure as depicted in Figure 5.12. There are a number of horizontal lines running across the upper level of the ostracon. These could represent the top section of the kiosk. The horizontal line in the mid-section of the ostracon could show painted wall decoration or a trellis hanging from the kiosk, as seen in Figure 5.12.

F.15: Petrie UC 33251 (Photograph Author's own)
Courtesy of Petrie Museum of Egyptian Archaeology.

Although fragmentary, the image is informative as it contains both a bed and a kiosk like structure. This is unique in the dataset. It has been drawn in outline only, using one tone, ochre. To the viewer's left an unidentified object is shown on the edge of the ostracon; the meaning of this is not apparent. It could represent a tall conical headdress, as seen on the attendant on ostracon EB.1.

3.6: Comparative evidence dataset

CE. 1

Present location	Stockholm MM 14006
Find spot	Unknown (From the Gayer-Anderson Collection)
Published	Peterson 1973: 76, Plate 27 Backhouse 2012: 37, Figure 9
Dimensions	11. 5 x 9 cm
Material	Limestone
Colour	Black
Verso	Text, badly erased

This ostracon with a jagged edge, has been broken into two but subsequently joined together. The image shows

CE.1: Stockholm MM 14006 (Photograph Author's own).

the goddess Isis in a kiosk, facing the viewer's right. The text immediately in front of her states 'The Great Isis, Mistress of the Sky, God...'. While the fragmentary text behind the goddess, to the viewer's left, is likely to be part of the epithet 'Mistress of the Two Lands' (Peterson 1973: 76). Isis wears a tripartite wig which is tied with a narrow fillet; the bow is visible at the rear of her head, which is surmounted by a crown. She is also attired in a broad collar, upper armlets and bracelets. She sits on a high-backed chair, which is throne like.

The goddess cradles a child in her arms; she may be cupping her breast to suckle the child. It is likely this is Horus, shown wearing a side lock of youth. The scene takes place under a roofed kiosk with two columns, possibly decorated with horizontal floral garlands; Peterson (1973:76) refers to this as a chapel. The text in front of the structure refers to '*Set Maat*', the ancient name of Deir el Medina – 'Place of Truth' and includes the names of private individuals including the 'chief man'. There is also some badly erased text on the verso, the exact meaning of which cannot be determined. Peterson (1973: 76) suggests the ostracon was a votive offering and noted depictions of Isis were rare at Deir el-Medina.

CE.2

Present location	Ashmolean Museum H.O. 49
Find spot	–
Published	Černý and Gardiner 1957: 2, Plates VII and VIIa
Dimensions	20.8 x 17.5 x 14 cm
Material	Limestone
Colour	Black

CE.2: Ashmolean Museum HO 49 (Photograph Author's own).

This near complete ostracon was given to the Ashmolean Museum by Alan Gardiner, who bought it from a dealer in Luxor in 1907 (Černý and Gardiner 1957: 2). As such it has no firm provenance, but it is believed to have a Theban origin, dating from the 18th or 19th Dynasty. Drawn in black outline and set on a baseline it shows the goddess Renenutet sitting on a throne turning to the viewer's right. She is represented in composite form with the head of a reared cobra and the body of a woman. She wears a *nemes* headdress and broad collar, but no dress is indicated. Sitting on her lap, supported by her left arm is a child; with her right arm she reaches out to the child and gives her left breast to it. Gardiner believed the child to be Nepri, the god of grain, who came to represent Osiris in his child form. In front of Renenutet, a standing male figure brings an offering, probably a piece of fruit; he wears a long kilt, but his head is missing. To the left and above the image are lines of hieratic text which contain a threat directed against some male being, most likely unrelated to the image (Černý and Gardiner 1957: 2).

CE.3

Present location	Louvre E 27661
Find spot	–
Published	Andreu 2002: 114, Figure 54
Dimensions	8.1 x 10. 5 cm
Material	Limestone
Colour	Black and red

This ostracon shows a woman sitting on a stool facing the viewer's left. Drawn on a black baseline, the scene is outlined in black with bright red fill. The seated woman cradles a child in her arms; the child has a long body suggesting it is not newly born. The woman is attired in a long robe; the outline of her body is visible beneath the robe, as is one foot. She wears a long black enveloping wig, tied with a fillet, surmounted with a cone, with a lotus flower to the front. The facial features

CE.3: Louvre E 27661 (Photograph Author's own).

of the woman are well defined; she has a hooked nose, a downturned mouth and a narrow almond shaped eye. She also wears jewellery, in the form of discus earrings and a broad collar; her attire suggests a well-groomed elite woman.

Facing the seated woman, a small servant figure stands. He has an elongated shaved head and wears a short kilt. His diminutive size is emphasised as he is positioned between two tall vase stands; a third stand is placed at the edge of the ostracon, to the viewer's left. Vase stands such as these have survived from ancient Egypt, for example EA 2470 in the British Museum (Killen 1980: 70, Figure 37). Each stand is topped by a different shaped vessel. Andreu (2002: 114) suggests these vessels contain the unguents and drinks offered and consumed at the celebrations of the birth of a child in an elite household. It is possible the vessel closest to the seated figure shows smoke rising, suggesting incense is being burnt. Similar vessels are seen on ostracon CE.6.

CE.4

Present location	Turin S.06287
Find spot	Deir el-Medina
Published	Turin Museum Online Catalogue
Dimensions	9 x 13 x. 2 cm
Material	Limestone
Colour	Ochre/red

This ostracon drawn in ochre/red shows a woman sitting on a stool, facing the viewer's right. She is attired in a complex wrap-around dress. She wears an enveloping wig, tied with a fillet, with a bow visible at the rear of her head. This is surmounted by a cone and has a lotus flower to the front. Sitting on her lap is a child, who appears to have one hand raised towards its mouth, in a gesture indicative of childhood. The child, who faces the viewer's left, has a long body and is not a newly born infant. Opposite the seated group stands a large bird with open wings. The Turin on-line catalogue identifies this as a duck; the bird is oversized in comparison to the woman and child. However, it is likely to be part of the original composition as it is drawn on the same baseline as the seated figure and uses the same tonal palette.

CE.4: Turin S.06287, © Museo Egizio, photograph by Franco Lovera.

CE.5

Present location	French Institute of Oriental Archaeology
Find spot	Deir el-Medina
Published	Vandier d'Abbadie 1937: 79 VA number 2383
Dimensions	11 x 8.5 cm
Material	Limestone
Colour	Blue/black, ochre and white

CE.5: IFAO VA 2383 (Photograph Author's own) © IFAO.

This badly preserved ostracon shows a woman sitting on a stool, outlined in ochre, with striped markings. This is likely to be created from a trunk of a palm tree, similar stools are depicted in kiosk scenes K.2-3. The woman faces the viewer's left; the tresses of her tripartite wig fall on her left shoulder. She wears a long white robe; the contours of her body, outlined in ochre, are just visible beneath the garment and her feet can be seen under the hem. She cradles a child in her arms. Opposite the seated figure a pair of hands appear in a gesture of offering. It is likely these belong to a standing companion, offering a vase and bowl or a mirror and kohl pot. The scene is unusual as the woman sits on a type of stool generally depicted in the kiosk scenes, but she wears a long robe commonly seen in the 'women on beds' dataset. It is likely this was drawn by an artist familiar with the motifs of the '*Scènes de Gynécées*' but who used them to create a more original composition.

CE.6

Present location	French Institute of Oriental Archaeology
Find spot	Deir el-Medina
Published	Vandier d'Abbadie 1937: 79, Plate XLIX VA Number 2336
Dimensions	-
Material	Limestone
Colour	Black and ochre

CE.6: IFAO VA 2336 (Vandier d'Abbadie 1937: 79, Plate XLIX) © IFAO.

This ostracon shows a woman sitting on an elaborate chair, facing the viewer's right. This indicates she is an elite woman. She holds a lotus flower in her left hand and a shallow bowl in her right. Her standing companion, shown opposite, pours water into the bowl from a tall vase. The feet of the two women would have touched, forming an arch, seen for example in WoB.36, indicating social intimacy. The facial features of the seated figure are destroyed but she wears a long black wig, the ends are still visible. She is attired in a complex wrap-around dress; the voluminous nature of which is illustrated by a series of pleats falling from the knot fastening beneath her breast and the translucent nature of the fabric is indicated on the sleeve, which reveals the arm beneath. In between and above the two women, the outline of a circular object is visible; it is likely to be a hanging floral collar or painted wall decoration. This suggests a festooned environment.

Many of the details of the standing figure are destroyed but it is probable a fillet was tied around her head, which was surmounted with a cone. Overall, it is likely she was dressed in a similar manner to her seated companion, clad in a complex wrap-around dress, suggesting the two women were social equals. To the viewer's right a stand containing three tall vessels is depicted, similar stands and vessels are seen on ostracon CE.3. The scene is outlined in ochre and black with the same colours used for limited fill. The composition is set on a baseline and is well balanced.

CE.7

Present location	French Institute of Oriental Archaeology
Find spot	Deir el-Medina, excavated 1930, '*Kom du Sud*'
Published	Vandier d'Abbadie 1937: 71, Plate LI VA number 2342
Dimensions	-
Material	Limestone
Colour	Black and ochre

CE.7: IFAO VA 2342 (Vandier d'Abbadie 1937: 71, Plate LI) © IFAO.

This partially erased ostracon shows a group of women giving and receiving gifts. It is likely the middle figure, facing the viewer's right, is sitting on a bed. In front of her stands a companion who offers her a bowl; Vandier d'Abbadie (1937:71) suggested this was filled with fruits. The seated woman raises a hand in a gesture of thanks or greeting. Behind her another female figure approaches; she carries a similar dish which contains a cone, in her other hand she holds what appears to be a broad collar necklace.

None of the facial features of the women have survived. However, they all wear long black wigs, tied with a fillet, with a lotus flower to the front; the outline of a cone is visible on the standing figure, seen to the viewer's left. It is likely that they all wore complex wrap-around dresses; the lower portion of two remains. The feet of the seated figure and her companion, to the viewer's left are touching, forming an arch, as seen for example on ostracon WoB.36. Above the procession of women, four bands of colour are visible, possibly depicting painted wall decoration; they frame the scene, which is contained by a baseline upon which the image is composed. Vandier d'Abbadie (1937: 82) believed this was a scene of toilette, a subset of the '*Scènes de Gynécées*'. The author considers this to be a scene of gift giving in a domestic setting.

CE.8

Present location	Cairo (Pre-selection for GEM) O.BTdK. 139
Find Spot	Valley of the Kings, near KV 18
Published	Dorn 2011: 259, Plates 130-131
Dimensions	25. 2 x 12.0 x 3.4 cm
Material	Limestone
Colour	Ochre/red

CE.8: O.BTdK. 139 (Cairo Pre-selection for GEM) © Andreas Dorn.

This ostracon, broken in two in antiquity and subsequently joined together, shows a young girl turning towards the viewer's left. She carries on her shoulder a large, circular vessel with a tall, flaring neck. She supports this with both hands, suggesting it is a heavy load. From her left hand hangs a lotus blossom and draped over her right shoulder is a papyrus umbel. Behind her walks a monkey on its hind legs; it reaches up to the girl's thigh with one paw and to her calf with the other. It is attached by a lead, which is held in the girl's left hand. The playful and intimate posture of the monkey suggests it is domesticated. Behind the girl, shown between her stride, walks a goat.

Drawn in a graceful manner, the young girl appears statuesque and long limbed. Two softly curved lines indicate the contours of her abdomen; only one breast is drawn, depicted in profile. Her facial features are reduced to one almond shaped eye with pupil, eyebrow and ear. She is shown with an elongated conical headdress, from which one long lock falls from the crown and another from her temple. Dorn (2011: 256) follows Vandier d'Abbadie (1957: 24) in suggesting this indicated the girl was a Syrian. The hairstyle is discussed in Section 5.3d. This ostracon is included in the comparative evidence dataset as the headdress/hairstyle is similar to that seen on the attendants shown on ostraca EB.1 and K.3. The image has been drawn on a base line, in ochre/red outline with no colour fill added.

CE.9

Present location	SCA Magazine near Carter House, Qurna, O.BRdK.140
Find spot	Valley of the Kings, near KV 18
Published	Dorn 2011: 257, Plates 132-133
Dimensions	25. 2 x 12.0 x 3.4 cm
Material	Limestone
Colour	Black and ochre/red

CE.9: O.BRdK.140 (SCA Magazine near Carter House, Qurna) © Andreas Dorn.

Two fragments remain of this ostracon broken in antiquity. In an ochre red frame, a young girl is shown, facing the viewer's left. Although badly damaged, given the similarity with CE.8, it is likely she held a large vessel above her head and was depicted with a similar conical headdress. As in CE.8, a monkey walks behind her, and a goat is shown in-between her stride. A papyrus umbel is depicted to the left of the standing figure.

This ostracon was clearly used for drawing exercises. The image of the young girl being inscribed latter, being the most prominent. There were also two chair legs drawn, one in ochre/red, in the upper frame; the other in black in the lower frame, where the image of a bull was also sketched.

CE.10

Present location	SCA Magazine near Carter House, Qurna, O.BRdK.141
Find spot	Valley of the Kings, near KV 18
Published	Dorn 2011: 258, Plates 134-135
Dimensions	19.3 x 9.9 x 3.2 cm
Material	Limestone
Colour	Black and ochre/red

This fragmentary ostracon, drawn in ochre and black outline, depicts a female head facing the viewer's left. She wears the same elaborate headdress/hairstyle as seen on ostraca CE.8, CE.11-12. This is discussed in Section 5.3d. Both temple locks are shown curling under the chin and a top lock is shown falling from the crown of the head. There is some sort of ornamentation on the girl's forehead; this was not present in any other depictions of the so called 'Syrians', it is perhaps a mistake or an idiosyncrasy of the artist. This appears to be a top knot or bobble. This was not so prominently depicted in other images of this genre but was suggested.

CE.11

Present location	SCA Magazine near Carter House, Qurna, O.BRdK. 142
Find spot	Valley of the Kings, Workmen's Hut (no.4)
Published	Dorn 2011: 257-258, Plates 134-135
Dimensions	17. 3 x 11.1 x 2.9 cm
Material	Limestone
Colour	Black and ochre/red
Verso	Worshipper

This badly worn ostracon shows a young girl wearing a similar elaborate headdress/hairstyle as seen on CE.8, CE.10 and CE.12. This is discussed in Section 5.3d. She carries a large vessel on her shoulder; she turns to the viewer's left and a goat walks beside her. Dorn

CE.10: O.BRdK.141 (SCA Magazine near Carter House, Qurna) © Andreas Dorn.

CE.11: O.BRdK. 142 (SCA Magazine near Carter House, Qurna) © Andreas Dorn.

(2011: 257-8) notes this may be a preliminary sketch as there are many fine lines on the girl's body, or this may represent a fine translucent garment. The latter would not be in keeping with depictions in this limited genre. It is more likely to be a preliminary sketch or practice piece given the depiction of a ram's head, 90 degrees counter-clockwise behind the girl's left leg. Furthermore, the verso has a sketch of a worshipper kneeling with arms raised in adoration (Dorn 2011: Plates 48-49). The numerous images depicted on this ostracon suggest it was used as a practice piece for artists sketches.

CE.12

Present location	Cairo (Pre-selection for GEM) O.BTdK.143
Find spot	Valley of the Kings, Workmen's Hut (no. 4)
Published	Dorn 2011: 257-258, Plates 136-137
Dimensions	19.1 x 15.2 x 3.0 cm
Material	Limestone
Colour	Black
Verso	Horus with double crown and hieroglyphs

Drawn in black outline, this ostracon depicts three naked young women. They wear elongated headdresses with long locks, which fall from their temples and the crown of their heads. The hairstyle is discussed in Section 5.3d. The girls all bend their legs at their knees and their feet appear raised, giving the impression of movement and balancing the weight of the vessels they carry. The central figure, facing the viewer's right, wears a broad collar and holds a large vessel with a tall neck. Her left arm has been drawn in three different positions, as the artist attempts to find the correct pose. It is possible the figure to the viewer's left was drawn first; this is paler in hue but takes the same posture as the central figure. As noted by Dorn (2011: 258), this figure lacks the definition of her companions. Subsequently, the central figure was drawn, in a more defined and darker tone. The poses of the two figures are so similar, implying one was a preliminary sketch. Opposite the central figure another female stands, facing the viewer's left. She attempts to support the vessel being carried by her companion, by placing both of her hands underneath it. The sketch captures a moment in time very effectively. The two figures are well balanced, suggesting they are the central motif of the ostracon. The abdomen is indicated on the two central figures by two curved lines. All three figures have dots on their thighs suggesting tattooing.

Below the baseline is a sketch, which Dorn (2011: 258) has identified as a male head facing the viewer's left.

CE.13

Present location	Cairo (Pre-selection for GEM) O.BTdK.144
Find spot	Valley of the Kings, near KV 18

CE.12: O.BTdK.143 Cairo (Pre-selection for GEM) © Andreas Dorn.

CE.13: O.BTdK.144 Cairo (Pre-selection for GEM) © Andreas Dorn.

Published	Dorn 2011: 256-257, Plates 138-139
Dimensions	16.1 x. 9.8 x 2.1 cm
Material	Limestone
Colour	Black

Drawn in black outline this ostracon shows the frontal depiction of a female figure, either standing or lying down. The left arm runs alongside the body, with the hand rotated inwards. The right arm is bent at the elbow and is held open above the navel. The pubic region and breasts are clearly indicated. Markings, most likely tattoos, are drawn on both thighs; these consist of three vertical, parallel lines, joined with a horizontal line at the top and bottom. The figure has no head and the feet lack definition. As Dorn (2011: 259) notes the depiction of headless women is unknown in the corpus of Egyptian art; he suggested the image may be of a 'lady on a bed' figurine.

This ostracon is included in the comparative evidence dataset due to the markings on the thighs, possibly of tattoos. These are similar to images found on the '*lit clos*' in house S.E.VIII as discussed in WP.I. Also, due to the link between the images in the '*Scénes de Gynécées*' and ladies on beds figurines, as proposed by scholars, initially Vandier d'Abbadie (1937: 85), then later Bruyère (1939: 144) and finally Pinch (1983) who explored this more fully.

CE.14

Present location	Cairo (Pre-selection for GEM) O.BTdK.145
Find spot	Valley of the Kings, near KV 18
Published	Dorn 2011: 259, Plates 138-139
Dimensions	16.2 x 12.0 x 2.6 cm
Material	Limestone
Colour	Ochre/red

CE.14: O.BTdK. 145 Cairo (Pre-selection for GEM)
© Andreas Dorn.

Drawn in ochre/red only, this ostracon depicts a female figure in outline. She is represented frontally and could be standing or lying down. She wears a long wig which reaches to the top of her breasts, which are indicated by fine lines; her pubic region and navel are also marked. Her right arm runs alongside her body while the left reaches across her chest to rest beneath her right breast. Dorn (2011: 259) suggests this may be a sketch of a fertility figurine, similar to CE.13, if so, these would be unique representations in the corpus of Egyptian art.

Chapter 4

'Scènes de Gynécées': The Corpus

4.1: Provenance

Of the 74 ostraca which form the primary evidence in this study 60 (81%) were found at Deir el-Medina. Figure 4.1 shows the details of each dataset. It is noteworthy that the only firm provenance for '*Scènes de Gynécées*' figured ostraca is from Deir el-Medina. The remaining 14 examples (19%) have no firm provenance.

Most of the ostraca from Deir el-Medina were excavated by Bruyère from 1922 onwards (Vandier d'Abbadie 1937: 1). They were found primarily in two locations. Firstly, in a heap of rubble at the foot of the south wall of the enclosure of the village; this built up during the normal occupation of the settlement (Bruyère 1952a: 60-61). This is referred to as the '*Kom du Sud*' and was excavated in 1930. Secondly, many were recovered from '*Le Grand Puits*' to the north of the village; this man-made pit was more than 50 m. deep and 35 m. wide. It is believed it was dug in the Ramesside period in an abortive attempt to reach the water-table (Bruyère 1953: 129). This was excavated from 1949-51. The abandoned pit subsequently became filled with debris in the Ramesside period. Bruyère believed heaps of garbage built up in the north and south locations as these were the only spots accessible for the accumulation of rubbish during the life of the village (Bruyère 1952a: 61). Vandier d'Abbadie (1937: 1) also stated that figured ostraca were found in the debris of houses and amongst the ruins of votive chapels. Many examples are recorded in the excavation reports for the village and the chapels, but these do not include any which depict the '*Scènes de Gynécées*'. It is possible one example (WoB.31) was found in the area associated with votive chapels; this ostracon was found during Bruyère's excavation in 1946 (Bruyère 1952a: 65-66, Figure 3) and is marked with N.E.T. which Toivari-Viitala (2014: 235-6) suggests came from '*au nord de l'enceinte du temple*', found in house J. One ostracon was found in a tomb, WoB.33 (Bruyère 1928: 22-23) and another more recently was found in the rubble of a workmen's hut, WoB.53 (Toivari-Viitala 2014). An additional example, not part of this study, a votive to Sobek (IFAO VA 2650), was found in house N.O. XVIII; it had plaster around the edges, suggesting it had been inserted into the wall (Bruyère 1939: 294).

The *Kom du Sud* is the most frequently recorded find spot for the '*Scènes de Gynécées*' figured ostraca, see Figure 4.2. This includes those excavated by the German team in 1913 (WoB.40-41, EB.1, F.11-12), as their excavation was close to this area, as noted by Toivari-Viitala (2014:235, n.12). Those marked '*Grand Puits*' are included in the number for the '*Kom du Grand Puits*'. There are no find spots recorded for the ostraca excavated by Schiaparelli. Three are in the 'women on beds' dataset (WoB.42-44) and one is in the comparative evidence dataset (CE.4). These are

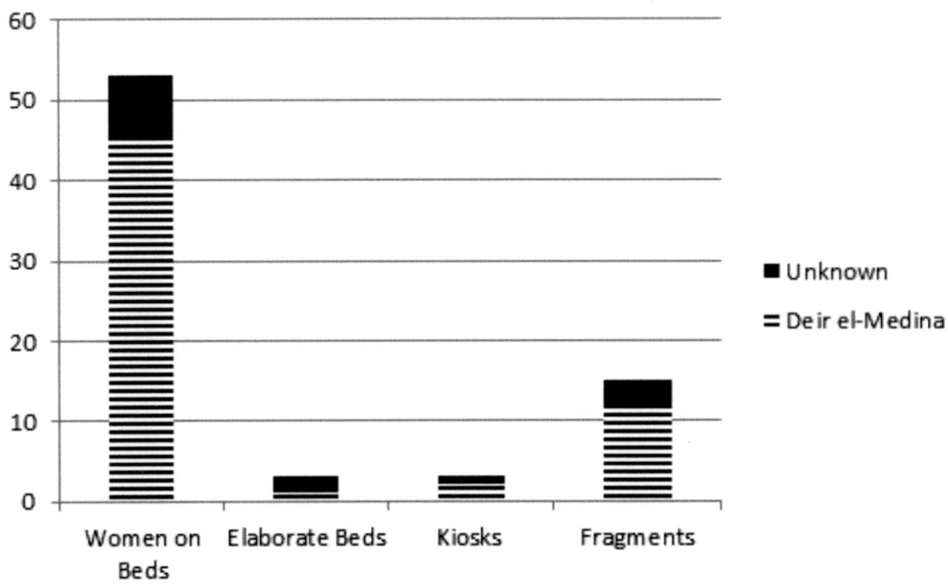

Figure 4.1: Provenance of ostraca which depict '*Scènes de Gynécées*' (Graph Author's own).

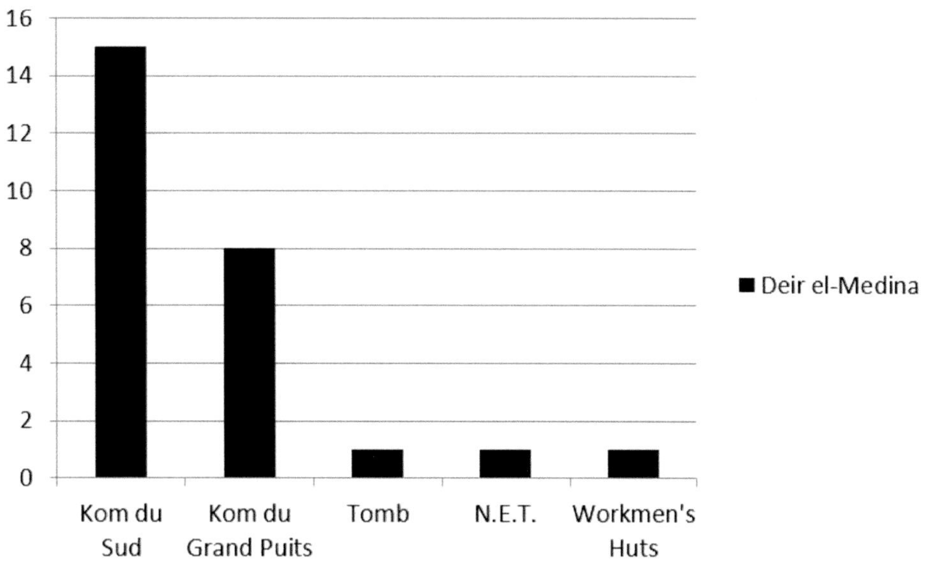

Figure 4.2: Recorded find spots of ostraca which depict '*Scènes de Gynécées*' found at Deir el-Medina (Graph Author's own).

now in Museo Egizio. With the exception of WoB.44, which was published by Trapani (2012:7, Figure 6), these are published only in the museum's online catalogue. Brunner-Traut (1955: 12) referred to six unpublished ostraca showing '*Scènes de Gynécées*' she saw in Museo Egizio; it has not been possible to locate all six examples.

The largest group of ostraca with no firm provenance are from the Gayer-Anderson Collection (WoB.45-48, EB.2). Gayer-Anderson (1881 – 1945) was a British surgeon who was seconded to the Egyptian Army in 1906, reaching the rank of Major in 1920, when he retired. He held a variety of prominent government positions including Oriental Secretary of the Residency in Cairo and the honorary title of Pasha (Bierbrier 2012: 210). Gayer-Anderson was an Orientalist who amassed a large collection of Egyptian antiquities; he favoured small objects such as pottery, jewellery, scarabs and figured ostraca. He returned to Britain in 1942, due to ill health. He presented over 7500 objects to the Fitzwilliam Museum in 1943 (The Fitzwilliam Museum 2016); this included 46 figured ostraca, published by Brunner-Traut (1979). The Medelshavmuseet, Stockholm purchased a significant number of figured ostraca from the Gayer-Anderson Collection in 1943, five of which are part of this study.

Several museums have a small number of ostraca, with no provenance, considered in this research. Four are currently located in Brussels Museum (WoB.51-52, F.13-14). A considerable number of figured ostraca came into their collection from the late 1920's onwards. Werbrouck (1953: 98, n.15) believed three of the four ostraca considered here, came 'without a doubt' from Deir el-Medina. An additional two examples were originally in Munich (WoB.49-50) but only one remains; WoB.49 was destroyed in the World War II. The Petrie Museum, London, also has two examples, one of which is in the 'elaborate beds' dataset (EB.3), and one of which is in the fragments dataset (F.15). One further example (K.2) was bought by the British Museum in 1843, which was also believed to be from Deir el-Medina (Demarée 2002: 9). The ostracon is so similar in style to F.11, which was found at Deir el-Medina, it is likely it was drawn by the same artist.

4.2: Dating

It is difficult to date the ostraca precisely due to their find spots. As Eyre (2013: 238-239, n. 42) notes the '*Kom du Sud*' is a very disturbed area. Some of the debris found in the '*Grand Puits*' and surrounding area was likely to be the result of a clearance in the north of the village carried out during building work on the temple to Hathor during the Ptolemaic period. Therefore, the figured ostraca can only be given a general date of the Ramesside period.

4.3: Comparative Evidence

A further 14 examples of figured ostraca have been included as comparative evidence; Figure 4.3 shows their provenance. It is noteworthy that four examples (CE.4-7) were also found at Deir el-Medina. These include images of nursing mothers and gift giving. A further seven examples were found in the Valley of the Kings, during excavations of the workmen's huts and waste dumps from earlier excavations south-east of Rameses X's tomb (Dorn 2011). These include images of servant girls and rare depictions of female figurines. Dorn (2011: 221) dates these from the second year of the reign of Rameses IV to the second year of the reign of Rameses V; therefore, comparable with the '*Scènes*

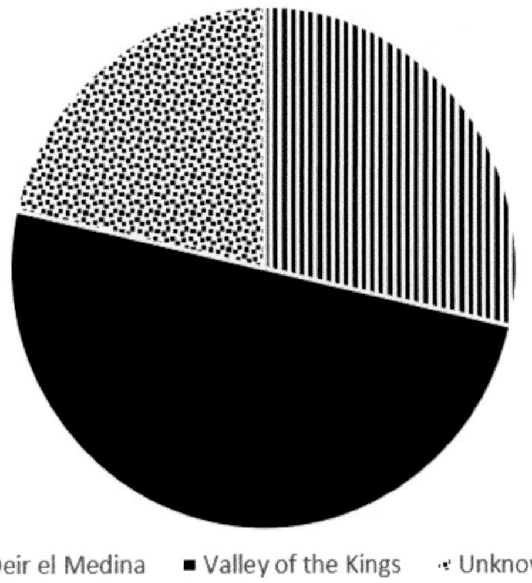

Figure 4.3: Provenance of ostraca which depict comparative data (Graph Author's own).

de Gynécées' figured ostraca. The provenance of three additional examples is unknown. Overall, the vast majority of figured ostraca considered in this study are from Deir el-Medina.

4.4: Material and Technique

Of the 74 ostraca which form the primary evidence of the study, 71 are fragments of limestone, while three are potsherds. All 14 examples in the comparative data group are drawn on fragments of limestone. The images on the potsherds are unusual/atypical, suggesting the choice of material was significant. WoB.13 shows a woman lying horizontally with a lizard before her face; while WoB.20 depicts a naked female, shown frontally, incorporated into the leg of the bed and WoB.31 illustrates a naked woman lying on a bed facing the viewer's left. Furthermore, images on two potsherds were drawn in outline only, perhaps reflecting the more porous nature of the material, making them unsuitable for more detailed images. Most ostraca were drawn with black and ochre/red outline and limited colour fill. As noted by Schäfer (translated by Baines 1986: 70) outline and fill is the norm for Egyptian art from about the 2nd - 3rd Dynasty, when Schäfer believed the foundations of Egyptian art were established. Earlier styles he suggested used colour with no outline or outline with no fill. Therefore, most ostraca which depict the '*Scènes de Gynécées*' are following the established principles of Egyptian art.

A small number of ostraca are drawn predominantly in outline only with limited fill, in the same colour as their outline. These include two potsherds (WoB.20 and WoB.31), two kiosk scenes (K.2-3), all three 'elaborate bed' scenes (EB.1-3) and two 'Women on Beds' scenes (WoB.2 and WoB.53). There are a further three examples in the 'Fragments' dataset. This includes F.11 and F.13, which were likely to have been part of a kiosk scene and F.15 which is a highly unusual scene, depicting a bed and possibly part of a kiosk or temporary internal structure. There is also some comparative data (CE.8-14) drawn in a mixture of ochre/red and black outline only, which depict young girls with distinctive non-Egyptian hairstyles. This suggests the style of drawing was chosen carefully with outline and limited fill (in the same colour) being preferred for kiosk scenes and elaborate bed scenes. Several of the scenes drawn in outline only are technically very accomplished, particularly the 'elaborate bed' scene (EB.2) and kiosk scene (K.2).

None of the '*Scènes de Gynécées*' figured ostraca clearly have multiple images drawn upon them. It is possible WoB.18 had been used for several compositions but this is not definitive. This suggests the '*Scènes de Gynécées*' were not drawing exercises but examples of narrative art, vignettes which tell a story, fiction or non-fiction or a combination of the real and imagined. Other examples of narrative art to come from Deir el-Medina include scenes of animal parody also drawn on ostraca, for example monkeys in satirical settings (Vandier d'Abbadie 1937: 54-69, Plates XXXVII-XLI). The only examples, in this study, of multiple images drawn upon one surface are found in the comparative evidence dataset (CE.9, CE.11 and CE.12). These ostraca, from the Valley of the Kings, depict servant girls, who are most likely non-Egyptian, drawn in outline only. It is possible that these were experimental designs made by one or a small number of craftsmen. However, similar hairstyles are seen on servants in the kiosk scenes (K.1 and K.3) and an 'elaborate bed' scene (EB.1), suggesting the imagery was meaningful to the royal artisans.

Many of the ostraca are broken and covered with scratches and cracks. It is likely this is due to the ravages of time; although it is possible that three examples had incision used as part of their decorative scheme (WoB.17, WoB.19 and WoB. 21). These pieces are iconographically consistent with others in the dataset; it is possible this was an idiosyncrasy of the artists concerned. Three further examples (WoB.23-24, 52) may have suffered smoke damage, suggesting they had been in the kitchen area; Bruyère (1939: 193) noted fragments of many '*laraires*' (household shrines) often located in the kitchen, were blackened by smoke.

4.5: Text

Only one ostracon depicting the '*Scènes de Gynécées*' had any text (K.3), although this is now badly faded and unreadable. Vandier d'Abbadie (1957: 28) noted it once said, 'to give beautiful plants and fruits offerings of the gardens and fields alike'. Many figured ostraca from Deir el-Medina do contain text, but the majority are votives, for example Figure 5.10. Text was integral to the function of votives as the name and plea of the dedicatee was vital. Two scenes of divine parallel (CE.1-2) also include text. One example (CE.1) shows Isis breast feeding a child; the text refers to the 'Place of Truth' and names individuals from the site (Peterson 1973: 76). The other example (CE.2) shows Renenutet nursing a child; the text refers to a threat against a man, most likely unrelated to the image (Černý and Gardiner 1957: 2). It is possible the ostraca depicting the '*Scènes de Gynécées*' did not contain any text due to the illiterate audience for whom they were created, probably the women of the village. The anepigraphic nature of the evidence may also relate to the type of scene depicted, possibly a secular celebration, not directly related to the gods. Furthermore, text may have been unnecessary as the participants were known to the artist and viewers.

4.6: The Inclusion of Children

Of the 53 ostraca in the 'women on beds' dataset 15 now contain an image of a child; two 'elaborate bed' scenes and all three kiosk scenes also include an infant. Due to the fragmentary nature of the evidence it is difficult to ascertain how many of the 'women on beds' scenes originally contained a depiction of a child. Only twelve complete scenes survive from the 'women on beds' and 'elaborate beds' datasets. This refers to those images in which both ends of the bed are visible. Seven of these show an infant; of the remainder, two lack clarity and the exact nature of the scene is impossible to determine. An additional two are atypical, one depicts the seated figure facing the viewer's left holding a large bouquet and no female attendants are shown (WoB.26). Another illustrates a woman lying down, facing the viewer's left (WoB.4); she appears to be naked, again with no female companions. Vandier d'Abbadie (1937: 84) did not believe this ostracon (WoB.4) belonged to the '*Scènes de Gynécées*' dataset. It has been included in this study as it meets the criteria of any image containing any part of a woman and a bed. Therefore, WoB.3 is the only 'standard' complete scene in the 'women on beds' dataset which does not include a child. This suggests the inclusion of children in the '*Scènes de Gynécées*' figured ostraca was the norm.

It is possible up to six children are shown to be male by the depiction of a penis. This includes two 'women on beds' scenes (WoB.1-2), possibly all three kiosk scenes (K.1-3) and one fragment which was probably from an 'elaborate bed' scene (F.12). However, it must be noted obviously, it is more difficult to identify a female child without the indicators of dress and adornment. While the children are not depicted with a great deal of uniformity, they do not appear to be newly born.

4.7: Orientation

Of the 56 ostraca in the 'women on beds' and 'elaborate beds' datasets, 41 show the main figure, the woman sitting on the bed, turning towards the viewer's right. In seven cases the image is unclear, and it is not possible to differentiate the orientation of the main figure. In all three kiosk scenes the nursing mother turns towards the viewer's right. In only six examples in the 'women on beds' dataset is the main figure depicted turning towards the viewer's left. A number of which have unusual features. These include WoB.4 and WoB.26, as discussed in Section 4.6, while WoB.7 is fragmentary and it is not possible to determine the exact nature of the scene. WoB.31 is a potsherd showing a naked woman lying on a bed and WoB.48 shows a figure without companions turning towards a large bouquet of flowers, possibly holding a cone of bread. Two children are depicted in these scenes, but no companions are present. In three of the scenes (WoB.4, 31, 48) the figures are not attired in the usual elaborate clothing. Whether naked or merely scantily clad, the contours of their body and/or skin tone are visible.

Numerous scholars have noted the preference for right-facing figures in Egyptian art (Schäfer translated by Baines 1986: 300; Robins 1994: 33). Schäfer acknowledged it was Erman who first sought to explain this (Erman and Ranke 1923, as cited in Schäfer, translated by Baines 1986: 300, n.51), suggesting when an Egyptian artist was free to choose the orientation of a figure, he made it face right. Robins (1994: 33) has suggested the preference may reflect the fact that most people are right-handed. Furthermore, she argues that in two-dimensional representations any accompanying text was normally orientated to face the same direction as figurative elements in a scene; thus, it is read from right to left. This would also be the direction in which a scribe wrote on a roll of papyrus, holding a brush in his right hand, he would begin at the right-hand edge of the papyrus moving left. These factors created an overriding preference for right-facing orientation in Egyptian representations.

Although the '*Scènes de Gynécées*' figured ostraca contain almost no text they show an overriding partiality for right-facing figures. Furthermore, most were drawn on a base line; only two examples show the participants on different levels. WoB.26 depicts a cat in the foreground; although Vandier d'Abbadie (1959: 187) suggested this was foreign to the scene. WoB.47 shows two servants and a large standing monkey on a different level than the bed; this scene is also unusual in terms of composition. One scene, (K.2), uses registers in which both scenes are stylistically and thematically linked. Overall, the artistic conventions employed suggest the '*Scènes de Gynécées*' figured ostraca were created following well known rules of representation and were not randomly conceived.

With regards to the placement of the child, in all three kiosk scenes and two 'elaborate bed' scenes (EB.1-2), the child is held by their mother. The seated woman also holds a child in WoB.38, F.12 and CE.3-5. Of the remaining images which include a child, three show the child behind the seated figure, resting against the footboard, while seven show the child lying on the bed in front of the mother. Generally, there is a preference for the placement of the child in front of the mother, including being held.

4.8: Dress and Decorum

Most of the women in the 'women on beds' scenes, with a small number of exceptions, wear what Vogelsang-Eastwood (1993: 106-111) defines as complex wrap-around dresses. She describes them as made from a large rectangle of cloth draped in various decorative manners. Occasionally, a second smaller length of cloth was used as a sash in order to secure the garment in place. Although we can only speculate on how the garments were worn in daily life, most depictions in the '*Scènes de Gynécées*' figured ostraca suggest it was tied over or just below the breast to form a large skirt, creating a top with wide bat-wing sleeves. The fringed edge of the fabric was frequently visible at the front. The dress often revealed the contours of the wearers' body, giving the impression that the fabric was translucent, although this may have been an artistic device employed to reveal the figure of the wearer. Janssen (1995: 383) suggests these elaborate styles, first seen in the 18th Dynasty, reflect status and rank, with more simple fashions giving way to more voluminous and fussy styles in the Ramesside period. The dresses used a large quantity of material, shown to be of high quality due to the thinness of the fabric. The depiction of the seated figure and her companions in similar styles of dress implies they were of a comparable status; also, their attire suggests the women were dressed in their finery, possibly for celebrations taking place in the home. The clothes show the wearer to be a Mistress of the House, not working outdoors.

4.9: Nakedness and 'Concealed Nudity'

There are a number of exceptions to this attire; in two of the kiosk scenes (K.1-2) the women wear only a cape or shawl around their shoulders and a broad collar. In the third kiosk scene (K.3), the seated woman wears a cape or shawl, broad collar and transparent robe which reveals the contours of her body. Two women in 'elaborate bed' scenes are similarly attired; EB.1 shows a woman who appears to wear only a broad collar, while in EB.2 the woman seems to wear only a cape or shawl. However, there are a number of 'women on beds' scenes which also suggest the women are naked; some are linked by left facing orientation. WoB.4 appears to show a naked woman but a sleeve is visible; this may be part of a cape or shawl, but no child is indicated. WoB.31 shows a naked woman lying on a bed drawn on a potsherd. WoB.48 appears to depict a naked woman turning towards the viewer's left. There are no companions in any of these scenes. Other indicators of nakedness are linked to status. For example, WoB.47 shows two servants who appear naked, while WoB.38 is an intriguing scene showing a nursing woman on a bed; the sleeve of her robe or shawl is visible but it is not possible to determine the remainder of her outfit. Her companions are dressed in translucent robes revealing the contours of their body, including their pubic regions and hip-girdles. This level of revelation and disclosure is not apparent on other secondary figures in the 'women on beds' scenes. Asher-Greve and Sweeney (2006: 140) refer to this as 'concealed nudity'. This suggests these were servants, possibly singers as Vandier d'Abbadie (1937: 84) suggested. Ostracon WoB.20 uniquely shows a female figure incorporated into the legs of the bed. Naked, wearing only cross-over beads with arms upraised she takes a similar pose as caryatid mirror handles, discussed in Section 5.4i, which it has been suggested also depict servants.

4.10: Summary and Conclusion

All the '*Scènes de Gynécées*' figured ostraca with a provenance, were found at Deir el-Medina, dated to the Ramesside period. Most are drawn on fragments of limestone with a black and ochre/red outline and some colour fill added. The scenes are composed on a baseline with a preference for right-facing figures. With one exception, (K.3), the '*Scènes de Gynécées*' are anepigraphic, possibly due to the nature of the audience. The god Bes is depicted frontally while all other actors are shown in profile. Therefore, the scenes have been created using the standard principles of Egyptian art.

Chapter 5

'*Scènes de Gynécées*': Repeat Motifs

A study of the corpus of the '*Scènes de Gynécées*' figured ostraca reveals repeat motifs which run through the 'women on beds', 'elaborate beds' and kiosk scenes. Individual themes will be examined below in order to understand the complex web of associations which link the images; comparisons with the material culture of New Kingdom Egypt will be made where appropriate.

5.1: Bes

Bes is the most prolific motif in the '*Scènes de Gynécées*' figured ostraca. He is depicted on 27 examples in the 'women on beds' and 'elaborate beds' datasets, incorporated into the feet of the bed in at least 25 examples. However, many of the ostraca are fragmentary and do not include complete scenes; upon close scrutiny it is apparent that only three 'women on beds' scenes which show the lower portion of the bed, do not include an image of Bes. There are a further seven depictions of Bes in the fragments dataset, all of which are likely to have been part of larger images of 'women on beds' scenes; all show the god incorporated into the feet of a bed. It is noteworthy, that when the god is depicted in this manner he is always shown with frontal facial features. There are only two possible profile facial depictions of the god in the evidence considered (WoB.11 and WoB.23).

5.1a: Iconography and Etymology

Bes is shown with varying degrees of detail, although always represented in a lively manner. He is generally depicted with his hands on his hips, with legs bent in a squatting pose. Frequently he stands and turns on the balls of his feet to suggest movement. He wears a short kilt, sometimes spotted, often with a sash around his waist, which ties at the front with a long belt which hangs to the floor; this suggests a loincloth and emphasises the region of his sexual organs. On several ostraca he is shown with a beard and mane, which give him a leonine appearance. Often, he wears a broad collar and the contours of his chest are rendered in a muscular manner. The depiction of Bes is to a degree paradoxical; he has menacing traits with a mane and a tall feathered headdress, but he is frequently shown with a large abdomen with rolls of fat and in more detailed depictions his tongue is shown protruding from his mouth. The juxtaposition between ferocious and comic elements led Romano (1980: 41) to suggest Bes lacks the dignity and presence of traditional Egyptian gods. Only one image in the 'women on beds' dataset includes alternative iconography for the god. Ostracon EB.1 shows Bes winged, making music and holding papyrus umbels; a similar image of Bes is found in the painted decoration of a house, see WP.7, Figure 2.22.

Much has been written on the origins and development of the image of Bes (Romano 1980) and on the etymology of the god's name (Meeks 1992). Scholars have noted the discrepancy between the first images of Bes, found on ivory wands from the Middle Kingdom, and the much later attestation of the name of Bes, found only from the 21st Dynasty, with no association of the two until the Ptolemaic period (Meeks 1992: 423; Romano 1980: 39-40). Furthermore, it has been noted that similar images have been used to represent at least eight deities including Aha, Soped and Tettetunu (Ballod 1913, 11-14, 24-26). A full analysis of the issues raised in wider scholarship is outside the remit of this study. This discussion will centre on why the depiction of the god known as Bes was a key feature in the 'women on beds' scenes. Dasen (1993) examined textual evidence and material culture in her analysis of the significance of dwarfs in ancient Egypt and Greece. She suggests Bes was a 'hypostases' of major deities whose role was as a protector in at least five spheres of human life, four of which are relevant to this study (Dasen 1993: 65).

5.1b: Protector of Women and Children

In textual sources Bes is called upon as a protector of women and children, demonstrated in spells to assist with childbirth. This is seen in *The Magical Texts of Papyri Leiden I*; Spell 30 calls for a 'dwarf of clay to be placed on the brow of a woman, who is giving birth while suffering' (Borghouts 1971: 29). Borghouts, in relation to the divine birth scene at Luxor temple, states both the dwarf (Bes) and the hippopotamus (Taweret) were sent from Ra. However, the images on the figured ostraca are post-birth; the women are dressed in their finery, receiving guests. This suggests Bes' protective role extended beyond birth into the wider domestic zone. The frontality of Bes is relevant here. Volokhine (2000: 7) argues frontal images speak directly to the viewer, in contrast to the majority of Egyptian profile representations; in the case of Bes his face is like a mask which has an apotropaic value. His visage is both monkey and lion like, with a grin that can be seen to represent fear, laughter or holding evil forces at bay (Volokhine 2000: 74). He is a guardian of the bed upon which women and children repose. It also explains his presence on the '*lit clos*', which may have been used for worship in the home, as discussed in Section 1.4.

5.1c: Domestic Space

Bes is also the most prolific motif on the surviving wall paintings found in the village. Representations of Bes were found in at least six houses (WP.I, WP.5-9). Bes is also found on wall paintings at Amarna, see Figures 2.24-5. Bes was clearly a popular motif in domestic space in New Kingdom Egypt, found in both the remains of settlement sites and depictions of domestic space, as illustrated on the figured ostraca. Similar representations of Bes are found in royal iconography. Bes is seen in the divine birth scenes of Hatshepsut at Deir el-Bahri, shown frontally next to Taweret under a couch with the legs of a lion (Naville 1896: Plate LI). Bes can also be seen as a protector of sleepers at night, as demonstrated by his appearance in Amenhotep III's bedchamber at Malkata. Figures of the god form a frieze on the west wall of the King's bed chamber. They stand above a series of representations of *ankh* and *sa* signs, delineating life and protection (Smith 1998: 104, Figures 287-288). This may also relate to a scene in the Eighteenth Dynasty tomb of Sennefer (TT 99), which shows an over-sized Bes next to a bed which is being prepared by a young woman, see Figure 5.1. Dasen (1993: 73) suggests statues of the god may have been set beside the bed in daily life, in a defensive capacity. It is noteworthy that Bruyère (1939: 101) recorded finding terracotta statues of Bes in the houses, rather than the tombs. They ranged in height from 5-20 cm; the god was depicted nude, dancing and with his hands on his hips.

5.1d: Protector of the Sleeping and the Dead

The protection of Bes extended to the nocturnal realm of sleep and to the realm of the dead. This is demonstrated in his depictions on numerous headrests, which were used in daily life and also deposited in the tomb. Taking the shape of the *akhet,* headrests were thought to ensure the sleeper would rise each morning like the sun (Hellinckx 2001); they were also believed to prevent the head of the deceased being removed as demonstrated in Spell 166 *Book of the Dead* (Allen 1974: 162). This combination of nocturnal and funerary protection is illustrated on the headrest of Qenherkhepeshef, a Scribe of the Tomb from Deir el-Medina. Made of limestone, it is likely to be a funerary item rather than made for use in daily life (Glanville 1934: 107). Bes is shown holding a spear in his right hand and brandishing a serpent in his left; serpents also fork from his mouth. The text expresses the hope for 'Good sleeping in the West, the Land of Righteousness, by the Royal Scribe Qenherkhepeshef, justified' (Glanville 1934: 106). In this capacity Bes is seen to be defending the deceased from evil spirits. This illustrates the link between sleep and death in ancient Egypt; both were seen as a time when people were vulnerable to attack from evil forces. As Szpakowska (2003a) notes from the New Kingdom onwards there is evidence that the Egyptians believed dreams were a portal between the living, the dead and the gods, as demonstrated in the New Kingdom dream manual, *Chester Beatty III* (Gardiner 1935). It is perhaps Bes' status as a '*demi-god*' or '*genie*', as suggested by Bruyère (1939: 93), that equipped the god to combat evil forces in daily life, in sleep and in the afterlife, as he is a combination of benevolent and malevolent power. There are also limited references to the god in *The Book of the Dead;* for example, Spells 28 and 163 which ask Bes to protect the body of the deceased (Allen 1974: 38, 159-160).

Figure 5.1: Scene from the Eighteenth Dynasty tomb of Sennefer (TT 99) (Bruyère 1939: 108, Figure 39) © IFAO.

5.1e: Music and Dance

It has been argued that images of Bes making music and dancing also had an apotropaic function (Piankoff 1937-1938; Romano 1980: 30-31). Pinch believed (2002: 118) Bes may have subsumed the characteristics of Hity, a dwarf god who drove away evil by stamping, dancing or beating a drum or tambour. Furthermore, Dasan (1993: 78) suggests music and dance were associated with celebrations of birth from the New Kingdom onwards. In the *Papyrus Westcar,* the goddesses who go to assist with the birth of Ruddedet change their appearance into dancing girls (Lichtheim 1973: 220). Dancers are frequently depicted wearing Bes tattoos, as discussed in Section 5.1f. Bes is shown making music on only one '*Scènes de Gynécées*' figured ostraca (EB.1) but wooden examples discussed in Section 5.1g show him playing the double flute.

5.1f: Tattoos

The image of the god Bes may also have had an amuletic function when applied to the body as a tattoo or temporary body art. No images of the '*Scénes de Gynécées*' ostraca show a wearer of a Bes tattoo. However, the dancer depicted in house S.E. VIII (WP.1) has the god inscribed on both thighs. Two fragmentary figurines from Deir el-Medina, now in the archive at IFAO, have incision marks on their thighs which could be depictions of the god Bes (IFAO 02574: IFAO 02638: Backhouse 2016: 501, 506). The marks are angular and schematic, similar in style to the manner in which Bes is represented on the '*Scènes de Gynécées*' figured ostraca, when incorporated into the foot of the bed. There is also a 'lady on a bed' figurine, with no provenance, which has markings suggestive of Bes tattoos on her thighs (British Museum EA 2371: Pinch 1983: Plate VI).

There are several contemporaneous depictions of musicians wearing Bes tattoos or body art, for example in the tomb of Nakhtamun (TT 341). This shows a young girl carrying an animal-headed lyre; she appears to be naked with the exception of two Bes tattoos on her thighs (Davies 1948: Plate 28). Bes is also depicted on the right thigh of a young girl playing a lute, which decorates a faience bowl now in Leiden Museum (Leiden AD 14: Friedman: 1998: 113). It has been suggested due to the imagery this originated in Deir el-Medina (Friedman 1998: 212). The association of Bes tattoos with dancers and musicians led Keimer (1948: 104) to suggest that Bes was their divine protector; however, he went on to argue tattoos were the mark of a prostitute, a courtesan or a 'libertine'. Unfortunately, Keimer used the work of Perdrizet (1921) to strengthen his argument; however, Perdrizet was examining Greek terracotta figurines, so there is a considerable time disparity. Even more problematic is Keimer's use of modern examples to confirm his assertion that tattoos are the markings of criminals, pimps and women of low morals (Keimer 1948: 105).

Pinch (1983: 412) also suggested Bes tattoos may have been worn as a charm to protect women in childbirth or to encourage conception. This would confirm Bruyère's (1939: 127) assertion that jewellery worn by figurines had talismanic power. Some scholars, for example Cherpion (2006: 20), have continued to stress that the wearers of Bes tattoos are '*dames aux moeurs dévergondées et libertines*', due to their nudity. Cherpion argues in ancient Egypt if adult women were portrayed naked it signified, they are '*prête à se donner*' either to their husband, lover or a client. Although she qualifies this by adding naked servant girls need special consideration. It is unlikely the wall painting, executed in the first room of house S.E. VIII (WP.I), depicted a prostitute, or by the same token, the hundreds of fragments of female figurines found at the village by Bruyère (1939: 109) all naked, represented prostitutes. By depicting the naked female form it is likely the Egyptians were celebrating something inherent in women, the fertility she encapsulated and therefore the potential for birth and rebirth.

No physical evidence of Bes tattoos has been found to date. Although, in 2014 Austin and Gobeil (2016) recorded at least 30 figural tattoos on a female mummy from Deir el-Medina. These were placed predominantly on her neck, back and shoulders, most were publicly visible. All were made prior to mummification as the shrinkage of the skin, which occurs as part of the process, has resulted in the distortion of some images (Austin and Gobeil 2016: 26). They include depictions of *wadjet* eyes, *nefer* symbols, Hathoric cows, *menat* necklaces and images of serpents. Austin and Gobeil (2016: 33) conclude 'the majority of the identified tattoos on this mummy evoke Hathoric designs.' They suggest this provided the deceased with a permanent connection to the goddess and that she may have been a dancer, or musician-priestess of Hathor. As reported in the scientific journal *Nature* the discoveries were made possible by the use of infrared imaging, which penetrated deeper into the skin than visible light imaging (Watson 2016: 155). This is a relatively new technique, which opens up the possibilities of more discoveries in the future, which may include Bes tattoos. The significant point to note is the use of tattoos to inscribe divine images.

In relation to figured ostraca from Deir el-Medina, there are depictions of tattoos, but these are confined to a dot motif. This includes the image of a dancer (IFAO VA 2868), see Figure 2.3 and images of servant girls, most likely non-Egyptian, see CE.12. It is possible two further figurines from Deir el-Medina (Louvre E 16506a, Louvre E 16506b: Backhouse 2016: 479-80) were depicted with tattoos. Both are handmade and have incised and applied decoration. Their bodies are covered in dot incisions; the motif is very prevalent and covers most of their bodies. The use of the dot motif in tattooing is known from the Middle Kingdom. It is found on many faience figurines, for example the figurine found by Winlock in the tomb of Neferhotep at Deir el-Bahri (Cairo JE 47710: Winlock 1942: 72). It is also seen on Middle Kingdom mummies found at Deir el-Bahri (Keimer 1948: Plates I-IX; Winlock 1942: 74) and Nubian C Group examples discovered by Firth (1927: 50) and more recently by Friedman (2004) at Hierakonpolis.

5.1g: New Kingdom Furniture

The discussion so far has centred on the symbolism attached to depictions of Bes in the '*Scènes de Gynécées*' figured ostraca and contemporaneous material culture. However, it is possible there were more practical reasons for the rendering of these scenes. Bruyère (1939: 98-101, Figures 32, 34) published four painted wooden figures of Bes in his excavation report of the village of Deir el-Medina, see Figure 5.2; he suggested these may have come from a piece of furniture. In three of these Bes is playing the double flute; while he has his hands on his hips in the other example. The Bes figures are standing on drums which were common elements of Egyptian furniture from the 1st Dynasty (Killen 1980: 23-63; Raven 2014: 194). Bes figures are also depicted standing on drums on ostracon EB.1. It has been noted by Raven (2014: 196-7) that as Bruyère did not specify a find spot, these wooden figures may have been bought in Luxor by the excavator, who believed they came from the site. These are now in Brussels Museum, listed in the register as 'probably from Deir el-Medina' (Raven 2014: 196).

After three similar examples were acquired by Leiden Museum, Raven (2014) undertook a study of similar objects in museum collections worldwide. He located 13 examples in total, many of which had passed through the international art market several times. None have a firm provenance, but Raven argues there are good reasons for suggesting many came from Deir el-Medina. Three (possibly four) came from the Michailidis Collection; Michailidis (1900 – 1973) was a Greek collector with an interest in hieroglyphs and Egyptian religion (Bierbrier 2012: 371). Michailidis (1963: 89) believed the Bes legs came from Deir el-Medina and he had other items from the village in his collection, for example *Ostraka Michaelides*, published by Goedicke and Wente (1962). After careful consideration Raven (2014: 202) suggests at least ten of the Bes legs originated from Deir el-Medina, while the other three were 'likely' to have come from the workmen's village or have a Theban provenance. He further notes 'the manner in which the god Bes is depicted on the bed legs has strong similarity to the god's iconography on other objects from Deir el-Medina, such as wall paintings, vase paintings or ostraca' (Raven 2014: 198).

The Leiden examples are all flat and unpainted on the rear. They have a rectangular socket at the level of the abdomen, which is surrounded by plaster, see Figures 5.3a-c. It is likely the headdress of Bes supported a rectangular frame and the legs were joined by mortise-and-tenon joints (Raven 2014: 195). Raven concludes that the upper edge of the frame stood 72-75 cm above the floor, which would be too tall for a comfortable seat. Furthermore, ordinary beds generally stood 18-44 cm from the floor; Raven (2014: 195) therefore,

Figure 5.2: Wooden figures of Bes, as published by Bruyère, Brussels E 7415a-b, E 7416a-b, (Bruyère 1939: 98, Figure 32) © IFAO.

Figures 5.3a-c: Wooden Bes legs, now in Leiden Museum, Leiden F 1964/1.4, Leiden F 1964/1.3, Leiden F 2011/2.1 (Courtesy of Maarten Raven) © Rijksmuseum van Oudheden.

suggests the Bes legs belonged to beds with a 'ritual' function. However, Raven notes the difficulties of the archaeological evidence. The condition of the Bes legs suggests they may have been deposited in tombs, although none were recorded by Bruyère in a funerary context. Furthermore, the only parallel artefact, a wooden figure 55 cm in height, was found in a cellar in house S.E.VIII (Bruyère 1939: 101, Figure 34) and was badly decayed.

5.1g: 'Women's Beds'

Regardless of their final placement, it is highly likely that beds with Bes feet were created and used in the village and were depicted on the figured ostraca. There are textual references which may describe the purchasing and commissioning of such items. Janssen's (1975: 180) study of economic transactions that took place in the village notes several exchanges of a 'woman's bed' (*ḥt'ti st),* as recorded in *O.Gardiner 9* and *O. Gardiner 105* (Černý and Gardiner 1957: Plates 24 and 53). There are further references to 'recompense for making a woman's bed' (*t3 myny n p3 ḥt'ti st'*) in *Ostraca Varille 13* (Grandet 2008: 168-170, Figure 3) and 'for the decoration of a woman's bed' in *O.Gardiner 9* (Černý and Gardiner 1957, Plate 24). As Janssen (1975: 182) noted the price indicated for the latter transaction is not for the cost of the bed but for the additional embellishment. The price for a 'woman's bed' was 3 *sniw* but the decoration of the bed cost a further 1 ½ *khar*. As suggested by Toivari-Viitala (2001: 177) 'women's beds' were differentiated from ordinary beds; she notes when a woman bought a bed it was not referred to as a 'woman's bed' simply a bed, as demonstrated in *O. British Museum 50737* (Demarée 2002: 35, Plate 138).

Material culture, textual evidence and visual representations suggest beds with Bes legs existed in the village. They may have been used for post-birth celebrations, as shown on the 'women on beds' scenes. Toivari-Viitala (2001:178) notes, as elaborate pieces of furniture it is likely they were used in subsequent births and possibly passed on from one generation to the next; she also raises the possibility that the beds were dismantled when not in use. The occasional use of these objects would account for the good state of preservation of the surviving Bes furniture legs.

There is further evidence of the use of Bes as a decorative motif on furniture in New Kingdom Egypt. A pair of wooden furniture legs in the collection of the Egypt Centre at Swansea University has Bes and Taweret painted on them, Figures 5.4 a-c. Serpents also flank the outside of the legs, providing an additional link to the images on the figured ostraca. Unfortunately, these objects have no known provenance. Similar association between two and three-dimensional representations is seen on a model bed found at Amarna, which may have been made for a figurine to repose on (Frankfort and Pendlebury 1933: 42). Bes and Taweret can be seen on the footboard, Figure 5.5. The association of Bes and beds is also found in the tomb of Yuya and Tuya (KV 46), which yielded some remarkably elaborate furniture (Davies 1907:36), see Figure 2.19.

5.1h: Linkage

The evidence suggests Bes was represented on the figured ostraca due to his protective capacity, principally of women and children in daily life but also of the wider domestic zone. His frontality may have been used to

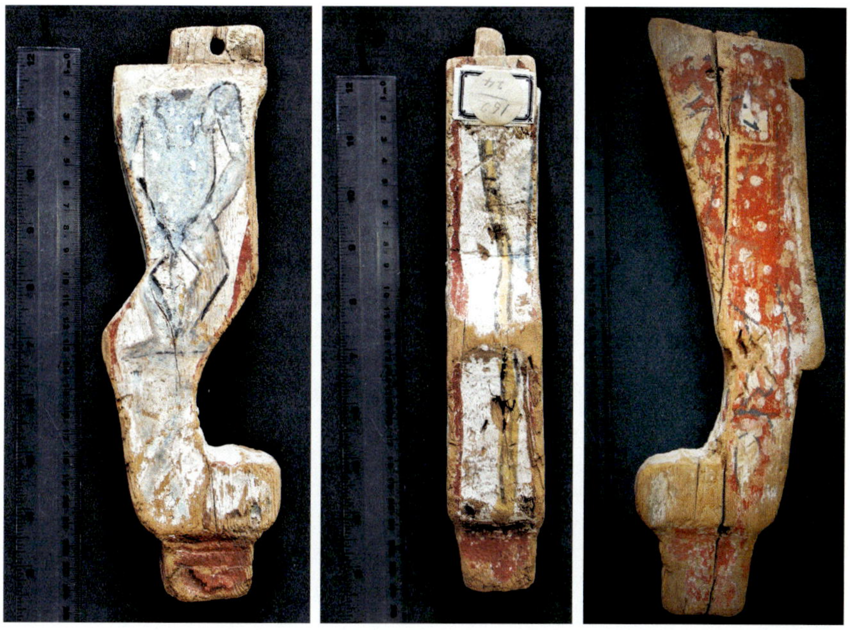

Figures 54a-c: Wooden furniture legs, with Bes, Taweret and serpent painted decoration, Swansea W 2052 a-c (Courtesy of Carolyn Graves-Brown) © Egypt Centre, Swansea University.

Figure 5.5: Terracotta model bed from Amarna, Petrie Museum UC 46891 (Photograph Author's own) Courtesy of Petrie Museum of Egyptian Archaeology.

speak directly to malevolent forces, confronting and holding them at bay. It is likely the beds depicted on the figured ostraca were used in daily life, in celebrations linked to the birth of a child, when the creation of a safe space for the mother and child was essential. The depiction of Bes may also reflect his association with music and dance, which may have been part of the festivities. Furthermore, the performative element may have had an apotropaic function in itself.

5.2: Serpent Imagery

A significant number of bed-frames shown in the 'women on beds' dataset contain a distinctive decorative motif. This is either a single wavy line drawn in black, for example (WoB.4) or a double wavy line with the addition of diagonal or spot markings, for example (WoB.29). These are seen on at least 24 bed-frames in the 'women on beds' dataset and three examples in the fragments dataset. These are likely to represent serpent imagery given the similarity to three-dimensional figurines, as discussed in Section 5.11a, images on stelae found at the Deir el-Medina and limited evidence of material culture from New Kingdom Egypt.

5.2a: Material Culture

One example of a bed from Deir el-Medina has been found which used serpents as a decorative motif. This was found in the tomb of Sennedjem (TT 1) and is now in Cairo Museum (JE 27254: El-Sabbahy 1999). The bed is made from two long side bars, joined by a cross bar at each end. No webbing was attached to the bed, which has no footboard. The bed is made of wood with two snakes painted along the side bars; their heads meet at the cross bar and their tails overlap, encircling the bed. The snakes are outlined in black; the bodies of the snakes are painted yellow with black spots used to indicate their skin pattern. Several ostraca use similar colours for the serpent motif (WoB.5, 21, 35). El-Sabbahy (1999: 14) suggests that the snakes on the bed form a circle offering magical protection to the deceased. The text is funereal in nature referring to Sennedjem as 'The Osiris, the Servant of the Lord of the Two Lands' (El-Sabbahy 1999: 14). It is likely Sennedjem's bed was a funerary bed. It is similar in form to Sennefer's bed, which was found in his tomb with his sarcophagus on top. Bruyère (1928: 60-61, Figure 31) believed Sennefer's bed had not been used in daily life as no webbing was attached. In relation to the images on the '*Scénes de Gynécées*' figured ostraca, this suggests the beds included imagery which also had funerary associations, possibly linked to rebirth and protection.

There is further evidence of beds with serpent motifs, seen on the wooden legs and frame now in the British Museum (EA 21574: Quirke 1992: 118, Figure 70). Around the wooden legs gold cobras are coiled, and ebony cobras run along the uprights of the footboard. It was originally thought that this was the remains of a royal throne belonging to Hatshepsut but is now believed they formed part of a bed or couch.

A number of wooden statues of snakes were also found at Deir el-Medina by Möller; these have been published by Weiss. One is still attached to its base but has its head missing (Berlin ÄMP 23877: Weiss 2015: 346, Catalogue number 10.6), two additional fragments show the body of the serpent detached from its base (Berlin ÄMP 21574, ÄMP 23874: Weiss 2015, 355-356, Catalogue numbers 10.21-2). These two examples have painted decoration of dots and a wavy line suggesting the skin of the serpent; this is similar to the imagery in the '*Scènes de Gynécées*' figured ostraca. These were all found in the area around the houses. A further example shows a curled snake (Berlin ÄMP 23875: Weiss 2015: 363, Catalogue number 10.37). This indicates the serpent was venerated in the home despite no clay serpent figurines being found at the site. Szpakowska has studied clay cobra figurines extensively (Szpakowska 2003b, 2012, 2015). She has found over 700 fragments in 14 sites, predominantly Ramesside settlement sites in the north of Egypt, her Levantine Empire and Libya (Szpakowska 2015: 275). The lack of serpent figurines with a Theban provenance may reflect regional preferences and relate to the predominance of the worship of Meretseger at the village.

5.2b: Significance of the Serpent

The serpent held an ambivalent position in Egyptian symbolism and mythology. They were often regarded as a source of chaos and disorder; as such they are depicted in numerous vignettes of *The Book of the Dead* being speared and cut. In the papyrus of Ani, in the vignette accompanying Spell 10, Ani is shown impaling a serpent which symbolises any force hostile to the dead (Faulkner 1985: 40). Although an oversimplifi-

Figure 5.6: Image from the anonymous TT 345 Deir el-Medina (Cherpion 1999: Plate 41) © IFAO.

cation, it is noteworthy that female serpent goddesses are generally viewed as protective and nurturing while many male serpent gods embody chaos and discord. Given the placement of the serpents on the bedframes and on three dimensional figurines, as discussed in Section 5.11a, it is likely they played a protective role, encircling the recumbent figure. As Szpakowska (2012: 40) notes snakes are often associated with powerful female goddesses, notably Weret-hekau, Isis, Nephthys, Mut, Neith, Wadjet, Meretseger, Renenutet and the Four Noble Ladies. Indeed, the link between serpents and goddesses 'was so strong that the sign of a rearing cobra becomes the standard and generic determinate for any goddess' (Szpakowska 2012: 40).

Possibly due to the shedding of their skins, snakes were also associated with transformation and rejuvenation. Spell 87, in *The Book of the Dead*, states 'I am a snake which is in the limits of the earth; I pass the night and am reborn, renewed and rejuvenated every day' (Faulkner 1985: 84). Cherpion (1999: 94) has suggested serpents were viewed as givers of life at Deir el-Medina. This is seen in the anonymous Theban Tomb 354, which shows a winged serpent running the length of the ceiling see Figure 5.6. Cherpion further argues the meaning for this is found in the tomb of Nefertari (QV 66) which contains similar imagery with the caption 'it gives life'. The feminine pronoun led Cherpion (1999: 94, n. 341) to suggest this could be Meretseger. This suggests the serpent motif was perhaps seen as a giver of life for eternity at Deir el-Medina, which demonstrates that the snake pattern in the '*Scènes de Gynécées*' figured ostraca should be viewed as life affirming and protective.

5.2c: Meretseger

It is possible the serpent motif in the '*Scènes de Gynécées*' figured ostraca and three-dimensional figurines from Deir el-Medina represented Meretseger. The goddess is most frequently depicted as a snake or a snake with the head of a woman with the head of a woman; although she is sometimes shown with the body of a woman and the head of a serpent or fully anthropomorphic (Bruyère 1929:108). Most noteworthy is her strong association with the Theban West Bank. She was often referred to as 'the Peak of the West', so personifying a topographic feature, the mountain known as el-Qurn. This rises behind the village of Deir el-Medina and dominates the skyline. However, Bruyère (1930: 193) suggested she was associated with the Theban West Bank in its entirety. She is very much linked to the natural environment, with her name evoking a quality of the locus, 'she who loves silence', suggesting she was a goddess of the necropoli, a place of peace, rest and tranquillity (Bruyère 1929: 16). Bruyère (1929: 7-8) believed the goddess was worshipped at a shrine close to the village, see Section 1.2f.

Meretseger is the deity most frequently depicted on stelae from Deir el-Medina (Exell 2006: 106). Many of which illustrate the goddess in snake form show a similarity in iconography to serpent imagery on the '*Scènes de Gynécées*' figured ostraca, particularly those stelae which show multiple images of the goddess, for example the stela of Wab, Mistress of the House, Figure 5.7. Significantly, Bruyère (1929: 122) suggested the goddess was depicted on these stelae numerous times to evoke the idea of eternity. Furthermore, he noted the goddess was often given the epithet 'Mistress of Generations and Manifestations without Number' (Bruyère 1929: 122). This would make her a highly suitable goddess to be depicted in the '*Scènes de Gynécées*' figured ostraca, which may show the celebrations surrounding the birth of a new child.

Meretseger is also depicted as a nurturing goddess at Deir el-Medina, associated with both the king and the workmen. A stela found in Chapel C in the rock cut shrine, shows the goddess suckling Rameses III (Bruyère 1929: 34-35, Plate XV). This stela includes the Theban triad of Amun, Meretseger and Horus, reflecting one of the epithets of the goddess as 'Divine Mother, Mother of the God' (Bruyère 1929: 133). Meretseger is assimilated with Hathor on the stela of Paser, which depicts both goddesses sitting opposite each other; in-between 14 serpents traverse from Meretseger towards Hathor, who is breastfeeding a child, see Figure 5.8. The text refers to Hathor as 'Mistress of the West and her beautiful name of Meretseger, Mistress of the Libyan Mountains', while Meretseger is referred to as 'Mistress of the West, Mistress of the Sky, Mistress of the Gods' (Bruyère 1952a:76-77, Figure 156). It is noteworthy that Yoyotte (2003) identified two forms of Meretseger, one as cosmic Hathor and the other as 'The Peak of The

Figure 5.7: Stela from Deir el-Medina, of the lady Wab, Turin 50060 (Photograph Author's own).

West', the local cult. On the Theban West Bank there was a synthesis of the two goddesses, for example there are graffiti at Deir el-Bahri temple which invoke Meretseger, while the majority are to Hathor (Marciniak 1974: 96) and the stela from Chapel C, discussed above, shows Meretseger's increasing role in royal cult.

Meretseger was clearly an important goddess to the residents of Deir el-Medina, associated with the local environment but it is likely she also took on some of the functions of great goddesses of ancient Egypt, particularly in relation to birth and rebirth. This is seen in the tomb of Neferrenpet (TT 336), where Meretseger, in human form, offers her breast to the tomb owner, shown as a child, see Figure 5.9 The text was damaged during the excavation, but it included references to Meretseger as 'Mistress of the Sky.... all of the gods, all provisions' (Bruyère 1926: 88). Later Bruyère (1929: 41) suggested the image represented the rebirth of the tomb owner, who had become a child again in another time. This clearly relates to her epithet of 'Mistress of many Births and Transformations' as noted by Bruyère (1929: 138).

Figure 5.9: Scene from the tomb of Neferrenpet, Deir el-Medina TT 336 (Bruyère 1926: 87, Figure 53) © IFAO.

Figure 5.8: Stela from Deir el-Medina, showing Meretseger and Hathor (Bruyère 1952: 76-77, Figure 156) © IFAO.

Figure 5.10: Ostracon dedicated to Meretseger from Deir el-Medina, Turin C.1659 (Photograph Author's own).

Bruyère found numerous lintels with depictions of Renenutet in the village, for example house S.E. II (Bruyère 1939: 267, Figure 139). However, Meretseger is frequently depicted on lintels and door jambs, for example in house N.O. XII (Bruyère 1939: 287, Plate XV, Number 6). Bruyère (1939: 193) noted many *'laraires'* were blackened due to smoke damage, as most were found in the kitchen area of houses. The association of serpents and food is also seen in the Ramesside Dream Manual (*P. Chester Beatty III*), which states if a man sees a serpent this is 'good as it means food' (Gardiner 1935: 12, Plate 5).

In addition to stelae and depictions in tombs there are a large number of ostraca found at Deir el-Medina which depict a serpent goddess (Vandier d'Abbadie 1937: 222-224, VA Numbers 2653-2664; Vander d'Abbadie 1959: 135–137, VA Numbers 3011-3018). Although levels of skill vary, the ostraca mostly show the goddess as a coiled serpent, sometimes wearing double plumes and a solar disc with her head turned towards a lotus flower or a table of offerings, Figure 5.10. Many are votives dedicated by workmen naming the goddess Meretseger. While not all ostraca contain a dedication, Meretseger is the only goddess who is named on serpent votives from Deir el-Medina.

5.2d: Renenutet

There is, however, one ostracon in the comparative evidence dataset which names Renenutet (CE.2). Although it has no firm provenance it is believed to have come from Thebes. Broekhuis (1971:149-150) notes Renenutet was a nurturer who was often depicted as a serpent, particularly as a cobra or a woman with the head of a snake; she is also associated with linen and woven fabric. Both Meretseger and Renenutet are seen as givers of life. Renenutet is attested at Deir el-Medina particularly on household shrines; Bruyère (1939: 193–196) refers to these as *'laraires'*. These are small shrines for domestic cult, consisting of a stone lintel, jambs and wooden doors; holes were drilled for the pivots of the wooden door leaves (which have not survived). They were generally found in fragments at the site. However, an almost complete example survives in the British Museum (EA 597: Bierbrier 1982: Plates 66-67). The left jamb was excavated by Schiaparelli and is Turin Museum (S.9506). This small shrine shows Inherkhau facing the viewer's left worshipping Renenutet and facing the viewer's right worshipping Ptah and Sobek.

Bruyère (1939: 196) recovered numerous fragmentary statues which he believed were once contained inside the domestic shrines. These included representations of the Theban triad, the Elephantine triad, Ptah, Amenhotep I and Ahmose Nefertari, Sobek, Taweret, Thoth in baboon form, and the serpents Meretseger and Renenutet. Bruyère (1939: 318) noted finding in house S.O. II a head of a uraeus in lapis lazuli, which he believed had been stored inside a household shrine.

5.2e: Serpent Cult

It would appear that serpent goddesses were firmly linked to domestic cult at Deir el-Medina. While both Meretseger and Renenutet are attested on household shrines far more stelae were dedicated solely to Meretseger than to Renenutet. This suggests that Meretseger was favoured more outside the home at Deir el-Medina, perhaps reflecting her association with Hathor and the great goddesses of Egypt, also her assimilation with the wider local landscape as 'The Peak of the West'. Similarly, with the figured ostraca, Renenutet is not named on any examples excavated from the site. It is likely the serpent imagery depicted on the bedframes in the *'Scènes de Gynécées'* figured ostraca is a schematic rendering of Renenutet or Meretseger, but the latter is more likely as she is represented on more stelae and named on figured ostraca found at the site. Meretseger was also linked to concepts of sustenance and rebirth, highly appropriate for her inclusion in the *'Scènes de Gynécées'* figured ostraca. It is probable real beds were decorated with serpent motifs, in association with the god Bes. Many examples of furniture depicted on the figured ostraca have been found, for example vase stands as illustrated on ostraca CE.3 (British Museum EA 2470: Killen 1980: 70, Plates 116-7). This suggests the furniture depicted on the figured ostraca existed in the village.

5.3: Kiosks

Only two ostraca (K.1-2) in the '*Scènes de Gynécées*' figured ostraca distinctly show a kiosk. These have papyri form columns with convolvulus leaves wrapped around them. A third ostracon (K.3) is likely to have included a similar structure. There are a further two fragmentary ostraca which almost certainly were from larger kiosk scenes (F.11 and F.13). Another fragmentary ostracon (F.3) is either from a kiosk or 'elaborate bed' scene. Although representations on the ostraca are limited, one of the most substantial wall paintings remaining at Deir el-Medina is likely to have depicted a kiosk scene, see WP.2. Furthermore, there are an additional eight ostraca in the 'women on beds' dataset which include a canopy-like feature stretching over the bed. Three show a vine with convolvulus leaves attached (WoB.41, 49-50), two are formed by convolvulus leaves only (WoB.48, 53), one is a tendril with flowers (WoB.45) and two do not include foliage (WoB.4, 37). A fragmentary example (F.14) shows a woman under a canopy formed by a tendril with flowers and bunches of grapes, described by Brunner-Traut (1955: 12) as a pergola of vine leaves, which she believed were also used to form kiosks. This suggests there is some linkage between the kiosk scenes, which appear to take place outdoors, and the 'women on beds' scenes, which take place inside the house.

5.3a: Birthing Pavilion

Brunner-Traut (1955: 17) suggested the kiosk represented the actual place women gave birth in. Spell 33 in *The Magical Text of the Papyri Leiden I* supports this assertion; it states 'Rejoicing, rejoicing in heaven! Birthgiving is accelerated! Come to me, Hathor, my mistress, in my fine pavilion, in this happy hour' (Borghouts 1971: 30). Brunner-Traut links these airy structures to birth houses, 'mammisi chapels' which were found at Greco-Roman temples. She notes both structures are outside more formal edifices and have plant-like columns. The symbolism attached to the mammisi chapel has been discussed by Badawy (1963). He suggested they evoked the birth of Horus in the papyrus thicket, as demonstrated in both text and image. This is seen in the inscription at Edfu on the facade of the ambulatory which states 'This is the place itself where the infant has been born by his mother, as did Isis for her son Horus in the hiding' (Badawy 1963: 81). Architecturally the naos is surrounded by composite columns forming an ambulatory; these columns derive from papyri form columns. Badawy (1963: 81) suggested they were 'an architectural transposition of the bush *(b3t)* round the child which protects Horus at Buto.' Clearly this is a mythical setting for a divine birth as women in ancient Egypt gave birth standing or squatting on mud bricks. One such brick has been found (Wegner 2009) dating to the Middle Kingdom. It is possible the kiosks created by papyri form columns, depicted on the figured ostraca, were symbolically generating a safe space for the mother and child, evoking the papyrus thicket.

Figure 5.11: Image from the Mammisi at Edfu, Hathor suckling Horus (Photograph Author's own).

Iconographically the scenes portrayed in the mammisi chapels show Horus being suckled by a mother goddess within a papyrus thicket, see Figure 5.11. This is generally Isis or Hathor, both goddesses associated with the maternity of kings. These are depicted on the uppermost register at the rear of the sanctuary. Badawy (1963: 84) argued this suggested a remoteness of time and space, as the images were based on the myth of the birth Horus at Chemmis on the edge of the Delta (Klasen 1952: 69). Although the mammisi chapels were created up to a thousand years after the drawing of the figured ostraca it is possible the same mythological framework underpinned their design.

5.3b: Internal Domestic Structures

While the depictions of kiosks in the '*Scènes de Gynécées*' figured ostraca is rare, convolvulus leaves are threaded

Figure 5.12: Tomb of Ay, Amarna, scenes of the harem (Davies 1908: 20, Plate XXVIII)
Image courtesy of the Egypt Exploration Society.

through many 'women on beds' scenes. It is possible they were used to create a pergola, a structure decorated for festive occasions or to provide seclusion. Brunner-Traut (1955: 18-19) noted that the 'ephemeral' pergola could be a replacement for a more permanent kiosk and could be erected anywhere. In dense settlements this could be on the roof or possibly inside the house. The tomb of Ay at Amarna contains images of what Davies (1908: 20) believed to be the harem, occupied by women engaged in music and dance. In a separate room, to the viewers right, a bed is shown between two papyri columns, hung between the columns is a banner or curtain, Figure 5.12. Although undecorated Brunner-Traut (1955: 19) believed this may have been a temporary pergola erected in a domestic setting. Brunner-Traut (1955: 12) noted in *Papyrus Westcar* that Ruddedet gave birth in a room at her home, she suggested that this was on a second storey as the maid is sent to the lower chamber (Lichtheim 1973: 220). Borghouts (1971: 165) asks if this upper storey room could be a pavilion erected on the roof. The small number of kiosk scenes may reflect the dense nature of the site of Deir el-Medina, which may have used more temporary structures erected indoors. It is possible decorative beds with Bes legs, were set up in the houses at Deir el-Medina for the birth but more likely for celebrations later. The rooms may have been decked with convolvulus leaves and floral collars to evoke the original outdoor location of the kiosks; or these may represent painted wall decoration.

5.3c: Dress and Decorum

While there are points of comparison in the 'women on beds' and the kiosks scenes, there are some distinct iconographical elements in the two datasets. The most striking feature is the attire of the main female protagonists. The women in the kiosk scenes are naked except for a broad collar and a cape/shawl around their shoulders; their hair is also arranged in a distinctive tripartite style. The women sitting on beds are mostly dressed in their finery; they wear complex wrap-around dresses and heavy wigs, tied with a fillet, often topped with a lotus flower and head cone. Furthermore, the iconography of the accompanying figures in both scenes is distinct. The female attendants in the kiosk scenes are naked and have an elongated hairstyle/headdress; the male figures also have an idiosyncratic hairstyle. It is possible the attendants in the kiosk scenes all offer the same objects – mirrors and kohl tubes. While the attendants in the 'women on beds' scenes are dressed in a similar manner to the main figure, indicating they are of equal status. They also offer a more diverse range of objects. This suggests the two datasets are depicting different events, although possibly linked by the birth of a child. Brunner-Traut (1955: 21) proposed that the kiosk scenes illustrate the period of purification, which *Papyrus Westcar* tells us was 14 days (Lichtheim 1973: 221). However, the 'women on beds' scenes show the lady of the house in her finery implying she has returned home.

Brunner-Traut (1955: 25) suggested that the distinctive hairstyle worn by women in the kiosk scenes is not a tripartite wig, as commonly referred to, for example by Peck and Ross (1978: 90) but is actually hair. She suggested that the images combine a frontal view of the hairstyle with a profile view of the woman. She argued the hair is arranged over a frame; the peg of which is visible on top of the head, from which ribbons are tied. To confirm this Brunner-Traut looked to the work of Soranus, a physician who lived in the 1st – 2nd Century AD and studied in Alexandria; he wrote a doctrine of gynaecology. He believed women's hair should be loosened to aid childbirth and they should not wear any tight or restrictive clothing (Soranus translated by Temkin 1991: 73-74). Brunner-Traut saw the tripartite hairstyle as neither a wig nor naturally falling hair but hair detached widely from the head in a special manner. She suggested that this hairstyle had significance for ancient Egyptians and played a role in the attire of women during childbirth.

While numerous female figurines dating to the Middle Kingdom have been found with a distinctive tripartite hairstyle, for example at Edfu (Michalowski *et al.* 1939: Plates XXIV, XXV), figurines with a peg on top of their

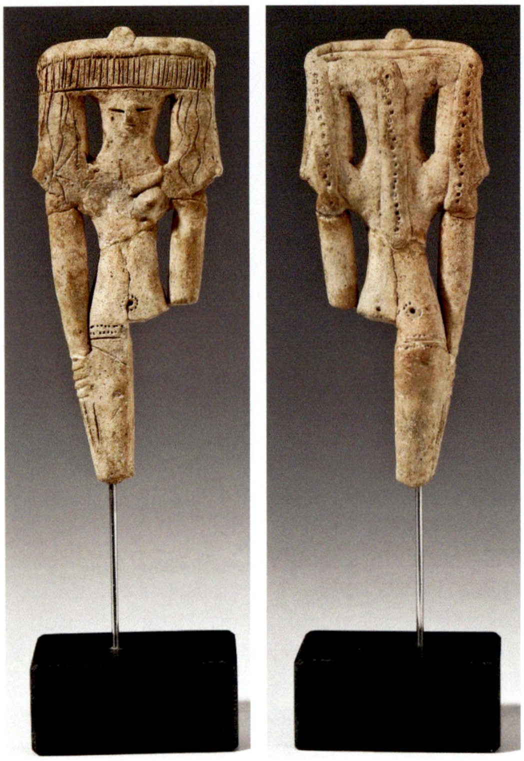

Figures 5.13a-b: Terracotta figurine, with heavy tripartite wig and top knot, Munich 1559, © State Museum of Egyptian Art, photograph by Marianne Franke.

head are extremely rare. Brunner-Traut (1955: 25, Figure 10) did note one example now in Munich, see Figures 5.13a-b, provenance unknown. Two further examples are cited by Bruyère (1939: 124, Figure 47) as from Gebelein, now in Cairo Museum (JE 41792: JE 41793). The head and upper body of a similar figurine is also in the Metropolitan Museum (MMA 17.6.74). Hayes (1959: 18) stated it was acquired at Koptos and describes it as wearing 'the divided, flaring coiffure surmounted by a fillet and a small cone'. Another possible example from el-Kab, unpublished, is at the Ashmolean Museum (1896.1908. E.3795). None of these figurines includes a depiction of a child or have any direct association with childbirth. By contrast, Ritner (2008: 174) sees the heavy tripartite hairstyle as unbraided, therefore removing all knots which might have magically hindered birth. He notes the hieroglyphic determinates for birth can also show dishevelled hair. Loose (1993: 288) also found two hieratic ostraca in Turin Museum that include the determinative of a woman with bound hair. In addition, it is used after the title '*iwr.ty*' 'Pregnant One' (Lopez 1978: Plate 46) and after the descriptor '*rnn.t-k*', 'she who feeds you' (Lopez 1978: Plate 98).

5.3d: Attendants

A distinctive element of the kiosk scenes is the attire of the servants which differentiates them from the main figure and from the attendants in the 'women on beds' scenes. In both K.1 and K.3 the attendants have similar hairstyles. In K.1 the female figure appears to have black hair tied up in a ponytail which curls at the end; Vandier d'Abbadie (1957: 23) referred to this a '*une mèche ondulée*'. Although, badly damaged in K.3 it appears that the attendant has a long lock falling from the top of their head and another falling from their temple, along the side of the face; Vandier d'Abbadie (1957: 23) referred to this as '*la mèche de la tempe*'. As only the outline is rendered it is possible the rest of their scalp was shaved or more probable, they wore a conical shaped headdress which allowed for the locks of hair to fall from their temple and crown. The headdress is also seen on ostracon EB.1 with the wearer offering a kohl tube and mirror to her companion. A similar rendition is found on F.13 with the wearer also proffering a mirror and kohl tube but the companion is now lost.

Four additional ostraca published by Dorn (2011:257-9) found in the Valley of the Kings also show women sporting this non-Egyptian style coiffeur (CE.8, 10-12). These depict young girls carrying large vessels; this suggests the wearers of this distinctive hairstyle were servants. Their nudity also prescribes them low status. Vandier d'Abbadie (1957: 24) suggested the hairstyle evoked the Syrian god Reshep or the leather helmets of warriors. Reshep wears a tall conical headdress, often described as a white crown; this is decorated with the head of a gazelle and tied with a ribbon. He is attested at Deir el-Medina, for example on the stela of Ramose (Turin C.1601: Fassone 2015: 217, Figure 285). The iconographic similarity led Vandier d'Abbadie (1957: 24) to assert the young girls are undoubtedly Syrian slaves. She also suggested the hairstyle was indicative of 'certain Syrian goddesses' who wear their hair in a similar manner. She refers to an image of the 'Mistress of Animals' published by Contenau (1931: 1070, Figure 739), see Figure 5.14. This ivory lid was found at Minet el-Beida and dates to c.1210 BC.

It has been noted that while the symmetrical style of the composition is common in Syrian and Mesopotamian art, the attire of the woman, her clothes and hairstyle were borrowed from motifs found in pre-Hellenistic art from Crete (Caubet: 2005-2011). This calls into question the link between this hairstyle and Syrian goddesses, although in subsequent scholarship this has been accepted (Dorn 2011: 257-9). The headdress/hairstyle suggests non-Egyptians and the nakedness indicates lower status but whether this can be assigned to Syrians is uncertain.

While their status as Syrian slaves is debatable, the kiosk scenes clearly show servants bringing objects for the toilette of the nursing mother. It is apparent this coiffeur was used to identify and distinguish a group of female attendants seen in nursing scenes and in scenes possibly related to domestic chores (CE.8-12).

Figure 5.14: Lid of pyxis decorated with the Mistress of Animals, Louvre AO 11601 (Rama, Cc-by-sa-2.0-fr).

The latter which depict girls carrying large vessels, may have represented preparations for celebrations in the home, relating to the birth of a child. Another theme in the kiosk scenes is the inclusion of male attendants, seen in K.2 and K.3. With the possible exception of the servant depicted on ostracon WoB.47, there are no male attendants in the 'women on beds' scenes. Furthermore, the two depicted in the kiosk scenes have distinctive hairstyles; both have a shaved head with long thick locks protruding. A similar hairstyle is depicted on an ostracon containing several diverse images, clearly used as a practice piece (Brussels E 6370: Werbrouck 1953: 99, Figure 11). It is possible these ostraca depict Nubians; the servant illustrated in K.2 wears a large hoop earring and the attendant in K.3 may have a mark of scarification on his face. However, the attendant in K.3 is shown in traditional Egyptian dress with a long double kilt and broad collar. The kiosk scenes include distinct groups of people, identified by their particular appearance, the significance of which is not clear but their association with nursing women is undeniable.

5.3e: Toilette Rituals

The kiosks scenes all include an element of toiletry, either a mirror and kohl tube are presented, or the mother's feet are washed in a unique scene in K.3. Vandier d'Abbadie (1957: 21, 26) assumed this to be a Nubian female attendant washing the feet of her mistress; however, there are no indications of sex from the depiction. Bruyère (1923: 122) made similar assertions regarding the remnants of the kiosk scene found in house WP.2, which he believed included Syrian and Nubian attendants in addition to Egyptian. These scenes may simply reflect the ethnic diversity of New Kingdom Egypt. The common theme in the kiosk scenes is the potential beautification of the mother, whether this is precipitated by the presentation of a mirror and kohl pot or the washing of feet. Loose (1993: 289) suggests this is the final stage in the rites of passage after giving birth, in which the mother is coaxed into preparing herself for re-entry into the community after her period of seclusion. Kemp (1979: 52-53) has also proposed the offering of mirrors may be part of purification rituals after birth. The significance of mirrors is discussed in Sections 5.4a-m.

5.3f: A Place of Intimacy and Rebirth

Textual evidence suggests kiosks were places women gave birth in or more likely spent a period of confinement in. In addition, in New Kingdom love poetry, kiosks were presented as places of intimacy and amorous liaisons. This is discussed more fully in Section 5.11d. A sense of the erotic is linked to the kiosk; the speaker says in *The Nakht-Sobek Songs*, 'Provide her with songs and dances, Wine and strong beer in her pavilion. You will arouse her passions, And fulfil them during the night' (Tobin 2003: 329). It is perhaps due to the secluded nature of the kiosk, outside the house and surrounded by lush vegetation, that desire and a sense of closeness is evoked. In *Papyrus Harris 500*, the girl speaks saying 'I am headed to the 'love garden', my bosom full of persea (branches), my hair laden with balm, I am a <noble woman>, I am Mistress of the Two Lands, when I am with you' (Fox 1985: 52).

It has been suggested that Egyptian love poetry should not be viewed as purely secular. Davis argues that when the ancient Egyptians composed the text 'they cast it in the traditional mould of their ancient mythological compositions' (Davis 1980: 112). She proposes therefore, the poetry should be viewed as 'divine fiction'. Talking of the *Cairo Love Songs* she suggests the whole poem can be viewed as a charm to maintain the cycle of love, which is an episode in a natural cycle (Davis 1980: 113). This is also seen in some examples of Amarna art, several of which show the royal couple with the princesses on their knees; these scenes of family intimacy, unprecedented prior to the Amarna period, take place in kiosk-like structures. A fragment, now in the Louvre, shows a unique degree of closeness between the royal couple (Louvre E.11624; Arnold 1996: 102, Figure 93). Unfortunately, only the lower portion of the scene remains; it depicts the couple taking repose under a reed kiosk. The King sits, facing the viewer's right, on an elaborate lion legged chair, resting his feet on a foot stool. The Queen is balanced on his knee, turning towards the viewer's right; the royal couple face each other. On the Queen's lap sit at least two children; only legs and arms are visible of the royal offspring.

Figure 5.15: Image from the royal tomb at Amarna, showing Meketaten, or her statue in a kiosk (Martin 1974: Plate 68) Image courtesy of the Egypt Exploration Society.

5.3g: Amarna Influence

It has also been noted by Arnold that the images on Amarna stelae are similar to wall paintings found at Deir el-Medina (Arnold 1996: 100). She suggests that in Amarna art Bes and Taweret were replaced with official Aten themes relating to creation and rebirth, with the King and Queen playing a crucial role in this. Furthermore, she argues it is likely most 'shrine stelae', which show images of the royal household in recreational settings, were placed inside the house and used in domestic worship. For example, the 'shrine stela' now in Berlin (Berlin 14145), has a layer of gypsum plaster on the back, suggesting it was placed in a wall niche. While the 'shrine stela' now in Cairo (JE 44865) has drill holes in the base which allowed wooden doors to be fitted (Arnold 1996:97). Therefore, it is possible that the '*Scènes de Gynécées*' figured ostraca, which show scenes of family life, similar to the 'shrine stelae', may have also held religious significance given the inclusion of the god Bes and very likely depictions of the goddess Meretseger.

Furthermore, the kiosks scenes may have been linked to the concept of rebirth. This is demonstrated most forcefully in a scene from the royal tomb at Amarna, Figure 5.15. This shows Meketaten, or her statue, standing in a kiosk like structure. Numerous scholars have suggested the princess died in childbirth (Robins 1997: 171; Tyldesley 1998: 71) due to the parallel scenes in the royal tomb which show a bed chamber, the death of a princess, the lamentations of the royal family and a newly born baby held by a female attendant (Bouriant, Legrain and Jéquier 1903: Plate IX). Alternatively, it has been suggested Meketaten was too young to have died in childbirth and the scenes are more likely to show her death, with the new-born child symbolising the wish for her rebirth (Arnold 1996: 115; Van Dijk 2009: 88). These scenes are difficult to interpret as little is known about the afterlife expectations in the Amarna royal family. Regardless of the status of Meketaten the kiosk clearly has connotations of rebirth.

The image of Meketaten, or her statue, in a kiosk with convolvulus leaves wrapped around the papyri form columns is undoubtedly similar to the kiosk scenes (K.1-2), which show a mother nursing a child. The desire for the rebirth of Meketaten is strengthened by the elaborate floral bouquet which stands in front of the princess. From the 18th Dynasty floral bouquets were designated as an *ankh* (Sugi 2002: 137). Linguistically *ankh* means to live. This relates to the life-giving qualities of the *ankh* particularly the giving of air and breath. The symbol of the *ankh* was also combined iconographically with bouquets in the New Kingdom. Five types were identified, some of which include the *ankh* sign while others are held by a personified *ankh* sign (Sugi 2002: 135). The representation from the royal tomb (Figure 5.15) suggests the floral bouquet, the *ankh,* is reaching towards the princess to give her the breath of life, necessary for her rebirth.

5.3h: Linkage

Textual evidence suggests the kiosk depicted on the figured ostraca may have represented the structures women gave birth in or more likely functioned as a place of seclusion where the mother and child spent a period of confinement post-birth. However, given the limited number of depictions of kiosk scenes it is unlikely that this was common practice at Deir el-Medina, possibly due to the dense nature of the settlement. It is more probable elaborate beds, with Bes feet, were set up in the home to create a safe and secure environment. The images of the kiosks may have been based on mythical associations of placing the mother and child under the protection of Isis, or Hathor, who it was believed gave birth to Horus in the marshes of Chemmis. A limited number of scenes show beds with vines or trellises trailing above or next to them; this may be a link to the papyrus thicket. The kiosks may have been endowed with connotations of rebirth as demonstrated in the Amarna tomb scene. The kiosk scenes, as depicted on the figured ostraca, may illustrate rituals of purification and beautification women underwent before returning to normal duties in the village, possibly during their period of confinement inside or outside the home. The links with the images of 'women on beds' suggests the representations of both were part of an extended narrative depicting different episodes in the same story.

5.4: Mirrors and Kohl Tubes

Mirrors and kohl tubes are prevalent motifs in the '*Scènes de Gynécées*' figured ostraca. They appear in the 'women on beds', 'elaborate beds' and kiosk scenes. In the 'women on beds' scenes they are shown under the bed in 11 representations; in nine instances they are depicted next to a tall kohl tube with applicator. A mirror is also possibly held by one woman to admire her appearance (WoB.41) and a mirror may also appear in the background of WoB.38. In the 'elaborate bed' scenes they are an object of presentation in one example, EB.1 and they appear in the background in another example, EB.2. They are also objects of presentation in two of the three kiosk scenes (K.1-2). As such they are a link between the main two datasets, 'women on beds' and kiosk scenes. Additionally, they are depicted on two fragmentary ostraca; F.3 is likely to be part of an 'elaborate bed 'or kiosk scene and F.13 is probably part of a kiosk scene.

5.4a: Burial Goods

Much has been written on the significance of mirrors (Derriks 2001: Lilyquist 1979). The discussion here will focus primarily on material culture and representations found at Deir el-Medina. Additional evidence will be considered only to contextualise this in relation to contemporaneous society. Bruyère (1937a: 75) found four mirrors in the Eastern Cemetery, most were discovered in close proximity to the body of the deceased and in association with women. Those with their handle still surviving are all papyri form in design. A mirror disc with handle, was found in tomb 1370 on the chest of the woman Maya, between the mummy wrappings; to the right of her head was a vase of kohl (Bruyère 1937a: 75, 157). A disc, without a handle, was discovered on the chest of a woman in tomb 1371, again between mummy wrappings. Inside the coffin, by her feet, were two sachets of galena, used to make kohl (Bruyère 1937a: 76, 158). In tomb 1380 a mirror, without a handle, was found in the coffin of a woman, near her right foot and objects of toiletry were scattered around the coffin; this included sachets of galena and an alabaster vase containing kohl with an ebony applicator (Bruyère 1937a: 76, 159). Bruyère (1937a: 76, 184-5) also found one mirror with a wooden handle in tomb 1382; this tomb contained the burial of two women and one man. Numerous vases of kohl, sachets of galena and ebony applicators sticks were also discovered in the tomb. One additional wooden mirror handle, lotus-form, was also excavated from '*Le Grand Puits*' (Bruyère 1953: 48-51).

5.4b: Textual Evidence: Deir el-Medina

Although Janssen (1975: 301) omits mirrors from his analysis of commodity prices at Deir el-Medina, due to ambiguity in the text, it is likely they were expensive objects. As Valbelle (1985: 250-251) notes, mirror discs were made of the same material as tools. The tools were strictly distributed to the workers and controlled by weight (Eyre 1980: 114, n. n). Valbelle further suggests mirrors used in the home would have been taken away when the village was abandoned at the end of the 20th Dynasty and many deposited in tombs may have been looted by tomb robbers in the 19th Century. There are very few textual references to mirrors in hieratic ostraca from Deir el-Medina (Valbelle 1985: 251). There is one example in the Ramesside Dream Manual, *P. Chester Beatty III* (Gardiner 1935: 9-23, Plates 5-12a) which was part of the collection of texts owned by Qenherkhepeshef, the necropolis scribe from Deir el-Medina during the reign of Rameses II. The text lists 226 dreams which are prescribed as either 'Followers of Seth', or describing the dreams of a moderate, well balanced, quiet man (Szpakowska 2007: 395). One prescription notes, 'If a man sees himself in a dream seeing his face in a mirror, bad, it means another wife' (Gardiner 1935: 6, Plates 6-7). Szpakowska (2007: 397) suggests that this relates to the association of mirrors with women. Dream manuals focus on images that were familiar to contemporary society, reinforcing social norms and codes of behaviour (Szpakowska 2007: 394). Mirrors are also linked to women in New Kingdom love poetry, as discussed in Section 5.11d.

5.4c: Tomb Scenes: Deir el-Medina

In addition to the material culture and textual references there are many depictions of mirrors in tombs from Deir el-Medina. They are normally shown under the seat of a significant female or under the funerary bed of the tomb owner. The earliest recorded depiction is found in the tomb of Amenemhat (TT 340) published by Bruyère (1926) and subsequently by Cherpion (1999). This shows a mirror and kohl pot under the chair of Amenemhat's wife and his mother (Bruyère 1926: Figure 43; Cherpion 1999: Plate 9), see Figure 5.16. Cherpion (1999: 31-35) dates this to the early 18th Dynasty and while stylistically the tombs of Deir el-Medina develop over time, the mirror remains a constant theme. A similar depiction is seen in Theban Tomb 354 with the tomb owner and his wife before a table of offerings; under the wife's chair is a papyri form mirror and basket, perhaps containing toiletry items (Cherpion 1999: Plate 27). Dated to the Ramesside period the identity of the tomb owner is unknown. Mirror and kohl pots are depicted twice under the seat of Merit in the polychrome tomb chapel of Kha and his wife (Vandier d'Abbadie and Jourdain 1939: Plates 1-111). An additional depiction is seen on the decorated coffer of the couple (Turin S.8212) found in their tomb (TT 8). This shows the deceased couple before a table of offerings, a mirror with a papyri form handle and a kohl pot with applicator stand under the chair of Merit (Vassilika 2010: 14, 88-89).

In the monochrome tombs, the image of the mirror under the chair of a significant female is recorded only in the tomb of Nakhtamon (TT 335). Here it is placed under the chair of his mother in-law; the disc takes a deep red hue (Bruyère 1926: 125, Figure 86). In the monochrome tombs mirrors are more frequently depicted under the funerary bed of the tomb owner, including Khabekhnet (TT 2; Bruyère 1952b: Plate VII) see Figure 5.17, Nakhtamon (TT 335: Bruyère 1926: 21, Figure 108), Neferrenpet (TT 336: Bruyère 1926: Figure 55) and Nebaenmaat (TT 219: Maystre 1936: Plate V).

In these scenes showing the funerary bed, Anubis is shown performing the opening of the mouth ceremony on the mummy of the deceased. The mummy either wears a cone on its head or cones are placed beneath the bed surmounting tall vases. Although the mirror is no longer linked by direct placement to the kohl pot/tube, in the scenes in the burial chamber, the link is maintained in a remarkable scene in the polychrome tomb of Ipuy (TT 217). This shows numerous craftsmen working on an elaborate catafalque, see Figure 5.18. A mirror is shown next to the bed; the handle takes the form of a *djed* pillar with upraised arms supporting the disc, suggestive of the sunrise scene, Spell 16, *The Book of the Dead* (British Museum EA 9001/1: Taylor 2010: 247). Next to the mirror are two workmen, one of whom is applying eye make-up, most probably kohl, to his colleague. This reiterates the association of mirrors and kohl, while linking the mirror disc, placed next to the bed, to the rising sun.

Figure 5.16: West wall, Eighteenth Dynasty tomb of Amenemhat, TT 340 Deir el-Medina (Cherpion 1999: Plate 9) © IFAO.

Figure 5.17: Burial chamber of Khabekhnet, TT 2, Deir el-Medina (Bruyère 1952: Plate VII) © IFAO.

Figure 5.18. Facsimile by Norman de Garis Davies, tomb of Ipuy, TT 217, Metropolitan Museum 30.4.116, Creative Commons CC0.1.0.

mainly in ochre and is lacking in detail. Baud (1935: 162) noted the scene was executed quickly, possibly suggesting an experimental nature. These two scenes may have been an early attempt to incorporate these motifs into tomb scenes, which did not develop.

However, scenes of hairdressing and toilette were deep-rooted in Egyptian culture and held significance far beyond the representation of daily life. These are seen from the Middle Kingdom onwards, for example Princess Kawit is shown sitting in a high-backed chair, having her hair arranged while holding a papyri form mirror on her sarcophagus (Cairo JE 47397) found by Naville (1907: Plate XX) at Deir el-Bahri, dating from the reign of Mentuhotep II. By the 18th Dynasty mirrors are frequently shown in tombs scenes, often accompanied by a kohl pot, placed under the chair of the tomb owner's wife, for example in the tomb of Menna (TT 69: Hartwig 2013:40-43, Figures 2.7a-b). Numerous additional examples are listed by Evrard-Derriks (1975-76) and Hartwig (2004: 90). It is upon this foundation the '*Scènes de Gynécées*' figured ostraca should be viewed.

5.4d: Comparative Tomb Scenes

Only two scenes found in contemporaneous tombs show comparable images to the 'women on beds' scene. They are located in the Dra Abu'l Naga necropolis, on the West Bank of Thebes. Split over two registers, the upper register in both scenes show a servant preparing a bed with a headrest. Toiletry items are stowed under the bed in the tomb of User (TT 260), which includes a mirror disc with papyri form handle and a kohl pot with applicator (Greenlees 1923: Plate XXI). In the lower register a procession of servants carry toiletry items, including a mirror, while one prepares the seat. The bottom register in the tomb of Neferrenpet (TT 140), Figure 5.19, shows two women similarly attired; one tends to the hair of her companion, who admires her reflection in a mirror (Baud 1935: Plate XXV). These scenes in the bedchamber, possibly showing toilette preparations, are unique in 18th Dynasty tomb scenes. Gauthier-Laurent (1935-38: 682, n. 2) suggested that they are thematically linked with the servant in the lower register of User's tomb preparing the chair for a woman to sit upon and the accessories are being brought to style her hair. User's tomb has been dated to the mid-18th Dynasty stylistically and also due to the removal of the name of Amun (Greenlees 1923: 131). It is possible this was painted by workers from Deir el-Medina who were experimenting with images which later formed the '*Scènes de Gynécées*'. The tomb of Neferrenpet, also dated to the mid-18th Dynasty (reign of Tuthmosis III or Amenhotep II), was drawn

Figure 5.19: Scene from the tomb of Neferrenpet, TT 140 (Baud 1935: Plate XXV) © IFAO.

5.4e: Etymology and Solar Association

Linguistically the word for mirror was *ankh* which also meant 'live' or 'life' in ancient Egypt (Faulkner 1962: 44). Bianchi (1985: 11) suggests this was not symbolic but merely echoed the function of the mirror, which caused the features of the beholder to live in the reflection. However, the careful placement of mirrors in the tombs at Deir el-Medina, their formulaic representations in tomb scenes and in the '*Scènes de Gynécées*' figured ostraca, suggest in addition to being functional objects used in daily life, mirrors were also highly emblematic and important funerary goods, represented in both two and three-dimensions in the tomb. Numerous scholars have suggested the mirror disc symbolised the sun in ancient Egypt, due to the reflective surface of the bronze disc (Bruyère 1937b: 75; Derriks 2001: 59). The association of mirrors with celestial bodies is seen in the ritual of the offering of mirrors depicted on Greco-Roman temples, when two mirrors symbolising the sun and moon were offered by the king to a variety of deities (Husson 1977). One example from Philae shows Tiberius presenting Isis, who is breast feeding Horus, a pair of mirrors (Husson 1977: 232, Document 75). This has similarities to the kiosk scenes (K.1-2), which show a mirror and a kohl tube being offered to a breast-feeding mother. As Husson (1977: 21) notes in the Greco-Roman period the mirror became an object of cult, an offering of the king's divinity. A full discussion of this later development is outside the remit of this study, but it illustrates the continuation and development of the solar association of mirror discs in ancient Egypt.

5.4f: Rebirth and Rejuvenation

All mirrors found in tombs at Deir el-Medina with a handle surviving were papyri form in design. Derriks (2001: 60) suggests this is evocative of birth and the renewal of life. She argues they evoke the papyrus thicket of the Delta where Hathor (or Isis) gave birth to and protected Horus (Klasen 1952: 69). The papyrus stem was also used to write the word *w3d* (Faulkner 1962:55); this was an ideogram, meaning papyrus plant but it also had connotations of freshness and vigour, and it was used to describe shades of blue/green (Baines 1985: 284; Robins 2001: 291). Papyrus column amulets were also depicted in the *Book of the Dead* (Spells 159-160) to ensure eternal rejuvenation (Faulkner 1985: 155). Therefore, the mirrors found at Deir el-Medina, combine two powerful symbols, the sun disc and the papyrus plant. Papyrus is strongly associated with Hathor; this is made explicit in the pulling or shaking of the papyrus ritual. This is first seen in the tomb of Queen Hetepheres II and her daughter Meresankh III in their Old Kingdom tomb at Giza (Dunham *et al.* 1974: 4, 10, Figure 4). This shows the Queen and her mother in a papyrus skiff pulling papyrus stems. The scene is accompanied by the caption 'She pulls papyrus for Hathor in the marshlands with her mother. They see everything which is in the marsh' as translated by Teeter (2010: 161). There has been much debate over the definition of the word *sŝŝ*, either meaning pulling or shaking. However, as the tomb scenes show the pulling of the papyri stems in the marshes, the former is favoured by some scholars (Teeter 2010: 161, n. 119).

5.4g: Hathoric Association

The ritual demonstrates that papyrus was an appropriate gift for the goddess Hathor. The link with the deity is manifest in the mirrors with papyri form handles, some of which also incorporate a Hathoric head. Most of these are extremely high-status objects made of gold, silver, electrum, precious and semi-precious stones. The handle is often inscribed to resemble a papyrus stem and umbel, which is surmounted by the face of Hathor, with cow ears. These were found from the Middle Kingdom onwards, for example the mirror of princess Sat-Hathor-Yunet (Cairo JE 44920), found at Lahun by Brunton (1920: 24-26, Plate XV) and they continue to be found in the New Kingdom, with two examples discovered in the tomb of the three foreign wives of Tuthmosis III (MMA 26.8.97 and 26.8.98: Lilyquist 2003: 16-17). There is also a more ancient link between Hathor and mirrors seen in the Old Kingdom mastaba of Mereruka at Saqqara. This shows the 'dance with mirrors' as discussed by Hickmann (1954-55). Part of a larger scene of dance and celebration, the vignette shows four young girls holding and presenting mirrors and clappers to each other (Hickmann 1954-55, Figure 2). The text accompanying this scene mentions the name Hathor and it has been assumed by scholars, for example Evrard-Derriks (1975-6: 226), that the dance was dedicated to the goddess.

5.4h: Mirror Handles

Mirror handles in the New Kingdom take on a variety of forms, some of which include motifs seen in the '*Scènes de Gynécées*' figured ostraca. There are a number of mirrors which incorporate the god Bes into their handle, although only one has a firm provenance found at the fort of Semna (Harvard University, Boston Museum of Fine Art 29.1198: Dunham and Janssen 1960: 54, Plate 129a). It is likely the mirror dated to the rule of Tuthmosis III when Egyptian activity reached a peak in the region (Lilyquist 1982:186). A caryatid mirror was found near the Bes example (Harvard University, Boston Museum of Fine Art 29.1197: Dunham and Janssen 1960: 84-5, Plate 129c). These two mirrors were found in a deposit below the Taharqa temple, along with a copper stand, two copper bowls, vases and a wooden kohl stick, suggesting they were votive offerings left in a sacred space. Mirrors incorporating a female figurine (caryatid) into the handle became popular in the 18th Dynasty. Derriks (2001) has catalogued 84, while

Lilyquist (2007: 96) notes there are at least a dozen more. During research for this study 14 such mirrors have been found with a firm provenance, all from the 18th Dynasty, see Table 1. Two were found in temples and 12 were found in tombs. No caryatid mirrors have been found in settlement sites.

5.4i: Caryatid Mirrors

Derriks (2001: 23-35) defines four types of caryatid mirror based on the capital. This includes lily and palm capitals, papyri form simple and extended; Figure 5.20 shows an example of the extended papyri form type; only papyri form (simple and extended) capitals have been found in excavated contexts. The caryatid figurine can be seen to rise and stretch its arms to hold the tips of the extended papyrus umbel; this gives the impression of the figurine presenting and offering the mirror to the viewer. Alternatively, the caryatid figurines may have their arms alongside their body, or they may have one arm stretching alongside their body and the other reaching across their chest, sometimes holding an object. A variety of objects are carried; a caryatid from Gurob holds a bird (Petrie 1890: 35, Plate XVIII), while an example from Buhen clutches a cat (Emery, Smith and Millard 1979: Plates 105, f, g, h.). These poses link the caryatids to standalone female figurines, many of which are in similar postures, numerous examples of these figurines were found at Deir el-Medina (Backhouse 2013: 28-29).

Figure 5.20: Caryatid mirror with extended papyri form handle, Manchester 10963, Image courtesy of Manchester Museum.

Figure 5.21: Wooden mirror handle from Gurob, Petrie UC 7913 (Photograph Author's own) Courtesy of Petrie Museum of Egyptian Archaeology.

A convergence of motifs popular in the '*Scènes de Gynécées*' figured ostraca are seen on two wooden mirror handles discovered at Gurob. The most unusual was found by Petrie (1891: 16-18, 36), who believed this to be a figurine of a queen. However, Lilyquist (2007: 98) suggests it was a mirror handle as a disc was found in the same tomb, which fits into the hole surmounting the head of the figurine. Furthermore, it is unlikely to be a queen given the overt nudity. The tomb is dated to the end of the reign of Rameses II by cartouches and pottery, demonstrating that the caryatid mirrors continued to be used in the Ramesside period. Remarkably, the figurine has a back panel upon which convolvulus leaves were inscribed. Another wooden caryatid figurine from Gurob was published by Thomas (1981: Plate 50); the female figure has two Bes tattoos incised into her thighs, see Figure 5.21, the find spot is unknown.

A number of scholars have considered who the caryatids represent, as outlined by Lilyquist (2007: 97). Williams (1992: 98) suggested that the figurines should be viewed as the goddess Hathor; he notes while some mirrors incorporate only the face of the goddess the caryatid mirrors include the whole figure. Alternatively, it has been proposed that the caryatids should be viewed as a *nefert,* one of the retinue of Hathor (Cleveland Museum of Art 1999: 301). Kozloff (1992: 354) made a similar suggestion regarding the female figurines incorporated into the wooden handles of so called 'cosmetic spoons'. As discussed by Kozloff (1992: 354) a *nefert* was commonly a musician or dancer associated with the cult of Hathor, depicted mostly in Old Kingdom tombs at Giza and Saqqara. While the association of mirrors and Hathor is evident both in material culture and tomb scenes, as discussed in Section 5.4g, there is no reason to assume the figurine handles represent the goddess. Hathor is never depicted completely naked nor without any divine attributes. Furthermore, the mirror handles are by nature frontal, in a rigid pose, with little association to music or dance, unlike the wooden spoons which can incorporate figurines in profile, suggesting movement. However, one caryatid considered in this study, Figure 5.21, does have Bes tattoos on her thighs. Similar tattoos were seen on images of musicians and dancers in New Kingdom Egypt, as discussed in Section 5.1f.

The most plausible suggestion to the identity of the caryatids has been made by Quack (2003 as cited in Lilyquist 2007: 97), who proposes that the women may be servants due to their hairstyles, tattoos and body type. Given the similarity to servants depicted in New Kingdom tomb scenes, for example the tomb of Nebamun (Parkinson 2008: Figure 95), which shows young girls serving banquet guests wearing only floral collars, hip-girdles, elaborate wigs, and earrings; this is a credible suggestion. The pose of the caryatids is also suggestive of a servant, some hold the tips of the extended papyri form umbel, presenting the mirror disc to the owner, and others proffer an object. Quack also proposed that the possible foreignness of the caryatids might indicate a lower status. Only one example with a provenance suggests a non-Egyptian female; the young girl has a partially smooth skull on the front, with back rivets which were intended to attach hair pieces. This was not a style attested in Egyptian material culture. The figurine has a short back, long legs with pronounced buttocks and Bes tattoos inscribed on each thigh (Khartoum National Museum 18595: Derrisk 2001: 188, Figure 73). It is noteworthy the iconography of the young girls who offer mirrors in the kiosk and 'elaborate bed' scenes (K.1, K.3, EB.1) also suggests these women were non-Egyptian due to their very particular conical hairstyle/headdresses as discussed in Section 5.3d.

However, the image of the naked servant girl has meaning beyond low rank and status. Robins (1996: 32-33) also notes the similarity between images of adolescent girls in tomb scenes and New Kingdom material culture, for example so called 'cosmetic spoons' and mirror handles. She links these representations to what she refers to as 'fertility figurines' (Robins 1996: 28-30). These are nude female figurines made in a variety of materials. The function of these nude female figurines is discussed in Section 5.11a. Robins (1996: 28) suggests that one of the key ideas to understanding these representations is that 'concepts of sexual union, fertility, birth into this world and into the next were indissolubly linked' in ancient Egypt. The daily cycle of the sun was viewed as the sun god impregnating the sky goddess every evening and being born anew each dawn. This was transposed into funerary art as the goddess Nut swallowing the sun which is shown travelling through her naked body to be born again in the morning. This is shown vividly in the tomb of Rameses VI (KV 9) (Piankoff 1954: Plates 186-196).

5.4j: Comparative Evidence

Mirrors were clearly linked to the concept of rebirth, due to their solar association. Given the ancient Egyptians correlation of birth and rebirth this ensured mirrors were associated with sexual activity. As discussed in Section 5.4a, mirrors were found mainly with women and had Hathoric connotations, as considered in Section 5.4g. The *Turin Erotic Papyrus 55001* illustrates vividly this correlation of themes. Two-thirds of the papyrus contains erotic imagery, broken down by Omlin (1973) into 12 scenes. The remainder of the papyrus contains scenes of animal parody. O'Connor (2011: 376) suggests these need to be considered together, as a satire ridiculing elevated models for the sake of amusement. Both the animal and human scenes are based on an inversion, with animals engaged in human activity and humans engaged in private activity in the public domain but also with couples mismatched in terms of age and physical attractiveness (O'Connor 2011: 362). The 12 vignettes, each depicting a couple and sometimes additional actors, would have been viewed singularly or in groups of two or three scenes, since the artefact is a roll which allows only a small section to be viewed at one time. This implies the images were well planned to form a compositional unity. It has been suggested that *The Turin Erotic Papyrus 55001* originated from Deir el-Medina due to the objects depicted (Omlin 1973: 73).

Figure 5.22: *Turin Erotic Papyrus*, Vignette 4, Turin 55001 (Photograph Author's own).

Most relevant to this discussion is vignette 4, which shows a young woman holding a mirror to apply her make-up. She sits upon an inverted Canaanite amphora revealing her genitalia to her aroused companion, Figure 5.22. This is one of the most sexually explicit scenes in Egyptian art. The female's body is drawn frontally, only her head is turned to the viewer's right; the mirror disc also faces the viewer. This scene makes plain the links between sex and rebirth, given the symbolism attached to the mirror disc and lotus flower, also a prominent motif in the '*Scènes de Gynécées*' discussed in Section 5.10b. In addition, the motif of beautification can also be seen as a prelude to sexual activity.

5.4k Kohl Pots/Tubes

In the '*Scènes de Gynécées*' figured ostraca mirrors were iconographically linked with kohl tubes. They appear together nine times in the 'women on beds' scenes, twice in kiosk scenes and in two 'elaborate bed' scenes. On the figured ostraca kohl is always shown in a tall tube with applicator stick; however, in tomb scenes at Deir el-Medina more diverse forms are depicted, for example the tomb of Amenemhat (TT 240) shows small squat pots with applicators, see Figure 5.16. Similar renditions of kohl pots are found in Eighteenth Dynasty tombs in the Theban necropolis, for example the tomb of Menna (TT 69: Hartwig 2013: 40-43, Figures 2.7a-b). It is evident a variety of containers were used for kohl at Deir el-Medina, as demonstrated by finds in the tombs; for example, tomb 1370 contained a basket full of various kohl pots and tubes, Figure 5.23. More luxurious receptacles were found in Merit's beauty case (Turin S.8479), which included vases and jars of alabaster, glass, faience and horn (Turin S.8480, 8481, 8483, 8484, 8486, 8487, 8490: Vassilika 2010: 45).

The composition of kohl has interested researchers for many years (Lucas 1930). More recent work has been undertaken by scientists at L'Oréal who analysed the composition of cosmetic powders preserved in 49 containers in the Louvre dating from 2000 – 1200 BC. They found two natural lead-based compounds, crushed ore of galena and cerussit (known as white lead or lead carbonate) (Walter *et al.* 1999). This expands upon earlier research by Lucas (1930: 41) which noted 64% of samples then recorded were galena, with the rest containing a variety of minerals, including oxide of copper, and iron.

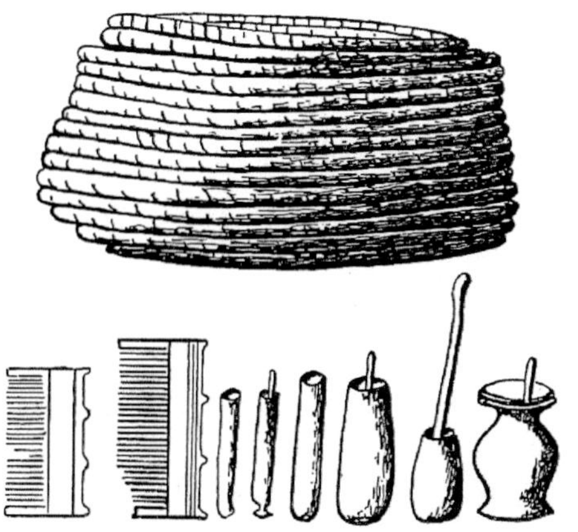

Figure 5.23: Toiletry items from tomb 1270, Deir el-Medina (Bruyère 1937a: 72, Figure 35) © IFAO.

Galena has been found in tombs and burials, throughout Pharaonic culture, in a variety of forms, including raw material, often left in small bags, stains on palettes and stones, and in a prepared state as kohl, either as a paste (now dried) or powder (Lucas 1930: 41). This suggests it was a desirable substance to be taken into the afterlife. Spell 125 in the *Book of the Dead* states that the deceased should enter the judgement hall and 'utter this spell pure, clean and clad in white garments and sandals, painted with black eye-paint and anointed with myrrh' (Faulkner 1985: 33-34). Manniche (1999: 136) notes that kohl was therefore an essential component in the process of justification and resurrection. The wearing of kohl was clearly seen as an ideal state, possibly equated with being pure and in the presence of the gods. In terms of application in daily life it was likely that the powder was poured into a tall vase or squat pot and applied using a moist applicator or mixed with fatty matter for medicinal application. *Papyrus Ebers* contains numerous spells for the treatment of eye diseases (Eb. 336-431: Bardinet 1995: 302-314). Many include minerals used in cosmetics, for example Eb.354 is a remedy to cleanse the eyes which contains galena, malachite, red ochre, honey and oil to be applied to the eye lids (Bardinet 1995: 305).

Although kohl is always shown in tall tubes in the '*Scènes de Gynécées*' figured ostraca, kohl pots in the New Kingdom take a variety of forms, several of which have links with the wider motifs of the '*Scènes de Gynécées*'. Many kohl pots incorporate the god Bes into the shape of the vessel; there are numerous examples in museums worldwide (Vandier d'Abbadie 1972: 55-59). Two remarkable kohl tubes in the Louvre (E 4851 and A.F. 6708) use a naked female figure as a decorative feature (Vandier d'Abbadie 1972: 70-71). One example (Louvre E 4851), a single tube dated stylistically to the 25th Dynasty, has a naked female figure on top of the tube, attending to the stopper. It is possible she is representing a servant. A triple kohl tube in the Cairo Museum (JE 44528) has a female figure in a long transparent robe inscribed into the main panels (Bénédite 1911: 32, Plate XIV). In one hand she holds a cup and in the other a bouquet. On the reverse another female figure holds a bouquet and a gazelle. Although this has no provenance it shows the association of gift bearing female figures and kohl tubes.

5.4l: The Offering of Mirrors and Kohl Tubes

The offering of mirrors and items associated with toilette is depicted from the Old Kingdom onwards.

Figure 5.24: Image from the tomb of Ukh-hotep, Meir (Blackman 1915: 24, Plate XV)
Image courtesy of the Egypt Exploration Society.

A small number of images are found in tomb scenes, these have been studied by Lilyquist (1979) and Derriks (2001: 6-14). Derriks (2001: 10) notes these may relate to rituals that were undertaken in 'the House of Morning' as described by Blackman (1918). Blackman (1918: 148) suggested this was a special chamber of the temple or palace which was 'a ceremonial toilet-chamber'. Here the king would undergo rituals each morning relating to his toiletry and purification to ensure he was reborn each morning like the sun god Ra. Blackman (1918: 156-157) suggested these rituals involved lustral washing, fumigating with incenses and the presenting of balls of natron on which to chew. Blackman went on to propose that these rituals were the same as those performed on the body of the dead king to ensure that he ascended to the heavens to join the gods; this included the offering of unguents, cosmetics and linen, referred to by Blackman as 'napkins.' For the purposes of this study, the key point to note, is the ceremonial significance of toilette rituals, which were linked to rebirth. It is possible, this is the basis for the importance of scenes of personal grooming, which often appear incongruous to modern viewers, for example the images of beautification on the sarcophagus of Princess Kawit, as discussed in Section 5.4d.

The presentation of a mirror in proximity to cosmetic pots and unguents can be seen as early as the 6th Dynasty. The tomb of Aba at Deir el Gebrâwi shows the tomb owner on the right of a false door. He sits on a couch beneath which are two papyri form mirrors and a third mirror is held by a dwarf. Behind the tomb owner are stacked eight vases of unguents. This is a remarkable scene showing the presentation of mirrors to the male tomb owner (Davies 1902: Plate 17). During the Middle Kingdom, there is a stronger association of mirrors and kohl. For example, the tomb of Ukh-hotep at Meir shows the tomb owner and his wife sitting before a table of offering stacked with bread and food, see Figure 5.24. Behind the seated couple a servant holds a mirror and vase of perfume in a gesture of offering. Above the table of offering is a row of seven vases of perfume and two bags which Blackman (1915: 24) suggested 'almost certainly' contained black and green eye paint.

A clear link between mirrors and kohl pots is seen on a Middle Kingdom coffin in Bologna Museum (Bologna 1958). This also depicts a mirror, a small round kohl pot with applicator and a tall fluted vase above a cosmetics chest; these objects are shown at the side of the false door (Lilyquist 1979: Figure 146). It must be noted the recipients of the mirrors and toiletry items are almost always deceased or royalty. For example, a Nineteenth Dynasty stela to Herumes in the British Museum (EA 1297) shows the lady Iouy making a libation and offering a mirror to a seated goddess, crowned with a sun disc and cow horns, named as 'Tura, Lady of Heaven' (Derriks 2001: 12, Figure 15). Budge (1909: 183) suggested the goddess was Hathor, while Derriks (2001: 12) considers it to be Taweret. Mirrors were also part of the gifts presented to Amenhotep III as depicted in the tomb of Ken-Amun (TT 162: Davies 1930: Plates XVII-XXIII). Aldred (1969) argued due to the magnitude of gifts offered these were not presented to mark New Year in the civil calendar but rather were gifts given after his rejuvenation at the *sed*-festival. Therefore, mirrors with their association with rebirth would be appropriate gifts. Evidence suggests mirrors were offered to the dead and to a limited degree goddesses and kings. While it is always assumed the '*Scènes de Gynécées*' figured ostraca depict the living, it must be acknowledged the scenes share some common motifs with representations created for perpetuity for the dead.

5.4m: Linkage

Mirrors provide the strongest link between two and three-dimensional representations in this study. They are depicted in the two main datasets in the '*Scènes de*

Site	Context	Publication
Abusir	Tomb *'puit des chiens'*	Bénédite 1907: 23, Plate 10.
Abusir	Tomb 2 Next to the face of the deceased	Bonnet 1928: 56, Plate 36.1.
Abydos El-Arabah	Tomb 166 Found with scarabs and pottery	Garstang 1901: 10, Plate 14.
Abydos	Tomb 949 Series of vaulted chambers entered from a common shaft	Garstang 1909: 129.
Aniba	Tomb 10	Steindorff 1937: 120, Plate 62.
Aniba	Tomb 91	Steindorff 1937: 120, Plate 62.
Buhen	North-west interior of the temple enclosure	Emery, Smith and Millard 1979: Plate 105, f, g, h.
Buhen	Tomb 25	Randall-MacIver and Woolley 1911: 140, Plate 62.
Buhen	Tomb 60	Randall-MacIver and Woolley 1911: 135, Plate 62.
Gurob	Tomb	Petrie 1890: 35, Plate XVIII.
Qustul	Tomb V 48	Leclant 1966: 152, Plate XXV.
Saint-Jean-d'Acre (Levant)	Tomb B2 Five burial pits dug into the sand, 3 skeletons	Ben-Arieh and Edelstein 1977: 29.
Semna	Tomb S524	Dunham and Janssen 1960: 84-5, Plate 129 c.
Semna	Temple Below Taharqa temple	Dunham and Janssen 1960: 54, Plate 128, c, d.

Table 1: Bronze caryatid mirrors with a firm context from New Kingdom Egypt

Gynécées'; they were also found as objects in tombs at Deir el-Medina and represented on tomb walls at the site. Furthermore, they are also depicted on a limited number of three-dimensional so-called 'ladies on beds' figurines from Deir el-Medina (Louvre E 14385, E 16515: Backhouse 2013: 32, Figures 2.17-8). They are linked to kohl pots/tubes, both on the figured ostraca, in tombs scenes and as objects found in tombs, often in close association with one another. This suggests mirrors and kohl pots/tubes can be seen as a united concept, with mirrors associated with rebirth and sexuality, while kohl is linked to the concepts of justification and also resurrection. The inclusion of mirrors in the '*Scènes de Gynécées*' figured ostraca highlights the complex nature of the scenes, incorporating many levels of meaning. The link to fertility and rebirth suggests the 'women on beds' scenes are not merely depicting celebrations that took place after the birth of a child but may also encompass the desire for rebirth. The presentation of mirrors and kohl pots may also relate to purification rituals that took place after the birth of a child and the grooming of the mother for re-entry into normal life.

5.5: Gift Giving and Presentation

A significant motif in the 'women on beds' scenes is the offering of objects by a companion to a seated figure. The companions are dressed in a similar manner to the seated figure, suggesting they are of equal status. This is seen 16 times in a variety of formats; this could be the presentation of gifts. The most common object to be offered is a shallow dish; this is given nine times, of which three dishes include a head cone. The dish is given in association with a tall vase four times. In four instances the seated figure acknowledges the receipt of gifts with a raised hand gesture, possibly a mark of thanks. There is some degree of exclusivity, the cones are never presented in association with a tall vase and cones are not acknowledged with a hand gesture. Water is poured from one tall vase into a bowl (WoB.34) and smoke or vapour is seen rising from one bowl, also presented with a tall vase (WoB.36). It is possible the dishes and vases contain gifts of food and drink.

Items of adornment and beautification are also offered. A floral collar is presented in WoB.42 and a mirror and kohl tube are proffered in EB.1. A lotus flower is tendered in WoB.43; this ostracon shows an exchange of gifts with the seated figure offering a bowl to the standing figure, who presents the lotus flower. Two kiosk scenes clearly show the tendering of a mirror and kohl tube (K.1-2); while in the third kiosk scene (K.3) it is not possible to identify the objects offered but the text suggests it was fruits and flowers. Again, there is an element of exclusivity; the mirror and kohl tubes are offered only in the kiosk and 'elaborate bed' scenes.

There are also a number of fragmentary offering scenes. F.2 shows a dish being tendered with water being poured into it; this is accompanied by a hand gesture from the recipient. Mirror and kohl tubes are also proffered in F.3 and F.13, both of which are likely to have come from an 'elaborate bed' or kiosk scene. There are additional examples of comparative data, CE.6-7 both show the presentation of objects to a seated figure.

5.5a: Comparative Data

Janssen's (1982, 1997) extensive study of hieratic ostraca from Deir el-Medina led him to suggest that on special occasions, for example the birth of a child or New Year's Day, the residents of Deir el-Medina offered each other small quantities of food, drink and some objects of daily life. This was based on recorded quantities of consumables and objects of daily life against a list of names as documented on a number of ostraca. The significance of the lists, as Janssen noted, is that the majority of people recorded are women. This research has been extended by Jauhiainen (2009), as part of her study on feasts and festivals in Ramesside Deir el-Medina; Jauhiainen suggests 16 documents can be interpreted as gift giving lists. A good example of which is *O. Petrie 31* (Černý and Gardiner 1957: Plate XXXV). The text, in three columns, lists nine women and three men who bring a variety of food stuff; everyone brings loaves of bread, while some also contribute cakes, meats, fish and fruit. Janssen (1997: 77) suggests 'The whole text with the black lines separating the entries makes the impression of having been noted down on the spur of the moment, that is, during the party itself, perhaps as the guests arrived', see Figure 5.25.

A more varied list is presented in *O. Cairo 25624* (Helck 1963: 457, n. 653). This consists of three columns which Janssen (1997: 71) suggested may constitute two separate lists. The first column contains nine names, only five of which are legible, three of which are women and two men. While every guest brings loaves of bread more diverse items are also recorded; this includes *mnt* jars, an ointment jar with *mrḥ* oil, wooden boxes, possibly a folding foot stool, a basket and two pairs of women's sandals. Janssen (1997: 72) suggests the recipient of the gifts may be a woman as 'women's sandals' are explicitly noted twice. Columns II and III note 21 items, all different in nature leading Janssen (1997: 72) to suggest they form one list. He further argued that as a woman was the recipient of the items in column II, it is likely she was also the recipient of the items in column III. Column II constitutes 'what he had given to Takse' on a specific day, IV *3ht* 29 of year 27 (of Rameses III), for a specific event 'the crossing of the water of the Mistress of the Interior', although Janssen is unsure of the nature of this event (Janssen 1997: 69-72).

Were these goods brought to a communal celebration to mark the birth of a child and if so, were the festivities depicted on the 'women on beds' scenes? As Janssen (1982: 254) noted, in many 'primitive and peasant' societies the only way families could accumulate the produce necessary for a festival or large celebration was by gift giving. One fragmentary ostracon (*O. Cairo CG 25705 + O.IFAO 01322 + O. Varille 38*) consisting of 13 fragments from a large vessel, records the contri-butions of 33 women and at least three men who brought food 'to the drinking – (party) of Hathor' (private person as indicated by seated female determi-native) (Janssen 1997:56). As Janssen notes, most guests brought loaves of various kinds while four also brought *mnt* jars, which probably contained beer.

Figure 5.25: Ostracon illustrating gift giving list, Petrie UC 39630 (Photograph Author's own) Courtesy of Petrie Museum of Egyptian Archaeology.

Jauhiainen (2009: 263) has differentiated the texts and identified a set of documents which she refers to as 'accounts of transfers'. She notes these documents 'record items given by the writer of the text to one or more persons on various occasions'. The main difference between the two sets of documents is that the gift giving lists are written by the receiver of the goods and record one occasion while the accounts transfers are written by the giver of the goods and record several donations, which can be from different points in time. One example (*O.IFAO. 1069*) records food and drink given to a man on four separate occasions. On the birth of his daughter he was given a wooden bed and a basket of food, which contained fish and meat, ten jars of beer, barley bread and some cosmetic oil (Grandet 2003: 124-6). Three days later he received various breads, beans, vegetables and reeds. When his daughter was 14 days old the man received more bread and broad beans. Finally, he received a quantity of goods for a big drinking party; this includes beer, bread, vegetables and more cosmetic oil (Grandet 2003: 124-6, 395-398). It seems unlikely that all these goods were given by one person to the unidentified man; they perhaps represent the contributions of one extended family.

Jauhiainen further notes there are five references to the transfer of goods in relation to the concept of *ḥsmn*. This is discussed by Toivari-Viitala (2001: 162-164); she concludes this may refer to menstruation or purification rites associated with birth, miscarriage or abortion. *Ostraka Michaelides 48* notes various kinds of food associated with private feasts, one of which was the purification of a daughter (Goedicke and Wente 1962: Plate LXXI). Another example, *Ostraka Berlin P 10631* refers to the giving of goods on the occasion of a woman coming out of *ḥsmn* (David 2010: 174). It is possible the kiosk scenes (K.1-3) depict women undergoing purification rituals in a place of confinement or seclusion after birth. That a special place for women existed is demonstrated in *Osraka OIM 13512*. This short ostracon is translated by Wilfong (1999: 420) as 'The day when these women came out [to/from the] place of the women while they were menstruating. They got as far as the rear of the house'. Wilfong translates *ḥsmn.t* as menstruating but Janssen (1980: 141-143) noted linguistically the verb *ḥsmn* is derived from the word for natron meaning to purify. Furthermore, Janssen found workmen were occasionally absent from work due to the *ḥsmn* of their wife or daughter. After studying the records available Janssen (1980: 142) argued the absences of the workmen due to the *ḥsmn* of their wives and daughters could not be accounted for by menstruation but only purification after birth or miscarriage.

5.5b: Gift Giving in Kiosk Scenes

The kiosk scenes are fundamentally different in nature to the 'women on beds' scenes. The former depict a nursing mother approached by a servant, indicated by different dress and hairstyles, suggesting unequal social status; the scenes show the offering of a mirror and kohl tube. Mirrors are unlikely to be gifts as metal objects would be too expensive, as discussed in Section 5.4b. It is more likely the mirror and kohl tube belonged to the seated woman and the servant was assisting in her toilette. The only 'women on beds' scene to show the offering of a mirror and kohl tube is an 'elaborate bed' scene (EB.1) and this is likely to be proffered by a servant, as indicated by her hairstyle.

5.5c: Linkage

It is possible the presentation of objects in the 'women on beds' scenes was a visual record of events similar to those recorded on the hieratic ostraca studied by Janssen and Jauhiainen. This suggests gift giving was part of the social pattern of Deir el-Medina. Sharing food and drink with neighbours, friends and family creates and maintains social relationships; moreover, the reciprocal nature binds a community together. This suggests the '*Scènes de Gynécées*' figured ostraca depicted events that took place in the village of Deir el-Medina; although no documents explicitly mention feasts taking place in the home. The objects offered in kiosk scenes are more likely to relate to preparation or rituals before the celebrations began.

5.6: Convolvulus Leaves

Another common motif in the '*Scènes de Gynécées*' figured ostraca is the depiction of stylised leaves on a vine, often oversized and interwoven throughout the scene. Vandier d'Abbadie referred to them predominantly as convolvulus but also as '*lancéolée*' (Vandier d'Abbadie 1937: 32; 1938: 28); this refers to the shape of the leaves, tapering from a round base to an apex. Brunner-Traut (1955: 17) described the plant as bindweed or morning glories. These leaves are depicted on at least 18 'women on beds' scenes, all three kiosk scenes and on at least three fragments.

5.6a: Botanical Identification

Stylised depictions of similar leaves are found from the Middle Kingdom to the Late Period (Aufrère and Lopex-Moncet 2001: 42). Many scholars have sought to classify the plant botanically, with the discussion focusing on ivy and convolvulus (Hugonot 1994; Loret 1892). The most comprehensive study has been produced by Aufrère and Lopex-Moncet (2001: 39-72). This includes a catalogue of scenes in which the plant is depicted, possible botanical identifications and a discussion on the symbolism attached to the imagery. They suggest the plant depicted is a type of convolvulus, which is difficult to distinguish from ivy. They note there is botanical evidence that convolvulus was used in funeral wreaths in ancient Egypt from the Middle Kingdom, as demonstrated by Newberry's analysis of the funeral wreaths discovered by Petrie at Hawara (Newberry 1890: 47-48).

Täckholm (1974: 425-430) in her study of the flora of contemporary Egypt has identified 23 varieties of the convolvulus plant. Those most similar to depictions from ancient Egypt are, *Convolvulus lantatus, Convolvulus arvensis, Convolvulus siculus and Convolvulus althaeodies.* Tackholm (1974: 425-430) describes it as an herb or shrub which can take a variety of forms, including trailers and twiners, which grow in diverse habitats. The flowers are funnel shaped and are found in a range of colours including blue, yellow, purple, pink and white. The stems may appear hairy and the leaves may be cleft or undivided, taking a heart or arrow shape. Figures 5.26 and 5.27 show modern examples of convolvulus, which are similar to those depicted in the '*Scènes de Gynécées*' figured ostraca. Boulos and Nadbil el-Hadidi (1984: 47) describe this perennial herb as 'One of the most widespread and persistent weeds in fields, gardens, roadsides, hedges, orchards, waste ground etc.' For the purpose of this discussion it will be assumed the stylised plants depicted in the '*Scènes de Gynécées*' figured ostraca are a type of convolvulus.

Figure 5.26: Convolvulus arvensis L.
(Image by Emilian Robert Vicol at Pixabay).

Figure 5.27: Convolvulus leaves
(Image by Thomas B at Pixabay).

5.6b: Wall Paintings

Convolvulus leaves are also a dominant motif in the wall paintings which survive at Deir el-Medina. They are a striking feature of the two most substantial examples, the image of the dancer, WP.1 and what is likely to be the remains of a kiosk scene, WP.2. The distinctive nature of the convolvulus leaves depicted in these two wall paintings led Bruyère (1939: 264) to suggest they were drawn by the same artist, who Bruyère believed had also painted the twentieth Dynasty tomb of Kynebu at Thebes (TT 113). It has subsequently been proposed Amenhotep, chief draftsman at Deir el-Medina, from year 2 of Rameses IV's reign, painted this tomb (Bác and Parkinson 2011: 42). Fragments of which survive at the British Museum, which show Ahmose Nefertari, in a kiosk encircled with convolvulus leaves (EA 37994). The depiction of convolvulus leaves is one of the strongest links between the '*Scènes de Gynécées*' figured ostraca and the wall paintings in the village of Deir el-Medina. This is seen most clearly with the depiction of kiosks on the ostraca and most likely on WP.2. However, a number of 'women on beds' scenes show convolvulus leaves forming a floral canopy over the bed, possibly entwined on a trellis (WoB.38, 41), while others show the leaves standing erect (WoB.40). However, it is possible that these are representations of the wall paintings, evoking the painted decoration of the houses.

Evidence from Amarna shows that columns, in the palace, both sandstone and limestone were painted with convolvulus leaves, Figure 5.28. Petrie (1894: 10) referred to these as 'vine columns' and believed the decoration to be unique in Egyptian art. He stated, 'Winding branches of a climbing vine twist around the column in wild confusion, their leaves turning in all directions and over lapping, with a pointed disregard of any symmetry or pattern.' Petrie believed the same style of decoration had been used for a large stela in the temple (Petrie 1894:10-1, Plate VIII). This depicted the royal family worshipping the Aten; a trellis of vines had topped the stela. The same abundance and free-form is seen in many of the depiction of convolvulus leaves in the 'women on beds' dataset. Convolvulus leaves and papyrus were also found on painted plaster fragments recovered from a second storey room in a house at Amarna (Kemp 1987: 26). Kemp suggested they may have belonged to a pilaster forming a painted panel behind a real bed. It is possible that convolvulus leaves were used to provide shade for kiosks in daily life; stylised depictions of these may be seen on the figured ostraca (K.1-3). They may also have been used to create temporary structures inside the home, forming canopies or trellises encircling the decorated bed. However, evidence from Amarna and Deir el-Medina suggests that convolvulus leaves were also a motif in wall decorations in domestic settings in New

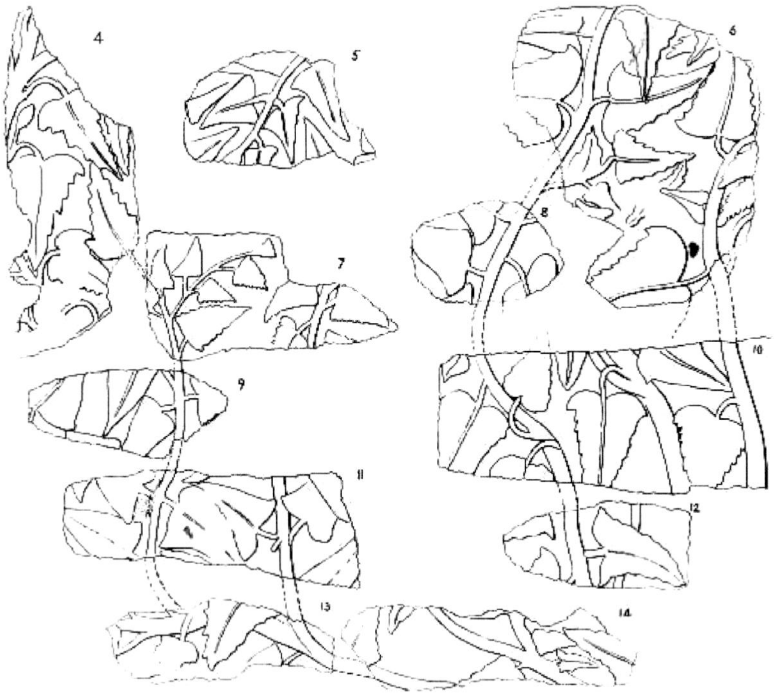

Figure 5.28: Illustrations of 'vine columns' from Amarna, as drawn by Petrie (Petrie 1894: Plate 2.9).

The link between Hathor and papyrus is well established and discussed in Section 5.4f. It must be noted that the papyrus and convolvulus plants generally belonged to different habitats, with the papyrus flourishing in the lush Delta region, while convolvulus was most commonly found in deserts, fields and on waste ground. Therefore, the association has to be through the symbolism attached to the plants not the natural environment. Hugonot (1994: 76) argues there was a monopoly of association between papyrus and convolvulus plants. He suggests when the two were intertwined and offered to a divinity the presentation was frequently made by women who often carried objects with Hathoric attributes. For example, at the Smaller Temple at Abu Simbel Nefertari holds a papyrus stem with convolvulus leaves and a Hathor headed *sistrum* (Desroches-Noblecourt 1968: Plate LII). These images create visual tags which connect convolvulus, papyrus and Hathor.

Convolvulus is also shown on numerous funerary papyri. In the papyrus of Ani, *The Book of the Dead,* Ani's wife Tutu is shown holding a papyrus stem with convolvulus wrapped around it, a Hathor headed *sistrum* and carrying a *menat* necklace. Ani, although dressed in his finery, does not hold any of these symbolically charged objects (British Museum EA 10470/19: Taylor 2010:36). Convolvulus, seen prolifically in tomb scenes and funerary papyri, is linked to rebirth most strongly in the image of Meketaten in the royal tomb at Amarna, discussed in Section 5.3g, Figure 5.15. It is possible in the representation of the convolvulus plant the ancient Egyptians sought the protection of Hathor in her many guises, who was revered particularly at Thebes, associated with the Western Necropolis. Theban Ramesside tombs include numerous depictions of convolvulus leaves in several modes of representation, as outlined by Aufrère and Lopex-Moncet (2001: 42-43). Convolvulus leaves are one of the dominant motifs in the Tomb of Amenemheb (TT 278) at Qurnet Murai, appearing in most scenes (Vandier d'Abbadie 1954). One of the most revealing scenes shows the deceased and his wife offering floral bouquets to Hathor, depicted in bovine form emerging from the Western Mountain, Figure 5.29. The bouquets include papyrus, mandrakes, poppies, lotus and convolvulus leaves. So close is the affinity with the goddess, the edge of the convolvulus leaves touch the double plumes of the

Kingdom Egypt. The discussion below will focus on why the plant was chosen and the meanings it held in contemporaneous society.

5.6c: Comparable Evidence

The most common depiction of convolvulus leaves is in New Kingdom tomb scenes. Aufrère and Lopex-Moncet (2001: 42-43) differentiated six types of scene which repeatedly include representations of the convolvulus plant. The first shows the convolvulus leaves in association with the papyrus plant, frequently wound around the stem. The second depicts the convolvulus leaves in isolation, commonly hanging from kiosks, which Aufrère and Lopex-Moncet (2001: 42) refer to as 'places of pleasure'. In the third type of scene the convolvulus leaves are objects of offering, often associated with papyrus. Fourthly, they are used in friezes to form garlands, particularly with their bell-shaped flowers and fifthly, the leaves are mounted in complex bouquets; both of these often also include the papyrus plant. Finally, convolvulus can be used as a 'floral metaphor', where the depiction is used as an emblem to suggest or symbolise another concept or object. It is noteworthy that the convolvulus plant is linked with the papyrus plant in three of the six types of scene.

5.6d: Hathoric Association

Aufrère and Lopex-Moncet (2001) and Hugonot (1994) suggest that convolvulus is strongly associated with Hathor due to its link with the papyrus plant.

Figure 5.29: Scene from the tomb of Amenemheb, TT 278
(Vandier d'Abbadie 1954: Plate XXVI) © IFAO.

goddess and her face. The frieze surmounting the scene also includes the bell-shaped flowers of the convolvulus plant, interspersed between lotus flowers and bunches of grapes.

5.6e: Solar Association

It has been suggested that the convolvulus plant also had solar symbolism; Aufrère and Lopex-Moncet (2001: 70) refer to this as the '*l'heliotropisme des liserons*'. They suggest the plant, which flowers in the summer, follows the solar cycle, opening for 3-4 hours in the morning and closing at sunset. Furthermore, Hugonot (1994: 80) notes the plant disappears in the winter and reappears in the spring, evoking spontaneous regeneration. This linking to the solar and annual cycle may account for the popularity of the plant in the Amarna period, seen in the 'vine columns' see Figure 5.28 and also on a fragment of a stela discovered by Petrie (1894: 10, Plate 2.9).

5.6f: Practical and Medicinal Applications

Dawson (1934: 186) suggested that *śnwtt,* as referred to by the ancient Egyptians, was a type of convolvulus due to the description in *Papyrus Ebers.* Ebbell (1937: 63) described this 'as an herb which grows on its bulb (lit. its belly)'. However, the link appears tenuous as Ebbell (1937: 133) believed *śnwtt* to be saffron. While *śnwtt* was used in medical applications it is not certain that convolvulus was known to the ancient Egyptians as *śnwtt.* However, Boulos (1983: 68), in his study of the use of plants in North Africa in modern times, found that convolvulus had a haemostatic property, that is they retarded the flow of blood. Miller (2009: 256) suggests convolvulus may have been used in daily life in ancient Egypt to stop postpartum haemorrhage and may have been depicted on the ostraca and walls of houses so the images could continue to magically ensure the health of new mothers. He proposed the plant may have been depicted in a funerary context as a healing plant, so associated with Osiris and his ability to reconstitute himself and to be reborn. The iconographic significance of the leaves may also lie in its botanical characteristics. Not only are convolvulus perennial but they are sturdy and resistant to removal due to long rhizomes which grow under or along the ground and send out stems or roots; these can reproduce without seeds by vegetative reproduction. One fragment is sufficient for the plant to regenerate; therefore, they may have had an association with fertility.

5.6g: Linkage

Convolvulus leaves provide one of the strongest links between the '*Scènes de Gynécées*' figured ostraca and wall paintings. They are also a dominant motif in Ramesside tomb scenes and funerary papyri, where they were strongly associated with Hathor. Convolvulus leaves may have been included in the '*Scènes de Gynécées*' figured ostraca to evoke the protection of the goddess for women and children in the domestic zone, especially post-birth, which was a vulnerable time. Additionally, as Hathor was strongly associated with the Theban necropolis, particularly the Western Mountain, the images may have also been created to seek the continued protection of the goddess in the afterlife and her assurance of rebirth.

5.7: Head Cones

Dome-shaped objects are depicted on the heads of men and women from the 18th Dynasty onwards. They are seen initially in tomb scenes, for example the Eighteenth Dynasty tomb of Amenemhat (TT 340) at Deir el-Medina (Cherpion 1999). The frequency of depictions of the cone increases throughout the New Kingdom and the mediums they are represented on extends to include coffins, mortuary papyri and three-dimensional female figurines. The cone continues to be depicted until the Ptolemaic period; a cone is illustrated on the head of Petosiris and his wife who lived under Persian rule (Lefebvre 1923: Plate XXV). In modern scholarship they have generally been referred to as 'perfume cones', although the nature and significance of the representations has been much debated; a good summary of the literature is provided by Padgham (2012: 9-14). In this study they will be referred to as head cones.

5.7a: Depictions in the 'Scènes de Gynécées'

Head cones are the most widely depicted motif in this study. In the '*Scènes de Gynécées*' figured ostraca they appear on the head of the main figure in the 'women on beds' dataset 13 times. However, many of the scenes are incomplete; there is only one ostracon (WoB.31), which clearly shows the crown of the head of the main protagonist without a cone. This ostracon is atypical, drawn on a potsherd, showing a woman lying down, facing the viewer's left. Cones appear on the head of ten companions in the 'women on beds' dataset. There are only three ostraca which clearly depict the crown of the head of the secondary figure undecorated, one of which (WoB.47) is atypical and may include naked male and female servants. In the 'women on beds' dataset there is also one representation of a child who appears to be wearing a head cone (WoB.2). This is a unique image in the dataset; the crowns of the head of numerous children are visible, without a cone.

In the 'women on beds' scenes cones also appear under or next to the bed in seven or eight examples. They are also offered as gifts to the seated figure in a further two examples (WoB.3, 33), in both cases the recipient of the cone is already wearing a cone. It is possible those depicted under the bed represent gifts previously received. Head cones also appear on two examples of comparative data (CE.3-4), both show seated women holding a child on their lap. Five further examples appear in the 'Fragments' dataset. While the cone is a pervasive motif in this study it has a degree of exclusivity. It is not represented in the kiosk scenes; nor is it worn by the servants with the conical headdresses, so called 'Syrians'. It is depicted only in the 'women on beds' scenes, one 'elaborate bed' scene and numerous three-dimensional figurines found at Deir el-Medina (Backhouse 2013: 29-33, 36, Figures 2.13-2.19).

5.7b: Theories

Scholarship falls into two main groups regarding the cone. The earlier theorists believed the cone was a block of fat impregnated with perfume oil which was worn on the head. It was suggested as this melted it conditioned the hair and released a pleasant aroma; one of the earliest exponents of this view was Erman (1885: 316-7). This belief held credence and was still accepted in modern scholarship for a considerable time (Freed 1982: 199-200). The second group of theorists maintained the cone was symbolic and did not represent a physical reality; this was argued most convincingly by Cherpion (1994). She noted numerous inconsistencies in terms of visual representations. Firstly, the cone is depicted on top of the wig, not directly on the hair of individuals, secondly the cones are also represented on shaven heads and thirdly they are shown on mummies, which are often depicted lying down. Finally, Cherpion (1994: 81-84) noted philologically there is no word to describe the cone or any archaeological evidence to support the physical existence of the cone. Cherpion followed Bruyère in suggesting the image of the cone is used to express an idea, not a physical object. Bruyère (1926: 71-72) believed the cone derived from two concepts. Firstly, the mound of sand, which was the original tomb and secondly, a cone of bread, watered with a libation to symbolise an offering. When depicted on the head of the deceased Bruyère suggested it represented survival, assured by the food necessary for the existence of the *ka*.

While Cherpion believed the cone to be symbolic, an abstract idea, she did maintain this was linked to perfume and anointing. She acknowledged that this view was expressed by Lisa Manniche in a talk given in Brussels in 1994 (Cherpion 1994: 86). For Cherpion perfume '*est un instrument du seduction et invite à l'amour*', and most significantly *'l'activité sexuelle est toujours une promesse de renaissance*' (Cherpion 1994: 79). Word play is key in understanding the concepts of anointing and perfume in Egyptian culture; this is discussed by both Cherpion (1994: 87) and Manniche (1999: 96). The Egyptian word *stj* means scent but also engender, beget or to pour. There are frequent references connecting perfume to sex in New Kingdom love poetry, as discussed in Section 5.11d. Furthermore, perfume is clearly associated with the gods; this is encapsulated in the divine conception of Hatshepsut. The text tells us that Queen Ahmose was awakened by the fragrance

Figure 5.30: Scene from the tomb of Nebamun and Ipuky, TT 181 (Davies 1925: Plate VII).

of the god Amun, and when 'his love passed into her limbs, which the fragrance of the god flooded; all his odours were from Punt' (Breasted 1906-7: 80, Section 196). Therefore, perfume connects both the carnal and divine realms. Perfume was also associated with the gods from early in Pharaonic history; for example Utterance 29 in the *Pyramid Text* states 'The perfume of the eye of Horus is on the King, it removes your efflux and protects you from the sweat of the hand of Seth' (Faulkner 1969: 6). Due to the linking of the cone with the concepts of perfume, anointing and the symbolism associated with these ideas, Cherpion (1994: 79) views the cone as '*gage de survie*'.

Cherpion has been criticised for overlooking the significance of anointing in Egyptian funerary beliefs (Thompson 1998). Anointing linked the deceased to the gods as the image of the deity was tendered daily as part of temple ritual, as outlined by Moret (1902). Furthermore, anointing helped preserve the physical integrity of the body through mummification and protected the deceased from the dangers of the afterlife. Tomb scenes show the offering of a cone to guests at the funerary banquet and anointing of guests; this is illustrated in the banquet scene in the tomb of Nebamun and Ipuky. Here one servant girl, holding a dish containing a cone, anoints a female guest, already wearing a cone; while another servant girl pours a liquid, from a small vase, into a shallow dish, held by a seated guest, see Figure 5.30. However, the '*Scènes de Gynécées*' figured ostraca show the cone only as an object of adornment and offering; there are no images of application or anointment. Although, it is possible to suggest the wearer of a cone, both in two and three-dimensional representations, has been previously anointed and therefore linked to the gods and was wearing the cone as an emblem of rebirth.

5.7c: Physical Evidence and New Interpretations

Evidence from Amarna suggests the cones were not merely symbolic. Excavations in the South Tombs Cemetery revealed cones of fat on the skulls of most interments; this took the form of either loose fragments of cones or the discolouration of hair or bones suggesting the melting of the cones (Kemp 2013: 5). While this confirms the cones were material objects it does not mean they were worn in life. Padgham (2012) has put forward a new interpretation of the cone. She notes that the cone is not depicted until the New Kingdom and appears most frequently in tomb scenes that show the male tomb owner in the opening of the mouth ceremony, the gold of honour ceremony and the banquet scene (Padgham 2012: 4). Contemporaneously *ba* birds also began to be depicted wearing cones, for example the tomb of Amenemope (TT 41: Assmann 1991, Plate XXVIIIb). This led Padgham (2012: 103) to suggests that the cone symbolised the *ba* receiving divine offerings on earth. She argues the *ba* of the deceased is shown receiving offerings in the opening of the mouth ceremony and in the banquet scene. However, in the gold of honour scene the *ba* of the living noble receives his necklace from the supreme solar deity. Padgham suggests the depiction of the cone is due to increased solar worship and changes in decorum. Previously the afterlife of non-royals had centred on the tomb and the *ka* but increasingly the *ba* gave the deceased freedom from the tomb.

In summary, Padgham (2012: 106) believes the cone is a symbol of the *ba* summoned to receive divine offerings. The new evidence from Amarna and the work of Padgham have significant implications for the interpretation of the '*Scènes de Gynécées*'. It is unlikely cones were worn in daily life but the evidence from Amarna suggests they were at least funerary goods. This does not discount Padgham's theory given that figures of *ba* birds were taken into the tomb as grave goods. The cones from Amarna may have been substitutes for the painted images in tombs, or simply encompassed the same wishes, to receive divine offerings in perpetuity.

In the '*Scènes de Gynécées*' figured ostraca it is possible the cones represent the *ba* of the women sitting on beds who are receiving gifts in a celebration or ceremony. It is likely the attendants depicted wearing a cone were members of the family or close friends, not servants, and the cone represents their *ba* seen in this temporary transformation, the giving of gifts. Also, this is a communal celebration in which they are partaking. As in the gold of valour ceremony the women may be living; there is no indication they are dead. It is apparent the cone had significance beyond adornment, given that cones are offered to recipients already decked with the head attire.

5.7d: Comparative Evidence

In addition, cones were also depicted in domestic decorative schemes, seen for example in a border of a painted pavement at Amarna, Figures 5.31-32. The central scene shows a lake teaming with fish, surrounded by lush vegetation. The cones are shown in dishes, decked with floral collars, with lotus flowers draped over them forming a border. Cherpion (1994: 85) notes the initial incongruity of the scene but suggests they symbolise rebirth. It is noteworthy the cones are depicted with lotus flowers and floral collars, both of which are significant motifs in the '*Scènes de Gynécées*', suggesting rebirth and rejuvenation, discussed in Sections 5.9 and 5.10. The offering of cones is also seen in a royal context on the small golden shrine of Tutankhamun (Cairo JE 61481: Eaton Krauss 1985: Plate XVIII). Here Ankhesenamun approaches the King with a dish containing a large cone, again this is decorated with a floral collar and lotus flowers. The King wears

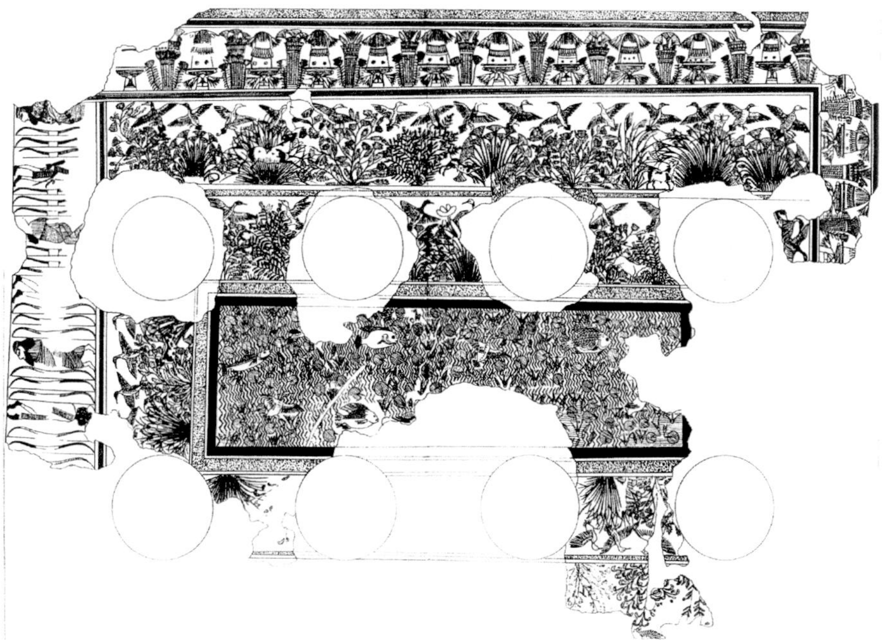

Figure 5.31: Painted pavement from the palace at Amarna, showing a lake lush with vegetation (Petrie 1894: Plate II).

Figure 5.32: Insert of painted pavement from Amarna, showing head cones decked with floral collars and lotus flowers (Petrie 1894: Plate II).

the blue crown, so the cone cannot be for adornment. It is noteworthy, the King is not referred to as an Osiris on the shine, so he is a living King receiving a gift from his wife.

5.7e: Linkage

There are many inconsistencies in the depiction of the cone in New Kingdom Egypt, with the inclusion in some representations but the exclusion in others. However, the cone appears to be depicted almost consistently on the 'women on beds' scenes. This is in contrast to other contemporaneous depictions of the female form, for example 'ladies on beds' figurines, which were found at Deir el Medina and throughout New Kingdom Egypt and her empire (Backhouse 2016: 425). The inclusion of the cone in both domestic decorative schemes and funeral scenes suggests it had a meaning beyond adornment. It appears to be linked to the receipt of offerings and gifts, perhaps gifts of nature in the case of the Amarna pavement. It may also indicate the recipient had been anointed, so linked to the gods.

5.8: Hair, Wigs and Scenes of Hairdressing

There are two main female hairstyles depicted in art in New Kingdom Egypt, tripartite and enveloping, both are represented in the '*Scènes de Gynécées*' figured ostraca. The former is divided into three parts, one of which falls down the back with two sections framing the face. This leaves the shoulders and often the ears visible. The enveloping style has no division and falls in a solid mass from the crown of the head, covering the shoulders. The difference between the two styles is demonstrated on ostracon WoB.5, which shows the seated figure wearing a tripartite style and her standing companion wearing an enveloping wig. The length of the hairstyles, which often reach waist or hip level, suggests they are depicted wearing wigs not natural hair.

5.8a: Evidence in Art

In the 'women on beds' scenes the hairstyle of 23 of the seated women can be identified; in 11 cases this is an enveloping wig, nine wear a tripartite wig, two don a short wig and one wears a headdress/scarf. With regard to their companions, 11 hairstyles are identifiable; all wear an enveloping wig. In the comparative evidence dataset three women are shown seated in a chair holding a child; two wear an enveloping wig while one wears a tripartite wig. An additional tripartite wig is seen on ostracon F.12 which depicts a nursing woman; which is likely to have belonged to an 'elaborate bed' scene. Only two women seated on a bed are shown wearing a short wig (WoB.26, 48); both these scenes are atypical and show the seated figure facing the viewer's left, holding an object in an outstretched hand, but no companions are present.

Both Haynes (1977) and Fletcher (1995) outlined the chronological development of female hairstyles in art in the New Kingdom. While there is some disagreement between the two scholars it is clear at the beginning of the 18th Dynasty the tripartite style was favoured but from the reign of Amenhotep II the enveloping style became popular. Throughout the New Kingdom both styles continued to be depicted with various frequencies. Although the enveloping wig is the most popular in the post-Amarna period, sometimes both styles are portrayed in the same tomb (Fletcher 1995: Figures 307, 503). However, by the 19th and 20th Dynasty the longer tripartite wig is most frequently represented in Egyptian art. Haynes (1977: 20) suggests tripartite wigs may have been favoured for venerated females as a mark of respect. It is possible this custom was adopted in the 'women on beds' scenes. Eleven seated figures are shown wearing an enveloping wig, while nine wear a tripartite wig. However, no attendants are clearly shown wearing a tripartite wig. It is possible the differentiation in wigs was used to show respect to the seated women as they received guests and gifts. The tripartite wig was therefore appropriate but not compulsory wear for the seated figure, but it was not appropriate for their guests. Hairstyles depicted in the kiosk scenes differ from those in the 'women on beds' scenes; these are discussed in Sections 5.3c-d.

5.8b: Physical Evidence

An example of an enveloping style wig was found in the tomb of Kha and Merit at Deir el-Medina (TT 8) (Turin S.8499: Vassilika 2010: 51). This was a high-status object, made of human hair, 54 cm in length; it has a central parting with long tresses which were plaited at the ends. This was stored in a wooden wig box inscribed with a funerary offering (Turin S.8493: Vassilika 2010: 52-53). It is possible that Merit kept her hair shorter and wore the wig for special occasions. Of the internments at Deir el-Medina, Bruyère (1937b: 141) noted the women often had their hair arranged in a tripartite style, either three large plaits, or numerous small plaits with a centre part. Bruyère also found loose hair in baskets and bags, for example tomb 1388 (Bruyère 1937b: 192). Fletcher (1995: 390) also recorded many examples of loose hair deposited in baskets and chests in tombs, both royal and non-royal, in the New Kingdom. While excavations at the South Tombs Cemetery at Amarna found no wigs, numerous extensions were discovered which were either braided or tied into the original hair (Kemp 2013: 19). Robins (1999: 63) has suggested women may have kept their natural hair long and wore wigs in addition because it 'embodied their sexuality and hence female gender identity.'

5.8c: Scenes of Hairdressing

Within the 'women on beds' scenes there are six possible depictions of hairdressing. The clearest indication is seen in WoB.33. This shows a woman sitting on a bed, behind her a companion stands with hands upraised to fix her coiffeur; while in front of her another companion stands, offering a dish containing a cone. Vandier d'Abbadie (1937: 82) suggested the cone was to be affixed after the hairdressing was complete. However, the seated figure already wears a cone, so the meaning of this gesture is beyond adornment. It may have signified the seated woman had been anointed. When considering hairdressing scenes, Gauthier-Laurent (1935-38) noted the limited number of images in Egyptian art. However, on consideration, these scenes of an intimate and personal part of daily life, initially appear incongruous to their context; many of which are found upon grave goods or tomb scenes. They appear first in the 10th or 11th Dynasty, for example the sarcophagus of Henouy (Berlin 13772: Gauthier-Laurent 1935-38: 764, Figure 1). This shows Henouy sitting on a stool holding a mirror in her hand, behind her an attendant fixes her hair; the scene was painted near the head of the mummy. Perhaps even more inharmonious are the images of hairdressing which are part of larger scenes, for example from the tomb of Sebeknekht at el-Kab, dated to the Second Intermediate Period c.1650-1550 BC. Figure 5.33 shows the tomb owner and his wife sharing a large seat under which objects of toiletry and dress are stowed.

In front of them a banquet is taking place. Behind the woman a small figure tends to her hair and a monkey offers her a small vase. It is unlikely a lady of the house would have had her hair dressed during a party; although the function of the image may have been to suggest preparations that took place previously. This may also have been the purpose of the images of hairdressing in the 'women on beds' scenes, or they may have funereal connotations as seen in the general repertoire of hairdressing scenes documented by Gauthier-Laurent (1935-38).

In terms of comparison to three-dimensional representations there is one 'lady on a bed' figurine which appears to show the recumbent figure having her hair dressed, Figure 5.34. Unfortunately, it has no provenance but stylistically it is dated to the 26th Dynasty; it does however show the continued association of women on beds and hairdressing. Derchain (1975a: 65) suggested the act of hairdressing indicated that sexual activity was to follow and noted the erotic nature of many scenes of hairdressing. Anthropologists have long recognised that the dressing and styling of hair is part of ritual behaviour often associated with rites of passage, mourning and sexual activity (Leach 1958). It is a method of communication, signalling a status or a state of being. It assumes a shared symbolic language between the actors and the audience. There is much evidence to support this in the context of ancient Egypt.

It is possible the scenes of hairdressing in the '*Scènes de Gynécées*' figured ostraca are depicting a rite of passage, the end of a period of confinement. Fletcher (1995: 53) suggests the distinctive tripartite hairstyles, with a top knot, seen in the kiosk scenes (K.1-3), depict women

Figure 3.33: Scene from the tomb of Sebeknekht at el-Kab (Tylor 1896: Plate VIII).

Figure 5.34: Limestone figurine, depiction a woman lying on a bed having her hair dressed, Petrie UC 8650 (Photograph Author's own) Courtesy of Petrie Museum of Egyptian Archaeology.

before they have completed their purification rites. Therefore, the 'women on beds' scenes, as illustrated on the figured ostraca, may show the women after they have undergone beautification and hairstyling in preparation for celebrations in the home to mark the birth of their child.

5.8d: Sexuality

Hair is linked to sexuality and beauty in ancient Egyptian culture. It is seen as alluring and enticing, as illustrated in numerous references in New Kingdom love poetry. For example, in *Papyrus Harris 500* hair is referred to as 'bait' and 'anointed with unguents' (Kitchen 1999: 357). The preparation of hair is often described as a prelude to romantic liaisons. *Papyrus Harris 500* describes how a young girl forgot to do her hair 'I went running off to seek you, And see! I forgot all about my hair... (But now) [...] I have adorned my hair, So that I may be perfect all the time' (Tobin 2003: 315). This is also illustrated in *The Tale of Two Brothers* but with stronger sexual connotations. Here the wife of Anubis is braiding her hair, she then suggests to her brother in-law, 'Come, let us spend an hour lying together', to which he replies she should 'loosen her braids' (Lichtheim 1976: 205). *The Tale of the Two Brothers* also recounts how the smell from a single lock of hair caused the pharaoh to fall in love with the unknown owner, so demonstrating the powerful combination of hair and perfume (Lichtheim 1976: 203-211). The importance of hair, particularly to the identity of women, is also demonstrated in numerous spells in *Papyrus Ebers*. This includes remedies to preserve the hair, remedies to make the hair grow and remedies to cause the hair to fall out, which should be applied to 'the head of a hated woman (i.e. a fellow wife)' (Ebbell 1937: 79-80).

5.8e: Divine Associations

Hair is also associated with goddesses, particularly Hathor. *Ramesseum Papyri XI* contains a spell in which Horus calls for the help of his mother Isis. He identifies various deities with parts of the body, Horus with his eye, Seth with his testicles and 'Hathor for her locks' (Gardiner 1955: 14). Goedicke (1970: 260) suggested Hathor was possibly the unnamed goddess in *The Story of the Herdsman*; he identified her by the epithets 'the Strong One' (*Wsrt*) and 'Mistress of the Two Lands' (*nbt-t3wy*). In the tale a shepherd meets a non-human female in the marshes; he is frightened due to the sight of her 'tresses', as translated by Parkinson (1997: 287). Parkinson goes on to note that 'tresses' of hair were often viewed as erotic, so linked to the scene, which takes place the next day. Here, when the herdsman meets her again, she is naked, and her hair is loose. It must be acknowledged not all scholars identify the goddess solely as Hathor. Schneider (2007: 316) argues the goddess has a twofold nature, depicted first as a predatory animal, whose hair is more akin to bristles, and secondly as a naked woman with loose hair. Therefore, Schneider (2007: 318) suggests this 'ferocious or distant goddess' may be Hathor; although alternatively, it could be Sekhmet, Mut, Tefnut or even a Libyan goddess. The important point for this research is the link between hair, eroticism and goddesses. Isis and Nephthys are also associated with hair, seen in the *Coffin Texts* were the hair of Isis is tied to the hair of Nephthys, Spell 168 (Faulkner 1977: 145). Naguib (1990: 23) has proposed this is a metaphor for the joining together of the two banks of the Nile to allow the deceased to cross the river without any danger.

5.8f: Mourning

The association of hair with mourning has been noted by numerous scholars (Fletcher 1995: 74-76; Millward 2012: 118). The word *i3kb*, which is translated as mourning, uses the determinate of a lock of hair (Faulkner 1962: 9). More particularly, *i3kb.t* is translated as mourning women, using the determinate of the lock of hair and a female figure with free-flowing hair. Mourning women are depicted with sweeping tresses in many New Kingdom tombs, for example the tomb of Ramose (TT 55: Davies 1941: 42, Plates XXXI-XXII, XXIV-XXV). Once again hair is used to mark a rite of passage.

5.8g: Linkage

Numerous scholars, from a wide range of disciplines, have commented on the unique nature of hair. Firth (1973: 262-3) noted hair is a very personal thing, a biological accessory, attached to the body and associated with growth, yet it is detachable and can be transferred to other people. It is renewable and to some degree an independent object. In relation to ancient Egypt, the ability for self-renewal may have linked hair to the concept of rebirth. This may explain the presence of loose hair in baskets and bags found in tombs at Deir el-Medina (Bruyère 1937b:192). Furthermore, as Firth (1973: 290) noted, hair is 'an intimate element of the personality' and it becomes a 'manipulable representation of the entire person' (Firth 1973: 296). The arrangement of hair and wigs functioned as identity markers in ancient Egypt indicating status, gender, age and possibly also life events and states of being. The 'women on beds' scenes show elite women dressed in their finery; the wearing of elaborate wigs was a key part of this, stressing their sexuality and by association their fertility, with possible links to the goddess Hathor.

5.9: Floral Collars and Broad Collars

Floral collars are a significant motif in the '*Scènes de Gynécées*' figured ostraca. They appear as wall decoration, objects of personal adornment and possibly as gifts. Although their representation is limited, they have links with material culture and are a widespread iconographic motif in contemporaneous tomb scenes. Floral collars are shown as circular wall decoration in at least five, possibly six, 'women on beds' scenes (WoB.1, 27, 40, 41, 50, EB.2) and one fragmentary ostracon (F.9). The imagery on WoB.41 is indistinct; the collar could be a wall hanging or an item of presentation. Broad collar necklaces are worn by nine women in the 'women on beds' scenes and 'elaborate bed' scenes. However, only three are likely to depict floral collars (WoB.6, 27, 49). A floral collar is also presented to a seated figure in WoB.42. The presentation of floral collars is common in banquet scenes in Eighteenth Dynasty tombs, for example the tomb of Rekhmire (TT 100). This shows floral collars being offered to guests who are already wearing the collar, suggesting the collar was not merely an object of adornment (Davies 1935: Plate, LXVIII). It is also likely the wall decoration depicted on a further five ostraca represented horizontal garlands, for example WoB.36. In addition, 'elaborate beds' (EB.1-3) may have also been decked with floral garlands as proposed by Schäfer (1916: 30).

5.9a: Painted Wall Decoration

Evidence from Amarna suggests floral collars and horizontal garlands were painted on the walls of houses as seen in Figures 5.35-6. Found in the Main City these wall decorations consisted of fruits, flowers, leaves and petals (Peet and Woolley 1923: 43-44). The festoons were surmounted by a horizontal garland of water lilies, some still in bud while others were open. Some festoons also had straps or ribbons attached and in one example, (House P.47.5), the straps ran down and supported a representation of a shrine (Peet and Woolley 1923: 44). It is apparent the garlands were part of elaborate painted decorations.

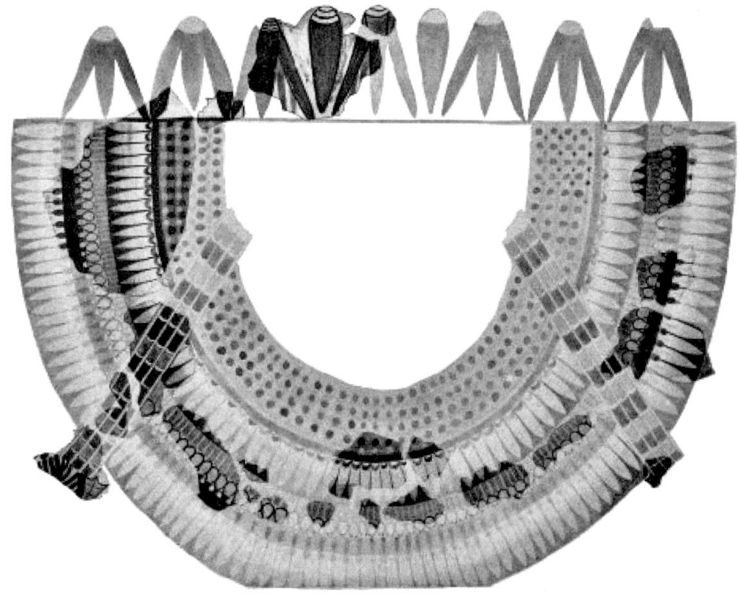

Figure 5.35: Painted wall decoration from the House of Ra'nŭfer, Amarna, House N. 49.18 (Peet and Woolley 1923: 43-44, Plate XV).

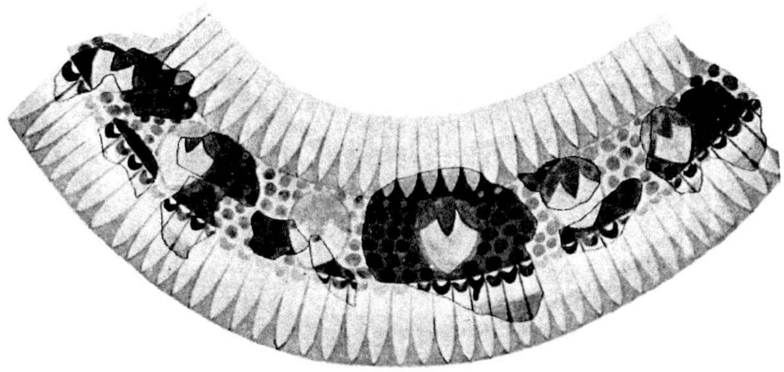

Figure 5.36: Additional painted wall decoration from the House of Ra'nŭfer, Amarna, House N. 49.18 (Peet and Woolley 1923: 43-44, Plate XV).

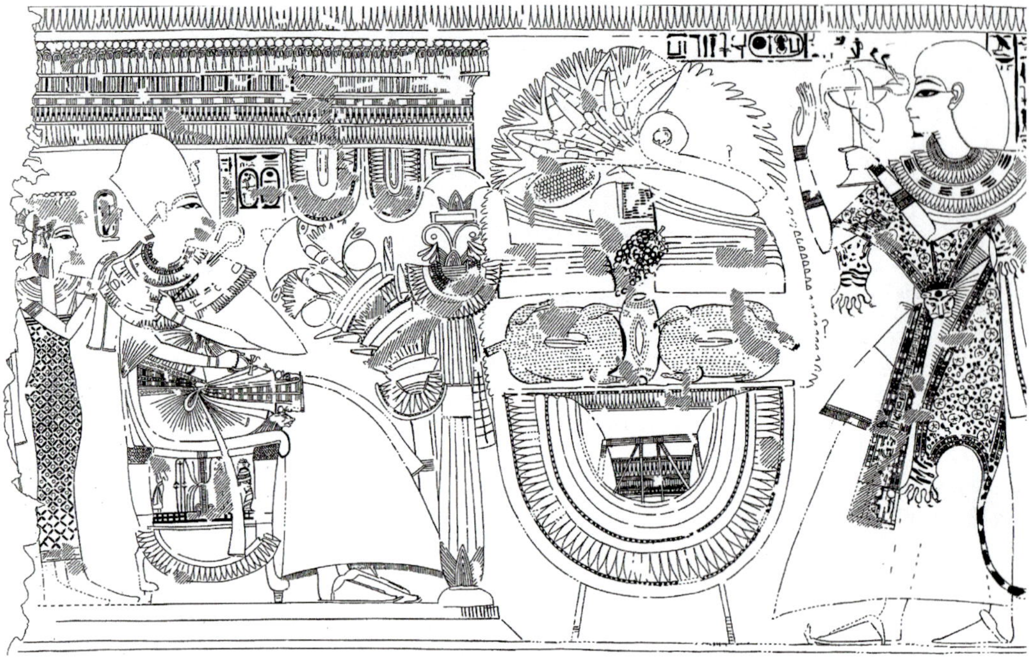

Figure 5.37: Scene from the tomb of Userhat, TT 51
(Davies 1927: Plate V).

5.9b: New Kingdom Tomb Scenes

Floral collars were also depicted in New Kingdom tomb scenes. One of the most prolific illustrations of collars is seen in the tomb of Userhat (TT 51), located at Sheikh Abd el-Qurna (Davies 1927). His tomb is resplendent in floral motifs, see Figure 5.37. Floral collars hang as wall decorations and items of personal adornment worn by the living, the dead, the royal and the divine. They are worn around the neck but also as fillets by numerous women depicted in the tomb; they also appear under the seat of the deified King. Furthermore, they adorn numerous tables of offerings and horizontal garlands also decorate wine jars and the boats journeying to Abydos. In addition, tall floral bouquets, incorporating floral collars, are also offered to the gods and stand before the living and the dead (Davies 1927: Plates V-XIV). The excessive nature of the iconography is noted by Davies (1927: 10) who calls them a 'tasteless addition'.

Floral collars were also a decorative motif on painted pottery in New Kingdom Egypt. It is noteworthy they are the dominant theme in the two main and distinct genres of vase painting of this time period. They are incorporated into blue painted ware from the 18th Dynasty, for example vases found at Malqata, Figure 5.38. These use floral motifs in a limited tonal palette. They are also a key feature in polychrome ware from the Ramesside period, which utilise vibrant hues, see Figure 5.39. In her study on polychrome pottery of the 19th Dynasty, Bell (1987) demonstrated that the majority of polychrome vases decorated with floral collars were from Deir el-Medina, with a small number from Gurob. Bell suggested that floral collars were linked to concepts of birth and rejuvenation, due to their association with large bouquets of flowers called *ankh*, which philologically refer to life. As discussed in Section 5.3g, Sugi (2002: 143) believes these bouquets were associated with the life-giving gifts of air and breath.

Figure 5.38: Blue ware vase from Malquta,
Metropolitan Museum of Art 11.215.462,
Creative Commons CC0.1.0.

Figure 5.39: Polychrome vase from the tomb of Sennedjem TT.1, Metropolitan Museum of Art 86.1.10, Creative Commons CC0.1.0.

These bouquets were offered to Amun in the Beautiful Festival of the Valley, in which the barques of Amun, Mut and Khonsu visited the temples of living and dead kings on the West Bank of Thebes. The procession was followed by the populace, who also visited the tombs of their ancestors. Food and drink were consumed, and guests may have been given floral collars. Bouquets known as *ankh* were presented to the tomb owner; it is possible these elaborate vessels were also offered. Schott (1953) details the depictions of the festival in Eighteenth Dynasty tombs but due to changes in tomb iconography, the representation of the festival diminishes in Ramesside tombs. Bell (1987: 56-57) suggests the polychrome vases, which are decorated with floral collars, were made by the workers of Deir el-Medina for use in the Beautiful Festival of the Valley. Figure 5.39 shows a jar found in the tomb of Sennedjem (TT 1) at Deir el-Medina; the tomb contained numerous similar jars (Bell 1987: 6-7). Several tombs at Deir el-Medina show the tomb owner and his wife being offered vases decorated with floral collars, for example the tomb of Ipuy (TT 217), Figure 5.40. The text informs us Ipuy is receiving a bouquet which has been proffered in the temple of Amun at Karnak (Davies 1927: 43). It is possible this is part of the Beautiful Festival of the Valley.

5.9d: Floral Collars: Physical Remains

In addition to being a significant iconographic motif floral collars were also left on coffins of the deceased. Tutankhamun had three floral wreaths (Newbury 1927: 189-96). This included a small wreath tied around the vulture and uraeus on the forehead of the second coffin, a pectoral garland on the breast of the second coffin and a floral garland on the third coffin. This trend continued in the Ramesside period with Ramses II being buried with 13 rows of floral garlands and single blue lotus flowers placed beneath the bands which sealed the mummy wrappings. The botanist Schweinfurth made drawings of the garlands; the physical remains of which are in the Agriculture Museum of Cairo and the *Herbier du Musée de Paris*, as noted by Manniche (1989:

Figure 5.40: Facsimile by Norman de Garis Davies (restored), scene from the tomb of Ipuy, TT217, Metropolitan Museum of Art 30.4.114, Creative Commons CC0.1.0.

30). This practise was not confined to royal burials but also seen in the tomb of Kha (TT 8), an architect from Deir el-Medina, which contained three collars of dried flowers, one on the inner sarcophagus (Turin S. 8319), one around the external sarcophagus (Turin S. 8430) and one around the neck of a wooden statue of Kha attached to a high back chair (Turin S.8335) (Vassilika 2010: 58-68).

5.9e: Philological Evidence

In the New Kingdom the floral collar could be referred to as *w3ḥ* or *m3ḥ* with a floral or collar determinative (Faulkner 1962: 54, 103) and used in the expression 'the collar of justification'. This was an emblem of Osiris and the vindicated dead. Bell cites the text on Tutankhamun's portable chest as evidence for the association of the collars with rebirth. This says 'May you take the *w3ḥ* collar of justification which was at the neck of Wenennnefer (that is Osiris) (so that) your limbs may become young and your heart may become strong (again) when you are examined/assessed by the Ennead' (Bell 1987: 57). The small wreath tied around the vulture and uraeus on the forehead of Tutankhamun's second coffin was referred to by Newberry as a 'wreath of justification' (Newberry 1927: 190). Bell goes on to suggest that the larger collar on the inner most coffin, referred to as 'the floral collaret' should also be understood as a collar of justification. Newberry (1927: 190) cited Spell 19 in *The Book of the Dead* which describes rites to be carried out over a wreath to be placed on a man's head. If the ritual is carried out correctly the man would become vindicated against his enemies living or dead and would become 'a follower of Osiris' (Allen 1974: 35).

5.9f: Broad Collar Necklaces

Board collars are worn by four women in the 'women on beds' dataset, two women in the 'elaborate beds' scenes and all three nursing women in the kiosk scenes. Collars also appear in a further three ostraca in the fragments dataset and are commonly depicted in the comparative evidence dataset. The collars are plain or comprised of circular bands; they do not have the detailed iconography of floral collars. Broad collars were the most frequently depicted item of jewellery throughout Egyptian history; they were worn by mortals and divinities, indiscriminate of gender. Two types were common, circular collars fasten together at the back of the neck; while semi-circular examples had a longer fastening cord and allowed the collar to rest on the shoulders (Lansing 1940: 66).

5.9g: Linkage

Contemporaneous material culture suggests floral collars were strongly linked to rebirth and rejuvenation, particularly at Thebes with their association with the Beautiful Festival of the Valley. This would make them an ideal decorative motif for houses, both real floral collars and painted wall decoration. It is possible floral garlands, both collars and horizontal, were hung during festival or times of private family celebrations. The presentation and offering of floral collar was a symbolic gesture linked to the concepts of rebirth and rejuvenation. The wearing of generic broad collars by women in the '*Scènes de Gynécées*' figured ostraca suggests they were dressed in their finery, again indicating a celebration or religious festival.

5.10: Lotus Flower Imagery

Eleven of the seated figures and six companion figures, in the 'women on beds' scenes are shown wearing what is traditionally referred to as a lotus flower. This is part of elaborate head adornment which includes a fillet and often a head cone; the flower is in bloom and takes the same orientation as the wearer. A lotus is also held by one companion figure in a gesture of offering towards a seated figure (WoB.43). The lotus is also seen in scenes of comparative data and fragments, this includes two nursing mothers scenes (CE.3-4), two scenes of presentation (CE.6-7) and three fragments (F.2-3,14).

5.10a: Botanical Identification

In botanical terms the flowers depicted are not lotus flowers, but two species of water lily. However, for the sake of continuity with previous scholarship this research will continue to use this descriptor. The flowers are two varieties of *Nymphaea* (water lilies). The most frequently represented in Egyptian art is the *Nymphaea cerulea* (blue lotus), which is found in still waters, Figure 5.41. The flower has small pointed petals, which are light blue in colour; these emerge from conical buds and the leaf has a smooth edge (Emboden 1981: 40). The flower blooms in the morning, from 7.30 am until before noon, for up to three days (Emboden

Figure 5.41: Nymphaea cerulean/Blue lotus (Creative Commons Attribution 2.0 Generic).

Figure 5.42: Nymphaea lotus/White lotus (Creative Commons Attribution 2.0 Generic).

1981: 41; Harer 1985: 52). This suggests scenes in which the flowers are depicted in bloom are taking place in the morning, if they are realistically represented, as cut flowers follow the normal cycle of those in their natural environment. The flower is fragrant, although there is much disagreement about the nature of the emission (Ossian 1999: 51).

The *Nymphaea lotus* (white lotus) is larger than the blue lotus with leaves spanning up to 20 cm in diameter, with a notched edge (Hepper 1990: 16). The petals are rounder and lie flatter upon the surface, Figure 5.42. It is also found in still water but favours deeper pools. In contrast to the blue lotus this flower blooms at night (Ossian 1999: 51).

5.10b: Creation and Rebirth

Lotus flowers are depicted widely in Egyptian art; they are worn as adornments, incorporated into floral bouquets, are part of funerary offerings and were used in architectural design (Ossian 1999: 49). Their ubiquitous presence is due to their role in creation myths, which link them to concepts of rebirth. For example, the creation myth of Heliopolis believed the self-engendered sun god Atum masturbated or sneezed creating Shu and Tefnut which led to the creation of the Ennead, illustrated in Spells 269 and 272 in the pyramid of Pepi II (Allen 2005: 269, 272). However, as noted by Gahlin (2007: 300) by the end of the 18th Dynasty the original appearance of Atum is replaced by the appearance of the blue lotus floating on the primordial waters, when the petals open the sun rises. This is referred to as 'the first appearance'. This is seen initially in Spell 335 of the *Coffin Texts* and then in Spell 17 in *The Book of the Dead.* This spell takes the title 'Spell for Emerging by Day' and as Allen (1988: 31) notes this becomes the title of *The Book of the Dead.*

From the Old Kingdom onwards the lotus flower was personified as the god Nefertum. In the pyramid of Unas Spell 160 states Unas 'will appear as Nefertum, as the lotus (translated by Allen as water lily) at the sun's nose when he emerges from the *Akhet* every day, the one at the sight of whom the gods become clear' (Allen 2005: 42). Anthes (1959: 176) suggests the lotus flower bestows life on Ra (as the sun) every morning and in doing so the moment of creation is reiterated. As Cherpion (1999: 94) notes, the lotus flower is a guarantor of eternity as the sun continues to be born anew each dawn; while for Germond (2008: 218) the lotus flower is one of the most important markers for rebirth.

In the New Kingdom the lotus flower allowed the deceased to join the gods in the Netherworld. Spells 80 and 81 in *The Book of the Dead* are both transformative spells with the deceased seeking to become a lotus. Spell 81 asks 'May you grant that I see the gods who lead the Netherworld, may there be given to me a seat in the realm of the dead in the presence of the Lords of the West, may I take my place in the Sacred Land' (Faulkner 1985: 79). The accompanying vignette, in the papyrus of Ani, shows the head of Ani emerging from a lotus flower, floating in a pond. Opposite a squatting god is shown wearing the sun disc; Faulkner (1985: 79) suggests this is the form Ani hopes to assume. These qualities make the flower a highly suitable item of adornment for figures shown in the 'women on beds' scenes, which are likely to represent the celebrations associated with the birth of a child, but which may also contain the desire for rebirth.

5.10c: New Kingdom Comparative Evidence

Lotus flowers were also incorporated into floral collars left on the coffins of the deceased in New Kingdom Egypt. For example, the three floral collars found on the coffins of Tutankhamun all included petals of the blue lotus flower (Newberry 1927: 232). In addition, one of the floral collars at the Metropolitan Museum (MMA 09.184. 314) found in the embalming cache of the King, also contains lotus petals (Arnold 2010: 74). These collars were linked to the concepts of rebirth and rejuvenation; as discussed in Sections 5.9a-g. The lotus is also a common motif in New Kingdom love poetry; the significance of this was discussed by Derchain (1975b). Both male and female lovers use the lotus in a metaphoric manner to bestow compliments onto their partners. In *Papyrus Harris 500* the boy says '[the mouth of] my sister is a lotus' (Fox 1985: 9). While in the *Cairo Love Songs* the girl speaks evocatively stating 'My god, my lotus' (Derchain 1975b: 70). It is suggested the male lover is equated to a god and a lotus to give him lustre (Derchain 1975b: 71). This also bestows upon him the power of creation, which could be a reference to sexual energy, fertility and birth/rebirth.

5.11: Linkage

A review of contemporaneous material culture and textual evidence reveals links to the '*Scènes de Gynécées*' figured ostraca. This includes figurines and figure vases; with the relationship between a mother and child providing the unify theme. New Kingdom Love Poetry also offers textual association and reiterates the concepts of eroticism and sexuality.

5.11a: Figurines

Both Vandier d'Abbadie (1937: 85) and Bruyère (1939: 144) suggested there was an analogy between the '*Scènes de Gynécées*' figured ostraca and 'ladies on beds' figurines. This was the basis of research for my PhD studies at the University of Liverpool (Backhouse 2016). The figurines were in fact the initial impetus for this work, which led to the consideration of the ostraca as objects in their own right. The study of the figurines formed a second volume of this work, the first is presented here on the ostraca. While it is hoped the publish a second volume, focusing on the 'ladies on beds' figurines at a later day, a summary is detailed below to establish and clarify the link between the 'ladies on beds' figurines and the '*Scènes de Gynécées*' figured ostraca.

Figurines from New Kingdom Egypt and her empire were examined; only figurines with a recorded provenance were considered. Research found 125 figurines; the majority of which were fragmentary, with only 19 complete or near complete examples (Backhouse 2016: 400). The study analysed the figurines in terms of context, assigning figurines to a primary context of daily life or funerary. Secondary contexts of daily life included settlement sites, industrial zones and temples. While secondary contexts for the funerary realm included tombs, surface debris and illegal digging in cemeteries.

Research discovered 61% of the 'ladies on beds' figurines were found in settlement sites of New Kingdom Egypt, particularly Gurob, Deir el-Medina and Memphis (Backhouse 2016: 549). Gurob was the site which yielded most figurines, with 26 found in a daily life context (settlement and industrial zones) and four from the funerary realm (Backhouse 2016: 402-405). A further 26 figurines were recorded from Deir el-Medina (Backhouse 2016: 405-406). While no 'ladies on beds' figurines have a definitive find spot in the village they were assigned a settlement context as Bruyère (1939: 109) stated most figurines were found in the rubble of the village. Furthermore, he noted he did not find any in the tombs of the 18th Dynasty, only standalone figurines (Bruyère 1933: 12). However, it is likely many more figurines were recovered from the site as Bruyère (1939: 109) detailed that he found hundreds of fragments of female figurines at Deir el-Medina, but this included standalone figurines also. For this research figurines from Deir el-Medina were studied and photographed at the Louvre and IFAO. Although, it is likely there are more in storage at Cairo Museum or in onsite magazines in the Theban region. Since the completion of this initial research figurines in Museo Egizio have also been examined and photographed for future study. They were not included in the initial research as they were not published by the excavator and only recently has any preliminary work been carried out on them (Trapani 2012). The third most lucrative site for figurines was Memphis; where 22 examples were found which dated from the New Kingdom. All of which were found in an area of settlement characterised by mud brick structures with narrow walls and clay floors (Giddy 1999: 3).

Given the predominance of figurines excavated from settlement sites, it is likely they were used in domestic cult. An analysis of contemporaneous material culture, particularly at Deir el-Medina, for example ancestor/anthropoid busts and *3ḫ iḳr n R'* stelae suggest this (Backhouse 2016: 35-41). The figurines were most likely offered to ancestors, who it was believed would intercede with the gods for the benefit of their living relatives. However, the 'ladies on beds' figurines clearly had a multi-functional use as 23% were found in a funerary context. Most of these were discovered in tombs, but a small number were found in surface debris or illegal digging in a cemetery. It is possible that they were used in daily life and then interred to assist with the rebirth of the deceased, or for the benefit of the living, hoping to tap into the *heka*, the power of the dead. Furthermore, five percent of figurines were found in a votive context – chiefly outside the Nile Valley and Delta, especially in temples linked to Hathor. This includes temples at Mirgissa, Serabit el-Khadim and Beth Shan (Backhouse 2016: 401). It is possible outside of Egypt the figurines were deemed appropriate gifts for the goddess and provided a connection with home.

As part of this study the work of Waraksa (2009) was examined. She argued that female figurines were ritual objects made to be broken; a theory based on 42 figurines recovered from the temple of Mut at Karnak and dated predominantly to the Late Period. She argued through a process of transference the illness or affliction leaves the patient and is absorbed into the figurine, which transforms into a goddess upon the vocalisation of a spell. The figurine is then disposed of. She suggests the generic image of a woman was chosen as it represents health (Waraksa 2009: 169). However, my research concluded that this proposition cannot be applied to the New Kingdom 'ladies on beds' figurines, due to their context and iconography (Backhouse 2016: 458).

With regard to the context no, New Kingdom 'ladies on beds figurines' were found in known refuse sites. Furthermore, Waraksa's study included only two 'ladies on beds' figurines dated to the New Kingdom. In addition, the iconography of the naked, nubile woman on a bed, with or without a child, was linked to fertility. The bed was recognised as a place of sexual activity in a variety of textual sources. In the divine realm this is seen in *The Contendings of Horus and Seth*. This charts the battle between the two gods for the throne of Osiris and describes how after a series of confrontations the two gods lie down upon a bed that was prepared for them. Seth aroused himself until he had an erection, which he then inserted between the thighs of Horus until he ejaculated (Wente 2003: 99). Few direct references to sexual activity survive from ancient Egypt; this is one of the most explicit in written form. In the mortal realm the link between the bed and sexual activity is demonstrated in New Kingdom love poetry, discussed in Section 5.11d. In addition, goddesses in ancient Egypt are rarely depicted naked, (with the exception of Nut), or without any divine attributes and they are never shown wearing head cones.

In terms of iconography there are a number of links between the '*Scènes de Gynécées*' figured ostraca and the 'ladies on beds' figurines. In the simplest terms the 'ladies on beds' figurines incorporate a female figure into a bed or plaque; together they form one object. The bed or plaque is a vehicle for supplementary motifs, in addition to the child, which often accompanies the woman. Both the serpent and to a lesser degree mirrors are depicted on the 'ladies on beds' figurines, both common themes in the '*Scènes de Gynécées*' figured ostraca. The most frequent motif is two wavy lines around the edge of the bed surrounding the figurine, suggesting serpent imagery. This was found on seven New Kingdom figurines, including a painted limestone example from Gurob and more numerous moulded clay examples from Deir el-Medina. The latter was the most frequent find spot for these figurines, accounting for six of the seven representations (Backhouse 2016: 426). A small number of 'ladies on beds' figurines also have a mirror depicted on the bed. It was found on three examples in this study. It is a rarity, yet it has a number of consistencies. It is always found to the left side of the woman (to the viewer's right) and a child is also included in the scene (Backhouse 2016: 427).

Overall, the study found the '*Scènes de Gynécées*' figured ostraca were a regional creation, limited to Deir el-Medina; while the 'ladies on beds' figurines were found throughout New Kingdom Egypt and her empire. This indicates the '*Scènes de Gynécées*' figured ostraca are part of a larger corpus of images of women, often depicted with a child or suggesting fertility through nubility. Iconographically the main difference between the two datasets (figurines and ostraca) is that the 'ladies on beds' figurines are naked, while most of the women represented in the '*Scènes de Gynécées*' figured ostraca are clothed. They may be depicting different parts of the same narrative, the story of motherhood and childbearing. The figurines represent the wish for a child and by association rebirth; while the ostraca show the celebrations associated with childbirth, which may also have apotropaic elements. Figure vases depicting a kneeling mother and child in various poses, produced in the mid-18th Dynasty appear to be a hybrid, combining iconographic elements of both (Bourriau 1987; Desroches-Noblecourt 1952).

5.11b: Figure Vases

Fourteen examples of so called 'figure vases' incorporating a kneeling mother and child, complete and fragmentary are known (Bourriau 1987: 94). The women depicted are attired in a shawl with their hair arranged in a simple fashion. However, they wear jewellery including bracelets and necklaces. Although no two objects are identical, the figure vases form a coherent group; the similarity in material and manufacture has led Bourriau (1987: 94) to suggest they were made in a single workshop spanning one or two generations. Furthermore, she views the vases as wholly Egyptian in source. While, Lilyquist (2005: 64-65) suggests they are of foreign origin arguing the shawl, hairstyle and jewellery are Asiatic in design. Regardless of the place of manufacture, the general consensus is that the vases were used to hold mother's milk (Brunner-Traut 1970; Bourriau 1987; Desroches-Noblecourt 1952). Mother's milk, particularly the milk of a woman who bore a male child, was viewed as a potent ingredient used in many medical preparations (Bardinet 1995: 574). One remedy in *Papyrus Ebers* (Eb.110) uses fat/oil, the milk of a woman who has borne a male child and moringa oil, to make an unguent (Bardinet 1995: 266). It is possible that any liquid poured into these vases was thought to take on the healing properties of mother's milk (Roehrig 2005: 234). The function of the vases as a receptacle for milk is clearly demonstrated, one example (Louvre A.F. 6.643) shows a kneeling woman squeezing her right breast, while holding a jar in her left hand to capture the milk (Robins 1993:81, Figure 27).

Only three examples have a firm context; one was found in a tomb at Abydos (British Museum EA 54694: Garstang 1909: 129, Plate XVI) and two were found in tomb 236 at Sedment (Ashmolean 1921.1290; Ashomolean 1921.1291). This suggests some figure vases and 'ladies on beds' figurines may have had a similar life history with both being used in daily life and then deposited in the tomb. Bourriau (1987: 94) notes 'Such vases would in themselves be powerful images of life and rebirth and animated by funerary magic they would have provided powerful protection for the dead in their journey to the next world.'

Figure 5.43: Stela of Pen-Amen, showing him as a child being nursed by this mother and as an adult, Louvre E 3447 (Photograph Author's own).

5.11c: Mother and Child

The image of a mother and child has a long history in Egyptian art with the fullest corpus found in the New Kingdom (Budin 2011: 30; Roehrig 2005: 234). As Budin's extensive study of images in the Bronze Age demonstrates the relationship is one of caring and nourishing; however, in Egypt this image has another level of meaning. From the Old Kingdom onward the king was often shown being suckled by a goddess. In the New Kingdom this is also represented on ostraca; one example in the Cleveland Museum of Art (87.156) shows Rameses II being suckled by a goddess in a kiosk (Cleveland Museum of Art 1999: 248-9). Leclant (1961: 263-67) argued the king was only shown being suckled on three occasions, his birth, his coronation and his rebirth. Therefore, in Egyptian iconography the image of the nursing mother and child is linked to rejuvenation, healing and resurrection (Roehrig 2005: 234).

There are a limited number of New Kingdom stelae which show the image of a nursing mother; these are discussed by Spieser (2012). Bruyère (1923: 126, Figure 3) had previously published the stela of Pen-Amen (Louvre E 3447) in his discussion on the wall paintings at Deir el-Medina. The upper register is shown in Figure 5.43. The stela shows Pen-Amen, a lector priest in the reign of Amenhotep I, as an adult standing before his seated mother, to whom he offers a lotus flower and also as a child being suckled (Spieser 2012: 25, Figure 3). In relation to the '*Scènes de Gynécées*' figured ostraca it is noteworthy that behind the image of Pen-Amen as a child, is a mirror and kohl pot. This image is clearly related to the rebirth of Pen-Amen, with the added symbolism of these emblematic objects, which are discussed in Section 5.4. In addition to the lotus flower offered by Pen-Amen, both women wear a flower on their head and the nursing figure also wears a head cone. Both head adornments (lotus flower and head cone) are significant motifs in the '*Scènes de Gynécées*' figured ostraca as discussed in Sections 5.9 and 5.10.

It is likely that the '*Scènes de Gynécées*' figured ostraca and the 'ladies on beds' figurines were created to express similar ideas. The figurines are found throughout Egypt and her empire in the New Kingdom. However, the only provenance for '*Scènes de Gynécées*' figured ostraca is from Deir el-Medina. Similarly, although only a few figure vases have a firm provenance, Bourriau (1987: 94) has suggested they were made in one workshop. It is possible the figure vases and '*Scènes de Gynécées*' figured ostraca were regional expressions of wider held beliefs linked to the image of the mother and child.

5.11d: New Kingdom Love Poetry

Hermann proposed a further link between the '*Scènes de Gynécées*' figured ostraca and 'ladies on beds' figurines, suggesting both reflected the imagery of New Kingdom love poetry. He believed the women were waiting for their lovers (Hermann 1959 as cited in Pinch 1993: 220). Given the inclusion of children on the figurines and the images on the ostraca, it is unlikely. However, there are a number of similarities between the figured ostraca and the love poetry. Some scholars refer to them as songs (Landgráfová and Navrátilová: 2009), with many believing they could be performed with musical accompaniment, although in structure and style they are similar to other genres of text (Eyre and Baines 1998: 106-7). The texts are here referred to as poems as they were transcribed and have been preserved as a text, but it is likely they had a performative element.

The provenance of the love poetry is the strongest link to the '*Scènes de Gynécées*' figured ostraca. As noted by Kitchen (1999: 315) there are four main collections of love poetry and a variety of fragments; all sources, with the possible exception of *Papyrus Harris 500,* were found at Deir el-Medina and almost all are Ramesside in date. Furthermore, Mathieu (2003: 127) who has studied the work of the scribes from Deir el-Medina, believes the residents of village were the authors of the texts. Mathieu (2003: 127) and Landgráfová and Navrátilová (2009: 220) argue the themes and genre of the love poetry reflect the education of scribes at Deir el-Medina, who worked with a rich corpus of texts. This educational background gave them the skills to transfer an oral tradition into a written form. In addition, most of the love songs are preserved on ostraca, a readily available source material at the village. The love poems are the direct speech of either a young man or woman; they are essentially monologues expressing their hopes and desires. They create a sense of intimacy and simplicity; these qualities are also seen in the '*Scènes de Gynécées*' figured ostraca. The protagonists refer to each other as brother (*sen*) or sister (*senet*), normal terms of endearment in Egyptian literature.

The two most frequent type of metaphors found in the poems are architectural and landscape (Landgráfová 2008: 72). These parallel the two most common settings found in the '*Scènes de Gynécées*' figured ostraca. Much of the love poetry is set in the bed chamber, which is depicted as a place of intimacy. In *Papyrus Harris 500*, the girl speaks asking, 'Would [you depart] in your fine clothing, While I am left with nothing but the bed sheets? (Tobin 2003: 309). Later the girl states, 'I found my lover on his bed, And my heart was more than happy' (Tobin 2003: 314). The bed was viewed as a place for sexual intercourse in ancient Egypt as discussed in Section 5.11a. Architectural metaphors are also used to suggest sexual activity, for example *Papyrus Harris 500* (stanza 7) 'The villa of my beloved: The entrance to her (room) is at the heart of the house, Her double doors are open, Their bolt is unlatched' (Tobin 2003: 311).

Many of the love poems are set outdoors in a lush garden landscape. For example, in the *Songs of Enlightenment,* the final section of the *Papyrus Harris 500,* each stanza begins with the name of a flower (Tobin 2003: 315-316); while in the *Songs of the Orchard (Turin Love Songs)* the trees speak (Tobin 2003: 319-321). This includes more particular references to the kiosk setting, the little sycamore says, 'Come and spend a moment among the girls, For the countryside is at its best, And there is a kiosk and a pavilion beneath me' (Tobin 2003: 321). The idyllic backdrop continues, 'Come and pass the day in happiness, Tomorrow, and the day after tomorrow, Even for three days, sitting beneath my shade' (Tobin 2003: 321). This creates a sense of eternity as three was used to indicate multiples in ancient Egypt.

However, it must be noted children do not feature in the love poems although they do appear in the '*Scènes de Gynécées*' figured ostraca. It is possible to 'read' the love poetry as a prelude to the figurative images. They suggest courtship and premarital relationships; although, there is also an element of idealisation. As noted by Landgráfová and Navrátilová (2009: 76), the presence of intimate areas in houses, for example the bed chamber (*ḥnky.t*), suggest larger houses with a clear differentiation of space. It is difficult to imagine this level of luxury in the walled village of Deir el-Medina. Furthermore, it must be acknowledged that scholars have expressed scepticism at the amount of freedom allowed the young people in the poems (Robins 1998: 110-111; Wimmer 2000: 29). This may be due to the imagination of the poets and romantic licence.

Both artistic genres, written and visual, use many similar motifs. The most prevalent notions are grooming, toilette and beautification. *The Cairo Love Songs* are translated by Fox (1980: 101) as two songs; the first he calls 'the crossing' and the second 'the wishing'. The second song is spoken by the boy who wishes he is the servant of his beloved, 'If only I were her Nubian maid, who attends upon her privately' (Fox 1980: 103). He further desires to launder her linen garments; he also vocalises 'Happy is her mirror [In] which she gazes' (Fox 1980: 103). One kiosk scene (K.3.) shows a small black figure bathing the feet of a nursing mother. Moreover, there are many more indicators of grooming and toilette in the figured ostraca, particularly the kiosk scenes with the presentation of mirrors and kohl tubes. These items are often represented under the bed in the 'women on beds' scenes, which may suggest previous use. The '*Scènes de Gynécées*' also include several possible scenes of hairdressing, discussed in Section 5.8c.

Furthermore, there are many references to perfuming the body in the love poetry, for example *The Cairo Love Songs* state 'Put fine linen on her body, While laying her bed with royal linen, Adorn [...] her body, Found like one sprinkled with perfume' (Tobin 2003: 318). While there has been much discussion on the significance of head cones, frequently represented in both the '*Scènes de Gynécées*' figured ostraca and 'ladies on beds' figurines, it is possible they symbolised the concept of anointing, although their link to perfume has been debated, see Section 5.7. In addition, nearly all the women in the 'women on beds' scenes are dressed in fine white linen robes. There are more general similarities between the visual and written culture, for example the emphasis on hair, a key feature in the '*Scènes de Gynécées*' and three-dimensional figurines, is referred to as alluring in the love poetry, see Section 5.8d.

5.11e: Eroticism and Morality

Contrary to the views of Brunner-Traut (1955) to fully understand the '*Scènes de Gynécées*' figured ostraca we must consider the erotic element of the scenes as advocated by Derchain (1975a: 65). Egyptian artists often encapsulated many levels of meaning and several moments of time into a single representation (Schäfer translated by Baines 1986: 277). On one level the 'women on beds' scenes are likely to show the celebrations relating to the birth of a child, while the kiosk scenes relate to the seclusion of the mother after the birth; although these are more likely to be symbolic than real structures. However, the depiction of the mother and child also relates to concepts of birth and rebirth which is based on sexual activity in this life and the next. Therefore, eroticism is fundamentally rooted in the '*Scènes de Gynécées*' figured ostraca. This is more apparent in the three-dimensional figurines, which show naked women lying on beds. These are discussed briefly in Section 5.11a, and more fully in the second volume of my PhD (Backhouse 2016), which it is hoped will be published at a later date. Keimer (1948: 99) confused eroticism with low morality but Bruyère (1939: 143) was correct to stress that the important element of these representations, both two and three-dimensional, is the maternal role of the women which is linked to the concepts of birth and rebirth.

5.12: Summary and Conclusion

Repeat motifs run through the two main datasets, 'women on beds' and kiosks, with some linkage provided by the 'elaborate beds' scenes. It is probable there is an association between the two main datasets suggesting the scenes depict different moments of the same narrative or different aspects. It is likely the 'women on beds' scenes showed celebrations in the home to mark the birth of a child. The domestic setting is decked with convolvulus leaves, floral collars and garlands, which may have been real or painted decoration. It is likely beds with Bes legs and serpent motifs existed in the village and were used during these festivities, perhaps thought to create a safe environment for the mother and child. The kiosk scenes may have shown the place of birth or more likely confinement after birth. However, due to the dense nature of the settlement at Deir el-Medina these images may be symbolic; with the concept of the kiosk recreated in the home with the use of convolvulus leaves forming a canopy. These may have been real trellis-like structures or painted decoration. The function of which was to evoke the papyrus thicket where Isis or Hathor gave birth to Horus and so place the mother and child under the protection of the goddesses.

As is common in Egyptian art, the images may have encompassed an additional level of meaning and were apotropaic themselves, placing the mother and child under the protection of Bes, Meretseger and Hathor, all deities symbolised in the scenes. Given the care and attention taken with some '*Scènes de Gynécées*' figured ostraca it is likely they were created for display in the home, possibly like small scale stelae. Such objects, with small 'fin like-feet' to enable them to stand were found in the Theban region dating to the Third Intermediate Period. These depict women in a boat, often playing a lute and/or grasping papyrus stems. The stelae were often accompanied by female figurines and votive beds (Teeter 2010: 159). Additionally, it is possible the '*Scènes de Gynécées*' also encompassed a desire for rebirth; one example (WoB. 33) was found in a tomb. This is also evident by the inclusion of items of toiletry in the 'women on beds', 'elaborate beds' and kiosk scenes, which are likely to have been linked to rituals for resurrection.

Chapter 6

Conclusions

6.1: The Remit

This study has provided a detailed examination of '*Scènes de Gynécées*' figured ostraca. These objects depict women sitting on beds in a domestic environment, many with a child, or nursing a child in a kiosk in an outdoor setting. Complete examples of these ostraca are the primary source of data; however, fragmentary examples, which seem to belong to the '*Scènes de Gynécées*' corpus have also been considered. This work represents the first systematic study of this material and it brings together ostraca from museums worldwide to form a corpus united contextually, thematically and stylistically.

6.2: The Deir el-Medina Context of '*Scènes de Gynécées*' Ostraca

The majority (81%) of these ostraca were found at Deir el-Medina, while the remainder have no known provenance. Since none of these ostraca have been recovered from any other site it is very likely that the '*Scènes de Gynécées*' motif was unique to Deir el-Medina. In order to provide a broader contextualisation of these ostraca a small number of comparative examples were also considered, including depictions of nursing goddesses, gift giving and images of servant girls. Although the numbers are small 28% of these scenes of comparative evidence were also found in or around the village of Deir el-Medina itself; while an additional 50% were found at the Valley of the Kings, in the area surrounding the tomb of Rameses X (KV 18) and in huts the workmen stayed in while working at the Valley of the Kings. Dorn (2011: 22) describes this latter area as 'Deir el-Medina reduced to the world of men'. The remaining 21% of comparative evidence has no known provenance. Therefore, there is a compelling case for believing that both the '*Scènes de Gynécées*' and comparative material were linked regional phenomena created by the workmen of Deir el-Medina. Evidence further suggests that, within the lifespan of the village, most if not all of this material was created during the Ramesside period.

6.3: Categorisation of the Figured Ostraca

The ostraca have been catalogued in five datasets. Firstly, 'women on beds' scenes, which shows any part of a woman and a bed; secondly, 'elaborate beds' scenes which depict women on beds decorated with elaborate frills, perhaps portraying floral garlands and kiosks scenes, which show women nursing children in temporary structures outdoors. Fragments of these images are also considered and scenes of comparative evidence. The detailed examination of this material has shown that common motifs run throughout the individual datasets, including the depiction of the god Bes, the inclusion of serpent imagery, scenes of gift giving, convolvulus leaves, and the inclusion of mirrors and kohl tubes. This suggests the images had shared meanings for their creators and viewers. Additionally, the depiction of mirrors and kohl tubes provides linkage between the 'women on beds', 'elaborate beds' and kiosk datasets. Mirrors and kohl tubes are shown under the bed in nine 'women on beds' scenes. While a mirror and possibly a kohl tube are depicted in the background of one 'elaborate bed' scene (EB.2) and a mirror and kohl tube are presented by a servant to a seated woman in another 'elaborate bed' scene (EB.1). Mirrors and kohl tubes are also presented by a servant to the nursing women in two kiosk scenes (K.1-2). The common iconographic motifs suggest that the images were part of the same chronicle united in theme. Narrative art should be understood as art which tells a story, real or imagined (Braun 2015). Given the inclusion of women, children and nursing mothers it likely the '*Scènes de Gynécées*' figured ostraca are depicting events following the birth of a child.

6.4: '*Scènes de Gynécées*' Ostraca and Bes-legged beds

An important link between the '*Scènes de Gynécées*' depictions and known material culture from New Kingdom Egypt is provided by evidence that the Bes-legged beds shown on the ostraca actually existed. The numerous Bes furniture legs documented by Raven (2014) are directly comparable to the Bes legs incorporated into the beds shown in the 'women on beds' and 'elaborate beds' scenes. This strongly suggests that wooden beds with Bes legs were used in the village. Hieratic texts from Deir el-Medina also refer to 'women's beds' which were more expensive due to the added decoration (Janssen 1975: 180-182). The pristine condition of the Bes legs recorded by Raven (2014) suggests they were reserved for special occasions, not everyday use.

6.5: '*Scènes de Gynécées*' Ostraca and Gift Giving

A review of both the material culture of New Kingdom Egypt and hieratic texts from Deir el-Medina strongly suggest that the 'women on beds' scenes depicted celebrations which took place in the home to commemorate the birth of a child, which included gift giving. The gift giving lists documented by Janssen (1983, 1997) record consumables, mainly bread, cakes, meats, fish, fruit and small household items, including sandals, baskets and boxes against a list of donors, many of whom were women. This research has demonstrated that these scenes of gift giving are likely to be depicted on the 'women on beds' scenes. These show women, dressed in their finery, wearing complex wrap-around dresses and heavy wigs, offering mainly bowls and vases to a seated figure, often shown with a child. The gift-givers and gift-receivers in these scenes are similarly attired, suggesting that they were of comparable status, while the intimacy depicted in the scenes – the touching of hands, feet and eye contact – might suggest bonds of kin and friendship.

6.6: '*Scènes de Gynécées*' Ostraca and Floral Decoration

The floral collars and convolvulus leaves shown in the background or threaded through the image in the 'women on beds' and 'elaborate beds' scenes are comparable to those depicted on wall paintings found at Deir el-Medina and Amarna. Therefore, it is impossible to determine if the floral decorations were hung as part of the celebrations in the home or were wall paintings within the houses. Nevertheless, the presence of a floral framing denotes a room decorated; it is likely the events shown on the '*Scènes de Gynécées*' figured ostraca took place in the first room of the house, where the only evidence of wall painting at Deir el-Medina has been found. This was discovered on the '*lit clos*', a mud brick structure generally believed to be a domestic altar, located predominantly in the first room of the house. This was the most public room of the home, so appropriate for a celebration (Koltsida 2007: 22-24).

6.7: Kiosk Scenes

Although only a comparatively small number of kiosk scenes have survived there is a high degree of standardisation in their representation. The scenes show a nursing woman wearing a heavy tripartite wig, sitting on a stool in a kiosk made of papyrus-columns, wrapped with convolvulus leaves. No physical evidence of such kiosks has been found, but this may be due to the ephemeral nature of the structure. There are limited textual references to suggest women gave birth in pavilions for example *The Magical Text of Papyri Leiden I* (Borghouts 1971: 30). However, there is evidence to indicate that women gave birth standing/ squatting on mud bricks (Wegner 2009). There is also a contemporaneous reference to a 'place of women', which has been interpreted as a place of confinement during menstruation or a place of purification after birth (O.OIM 13512: Wilfong 1999). Given the limited evidence, it is likely the structures depicted on the figured ostraca were symbolic, evoking the birth of Horus in the marshes of Chemmis, as later depicted on mammisi chapels in the Greco-Roman period (Badawy 1963). It is possible the kiosk scenes had an apotropaic function for the new mother and child by eliciting the protection of Isis, or Hathor, who nurtured Horus in the papyrus thicket of the Delta. However, a further eight 'women on beds' scenes show a canopy-like structure over the bed, five of which include convolvulus leaves. These kiosk-like structures may have been set up in the home to provide seclusion and protection for the mother and child, so demonstrating the link between the two main datasets, 'women on beds' and kiosk scenes.

The kiosk scenes are the closest link between the '*Scènes de Gynécées*' figured ostraca and wall paintings found in the village. The kiosk is depicted clearly on two ostraca and two fragmentary examples; a partial image of a kiosk was also found painted on the '*lit clos*' in house S.E.I. The god Bes is also a prominent motif on both the '*Scènes de Gynécées*' figured ostraca depicted on 27 examples and on six '*lit clos*'.

6.8: Figured Ostraca as Practice Pieces

There is nothing to suggest the '*Scènes de Gynécées*' figured ostraca were practice pieces for the wall paintings. There are no grid lines used on the ostraca or any signs of the correction of outlines; there are corrections only in the comparative evidence dataset (CE.12). It is evident that both the wall paintings and the '*Scènes de Gynécées*' figured ostraca depicted comparable themes, using similar iconographic motifs, including the god Bes, convolvulus leaves and kiosks. While previous scholarship has suggested the figured ostraca were practice pieces for wall paintings, tombs or temples (Brunner-Traut 1956: 64-65; Borchardt 1919; Maspero 1912: 168-9), the evidence presented here indicates that some at least were finished objects in their own right. It is possible that these were created to be displayed like small scale stelae in the home.

6.9: Figured Ostraca and Layered Meaning

This study has demonstrated that the 'women on beds' and 'elaborate beds' scenes are likely to have been drawn as a commemoration at the birth of a child and the subsequent celebrations. However, one example was found in a tomb (WoB.33), so they may have had a more complex life history. As is common in Egyptian art these scenes may have contained more than one meaning. The commemoration of a birth may have also encompassed a desire for rebirth, illustrated by the inclusion of items of toiletry, such as mirrors and kohl tubes under the bed, which are often seen in New Kingdom tomb scenes. The significance of toiletry rituals is discussed by Blackman (1918), who suggests the toiletry rituals which the king underwent each morning linked him to the sun god Ra and ensured his daily rebirth. The 'women on beds' and 'elaborate beds' scenes provide insights into aspects of daily life in the village. The images are important as no texts directly refer to feasts celebrated in the home (Jauhiainen 2009: 296). Therefore, they provide new information and a visual link to the gift giving lists as published by Janssen (1982, 1997) and Jauhiainen (2009).

6.10: Linkage

This study also considered the link between the '*Scènes de Gynécées*' figured ostraca and the material culture of New Kingdom Egypt, particularly 'ladies on beds' figurines and figure vases. The evidence demonstrated the '*Scènes de Gynécées*' figured ostraca were a regional creation, limited to Deir el-Medina; while the 'ladies on beds' figurines were found throughout Egypt and her empire. The figure vases may also have been a regional creation from a single workshop over one or two generations. The ostraca, figurines and figure vases all express aspects of the relationship between the mother and child; therefore, they represent different episodes of the same narrative. The figurines represent the wish for a child, the ostraca illustrate celebrations/rituals after the birth of a child and figure vases provided sustenance and protection for the child. However, while all three types of object were found predominantly in daily life contexts, a limited number were found in tombs; suggesting they were multifunctional, with a complex life history. Together they elucidate the link between birth and rebirth in ancient Egypt.

6.11: Summary Conclusion

The '*Scènes de Gynécées*' figured ostraca are part of a larger corpus of images of women. They illustrate the importance of progeny to the ancient Egyptians and provide valuable insights into daily life in the village of Deir el-Medina. This study also furthers our knowledge of regional art, created utilising available resources and skills.

Bibliography

Aldred, C. 1969. The 'New Year' gifts to the Pharaoh. *Journal of Egyptian Archaeology* 55: 73-81.

Allen, T. G. 1974. *The Book of the Dead or Going Forth by Day*. Chicago: Oriental Institute Publications.

Allen, T. G. 1988. *Genesis in Egypt: The Philosophy of Ancient Egyptian Creation Accounts*. New Haven: Yale University Press.

Allen, T. G. 2005. *The Ancient Egyptian Pyramid Texts*. Leiden: Brill.

Andreu, G. 2002. *Les artistes de pharaon: Deir el-Médineh et la Vallée des Rois*. Paris: Réunion des Musées Nationaux.

Andreu-Lanoë, G. (ed.) 2013. *L'art du contour; Le dessin dans l'Égypte ancienne*. Paris: Louvre Éditions.

Anthes, R. 1943. Die Deutschen grabungen auf der Westseite von Theban in den jahren 1911 und 1913. *Mitteilungen des Deutschen Archäologischen Instituts, Abteilung Kairo* 12: 1-68.

Anthes, R. 1959. Egyptian theology in the third millennium B.C. *Journal of Near Eastern Studies* 8 (13): 169-212.

Arnold, D. 1996. *The Royal Women of Amarna: Images of Beauty from Ancient Egypt*. New York: Metropolitan Museum of Art.

Arnold, D. 2010. Updating Winlock: An appendix of recent scholarship, in H. E. Winlock *Tutankhamun's Funeral*: 67-79. New York: Metropolitan Museum of Art.

Asher-Greve, J.M. and D. Sweeney 2006. On nakedness, nudity, and gender in Egyptian and Mesopotamian Art, in S. Schroer (ed.) *Images and Gender: Contributions to the Hermeneutics of Reading Ancient Art*: 25-176. Fribourg Göttingen: Academic Press.

Assmann, J. 1991. *Das Grab des Amenemope (TT 41)*. Mainz: von Zabern.

Aufrére, S. H. and A. Lopex-Moncet 2001. Representations végétales énigmatique de nouvel empire: La<<liane>> à feuilles sagittées, in S. Aufrére (ed.) *Encyclopédie religieuse de l'univers vegetal: croyances phytoreligieuses de l'égypte ancienne. Montpellier:* 39-78. Université Valéry-Montpellier III.

Austin, A. and C. Gobeil 2016. Embodying the divine: A tattooed female from Deir el-Medina. *Bulletin de l'Institut Français d'Archéologie Orientale* 116: 23-46.

Bács, T. and R. Parkinson 2011. Wall-painting from the tomb of Kynebu at Luxor. *Egyptian Archaeology* 39: 41-43.

Backhouse, J. 2010. Figured ostraca from Deir el-Medina, in H. Abu. El Gawad, N. Andrews, M. Correas-Amador, V. Tamorri and J. Taylor (eds) *Current Research in Egyptology 2011:* 23-39. Oxford: Oxbow Books.

Backhouse, J. 2013. Female figurines from Deir el-Medina: A review of evidence for their iconography and function, in C. Graves, G. Hefferman, L. McGarrity, E. Millward, and M. S. Bealby (eds) *Current Research in Egyptology 2012:* 22-40. Oxford: Oxbow Books.

Backhouse, J. 2016. '*Scènes de Gynécées*' Figured Ostraca: Their Relationship to the Material Culture of New Kingdom Egypt. Unpublished PhD dissertation, University of Liverpool.

Badawy, A. 1963. The architectural symbolism of the mammisi-chapel in Egypt. *Chronique d'Égypte* 38: 78-90.

Baines, J. 1985. Color terminology and color classification: Ancient Egyptian color terminology and polychromy. *American Anthropologist* 87(2): 282-297.

Baines, J. and J. Malek 2000. *Cultural Atlas of Ancient Egypt*. Oxford: Andromeda Limited.

Ballod, F. 1913. *Prolegomena zur Geschichte der zwerghaften Götter in Ägypten*. Moskau: H. Liessner and D. Sobko.

Baraise, É. 1914. Compte rendu des travaux exécutés à Deir el Médineh. *Annales du Service des Antiquités de l'Égypte* 13: 19-42.

Bardinet, T. 1995. *Les papyrus médicaux de l'Égypte pharaonique*. Lyon: Fayard.

Baud, M. 1935. *Les dessins ébauchés de la nécropole au temps du nouvel empire*. Cairo: Institut Français d'Archéologie Orientale.

Bell, M. 1987. Regional variations in polychrome pottery of the 19th Dynasty. *Cahiers de la Céramique Égyptienne* 1: 49-76.

Ben-Arieh, S. and G. Edelstein 1977. Akko tombs near the Persian Garden. *Atiqot* 12: 1-44.

Bénédite, G. 1907. *Catalogue général des antiquités égyptienne du Musée du Caire: Nos 44001-44102: Mirrors*. Cairo: Institut Français d'Archéologie Orientale.

Bianchi, S. R. 1985. Reflections of the sky's eyes. *Source Notes in the History of Art* 4 (2-3): 10-18.

Bierbrier, M. L. 1982a. *The Tomb Builders of Pharaoh*. London: British Museum Publications.

Bierbrier, M. L. 1982b. *Hieroglyphic Texts from Egyptian Stelae, etc. in the British Museum. Part 10 (issued by the Department of Egyptian Antiquities)*. London: British Museum Press.

Bierbrier, M. L. (ed.) 2012. *Who was Who in Egyptology*, 4th Revised Edition. London: The Egypt Exploration Society.

Blackman, A. M. 1915. *The Rock Tombs of Meir*, Volume II. London: Egypt Exploration Fund.

Blackman, A. M. 1918. The house of morning. *Journal of Egyptian Archaeology* 5: 148-165.

Bomann, A. 1991. *The Private Chapel in Ancient Egypt*. London: Kegan Paul International.

Bonnet, C. and D. Valbelle 1975. Le village de Deir el-Médineh: reprise de l'étude. *Bulletin de l'Institut Français d'Archéologie Orientale* 75: 429-446.

Bonnet, C. and D. Valbelle 1976. Le village de Deir el-Médineh: étude archéologique. *Bulletin de l'Institut Français d'Archéologie Orientale* 76: 317-342.

Bonnet, H. 1928. *Ein frühgeschichtliches Gräberfeld bei Abusir*. Leipzig: J.C. Hinrichs.

Borchardt, L. 1910. Studien und Entwürfe altägyptischer Künstler. *Kunst und Künstler* 8: 34-42.

Borghouts, J. F. 1971. *The Magical Texts of Papyrus Leiden I 348*. Leiden: Brill.

Boulos, L. and M. Nabil el-Hadidi 1984. *The Weed Flora of Egypt*. Cairo: American University in Cairo.

Boulos, L. 1983. *Medicinal Plants of North Africa*. Michigan: Reference Publications.

Bouriant, G., G. Legrain and G. Jéquier 1903. *Monuments pour server à l'étude du culte d'Atonou en Égypte*. Cairo: Institut Français d'Archéologie Orientale.

Bourriau, J. 1987. Pottery figure vases of the New Kingdom. *Cahiers de la Céramique Égyptienne* 1: 81-96, Plates XXVI-XXXI.

Braun, N. S. 2015. Narrative, in M. K. Hartwig (ed.) *A Companion to Ancient Egyptian Art*: 344-359. Chichester: Wiley: Blackwell.

Breasted, J. H. 1906-7. *Ancient Records of Egypt: Volume II New Kingdom*. Chicago: Oriental Institute Publications.

Broekhuis, J. 1971. *De Godin Renenwetet*. Assen: Van Gorcum.

Brunner-Traut, E. 1955. Die wochenlaube. *Mitteilungen des Instituts für Orientforschung* 3: 11-30.

Brunner-Traut, E. 1956. *Die altägyptischen Sherbenbilder (Bildostraka) der Deutschen Museen und Sammlungen*. Wiesbaden: Steiner.

Brunner-Traut, E. 1970. Das Muttermilchkrüglein: Ammen mit Stillumhang und Mondamulett. *Die Welts des Orients* 5: 145-164.

Brunner-Traut, E. 1979. *Egyptian Artists' Sketches: Figured Ostraka from the Gayer-Anderson Collection in the Fitzwilliam Museum, Cambridge*. Istanbul: Nederlands Historish-Archaeologische Instituut te Istanbul.

Brunton, G. 1920. *Lahun I: The Treasure*. London: British School of Archaeology in Egypt.

Bruyère, B. 1923. Un fragment de fresque de Deir el Médineh. *Bulletin de l'Institut Français d'Archéologie Orientale* 22: 121-133.

Bruyère, B. 1926. *Rapport sur les fouilles de Deir el Médineh (1924-1925)*. Cairo: Institut Français d'Archéologie Orientale.

Bruyère, B. 1928. *Rapport sur les fouilles de Deir el Médineh (1927)*. Cairo: Institut Français d'Archéologie Orientale.

Bruyère, B. 1929. *Mert Seger à Deir el Médineh*, Volume I. Cairo: Institut Français d'Archéologie Orientale.

Bruyère, B. 1930. *Mert Seger à Deir el Médineh*, Volume II. Cairo: Institut Français d'Archéologie Orientale.

Bruyère, B. 1933. *Rapport sur les fouilles de Deir el Médineh (1930)*. Cairo: Institut Français d'Archéologie Orientale.

Bruyère, B. 1936. La nécropole de Deir el Médineh. *Chronique d'Égypte* 11-12: 329-340.

Bruyère, B. 1937a. *Rapport sur les fouilles de Deir el Médineh (1933-34): La nécropole de l'ouest*. Cairo: Institut Français d'Archéologie Orientale.

Bruyère, B. 1937b. *Rapport sur les fouilles de Deir el Médineh (1934-35): La nécropole de l'est*. Cairo: Institut Français d'Archéologie Orientale.

Bruyère, B. 1939. *Rapport sur les fouilles de Deir el Médineh (1934-1935)*. Cairo: Institut Français d'Archéologie Orientale.

Bruyère, B. 1952a. *Rapport sur les fouilles de Deir el Médineh (1945-1946 et 1946-1947)*. Cairo: Institut Français d'Archéologie Orientale.

Bruyère, B. 1952b. *Tombes thébaines de Deir el Médineh à decoration monochrome*. Cairo: Institut Français d'Archéologie Orientale.

Bruyère, B. 1953. *Rapport sur les fouilles de Deir el Médineh (1948-1951)*. Cairo: Institut Français d'Archéologie Orientale.

Bruyère B. 1959. *La tombe no 1 de Sen-nedjem à Deir el Médineh*. Cairo: Institut Français d'Archéologie Orientale.

Budge, E. A. W. 1909. *A Guide to the Egyptian Galleries (Sculpture)*. London: British Museum Department of Egyptian and Assyrian Antiquities.

Budlin, S. L. 2011. *Images of Women and Child from the Bronze Age*. Cambridge: Cambridge University Press.

Caubet, A. (2005-2011) Lid of a Pyxis with Mistress of Animals. [Online] Paris: Louvre. Available from: http://www.louvre.fr/en/oeuvre-notices/lid-pyxis-mistress-animals (Accessed 10 March 2015).

Černý, J. 1927. Le culte d'Amenophis I chez les ouvriers de la nécropole thébaine. *Bulletin de l'Institut Français d'Archéologie Orientale* 27: 159-203.

Černý, J. 1935. *Catalogue général des antiquités égyptienne du Musée du Caire: ostraca hieratiques*. Cairo: Institut Français d'Archéologie Orientale.

Černý, J. and A. H. Gardiner 1957. *Hieratic Ostraca*, Volume I. Oxford: Griffith Institute.

Cherpion, N. 1994. Le 'cône d'onguent', gage de survie. *Bulletin de l'Institut Français d'Archéologie Orientale* 94: 79-106.

Cherpion, N. 1999. *Deux tombes de la XVIIIe dynastie à Deir el-Medina: Nos 340 (Amenemhat) et 354 (anonyme)*. Cairo: Institut Français d'Archéologie Orientale.

Cherpion, N. 2006. La danseuse de Deir el-Medina et les prétendus << lits clos>> du village. *Revue des archéologues, historiens d'art et musicologues de l'Université Catholique de Louvain (UCL)* 4: 11-26.

Cleveland Museum of Art 1999. *Catalogue of Egyptian Art; The Cleveland Museum of Art*. New York: Hudson Hills Press.

Contenau, G. 1931. *Manuel d'archéologie orientale depuis les origins jusqu'à l'époque d'Alexandre, Le Volume II: Histoire de l'art*. Paris: Picard.

Cooney, K. M. 2012. Apprenticeship and figured ostraca from the ancient Egyptian village of Deir el-Medina, in W. Wendrich (ed.) *Archaeology and Apprenticeship: Body Knowledge, Identity, and Communities of Practice*: 145-170. Tucson: University of Arizona Press.

Dasen, V. 1993. *Dwarfs in Ancient Egypt and Greece*. Oxford: Clarendon Press.

David, A. 2010. *The Legal Register of Ramesside Private Law Instruments*. Wiesbaden: Harrassowitz.

Davies, B. G. 1999. *Who's Who at Deir el-Medina: A Prosopographic Study of the Royal Workmen's Community*. Leiden: Nederlands Instituut Voor Het Nabije Oosten.

Davies, N. de G. 1902. *The Rock Tombs of Deir el-Gebrâwi I*. London: Egypt Exploration Fund.

Davies, N. de G. 1908. *The Rock Tombs of El Amarna: Part VIi*. London: Egypt Exploration Fund.

Davies, N. de G. 1917a. Drawings on limestone flakes. *Journal of Egyptian Archaeology* 4: 234-240.

Davies, N. de G. 1917b. *The Tomb of Nakht at Thebes*. New York: Metropolitan Museum of Art.

Davies, N. de G. 1925. *The Tomb of Two Sculptors at Thebes*. New York: Metropolitan Museum of Art.

Davies, N. de G. 1927. *Two Ramesside Tombs at Thebes*. New York: Metropolitan Museum of Art.

Davies, N. de G. 1930. *The Tomb of Ken-Amūn at Thebes*. New York: Metropolitan Museum of Art.

Davies, N. de G. 1935. *Paintings from the Tomb of Rekh-mi-Re at Thebes*. New York: Metropolitan Museum of Art.

Davies, N. de G. 1941. *The Tomb of the Vizier Ramose*. London: Egypt Exploration Society.

Davies, N. de G. 1948. *Seven Private Tombs at Kurnah*. London: Egypt Exploration Society.

Davis, T. M. 1907. *The Tomb of Iouiya and Touiyou*. London: Constable.

Davis, V. L. 1980. Remarks on Michael V. Fox's 'The Cairo Love Songs'. *Journal of the American Oriental Society* 100: 111-114.

Dawson, W. R. 1934. Studies in the Egyptian medical texts – IV. *Journal of Egyptian Archaeology* 20: 185-8.

Demarée, R. J. 2002. *Ramesside Ostraca*. London: British Museum Publications.

Derchain, P. 1975a. La peruque et le cristal. *Studien zur Altägyptischen Kultur* 2: 55-74.

Derchain, P. 1975b. Le lotus, la mandragore et le perséa. *Chronique d'Égypte* 5: 65-86.

Derriks, C. 2001. *Les miroirs cariatides égyptiens en bronze: typologie, chronologie et symbolique*. Mainz: von Zabern.

Desroches-Noblecourt, C. 1952. Pots anthropomorphes et recettes magico-médicales dans l'Égypte ancienne. *Revue d'Égyptologie* 9: 58-67.

Desroches-Noblecourt, C. 1968. *Le petit temple d'Abou Simbel*. Cairo: Ministère de la culture.

Dorn, A. 2011. *Arbeiterhütten im Tal der Könige: Ein Beitrag zur altägyptischen Sozialgeschichte aufgrund von neuem Quellenmaterial aus der Mitte der 20. Dynastie (ca. 1150 v. Chr.). Volume I – Text and Catalogue: Volume II – Plates*. Basel: Schwabe.

Dunham, D., W. K. Simpson, G. A. Reisner and W. S. Smith (1974) *The Mastaba of Queen Mersyankh III, G7530-7540*. Boston: Harvard University-Museum of Fine Arts.

Dunham, D. and J. M. A. Janssen 1960. *Second Cataract Forts I; Semna Kumma*. Boston: Museum of Fine Arts.

Eaton-Krauss, M. 1985. *The Small Golden Shrine from the Tomb of Tutankhamun*. Oxford. Griffith Institute.

Ebbell, G. M. 1937. *The Papyrus Ebers*. Copenhagen: Levin and Munksgaard.

El-Sabbahy, A. F. 1999. A funerary bed from the tomb of Sen-nedjem. *Discussions in Egyptology* 43: 13-18.

Emboden, W. A. 1981. Transcultural use of narcotic water lilies in ancient Egyptian and Maya drug ritual. *Journal of Ethnopharmacology* 3: 39-83.

Emery, W. B., H. S. Smith and A. Millard 1979. *The Fortress of Buhen: The Archaeological Report*. London: Egypt Exploration Society.

Erman, A. 1885. *Aegypten und aegyptisches Leben im Alterthum, geschidert von Adolf Erman*. Tübingen: H. Laupp'schen Buchhandlung.

Evrard-Derricks, C. 1975-76. Le miroir représenté sur les peintures et bas-reliefs égyptiennes. *Orientalia Lovaniensia Periodica* 6/7: 223-229.

Exell, K. 2006. A Social and Historical Interpretation of Ramesside Period Votive Stelae. Unpublished PhD dissertation, University of Durham.

Eyre, C. 1980. An accounts papyrus from Thebes. *Journal of Egyptian Archaeology* 66: 109-119.

Eyre, C. 1987. Work in the New Kingdom, in M. A. Powell (ed.) *Labour in the Ancient Near East*: 167-221. New Haven: American Oriental Society.

Eyre, C. 2013. *The Use of Documents in Pharaonic Egypt*. Oxford: Oxford University Press.

Eyre, C. and J. Baines 1989. Orality and literacy in ancient Egypt, in K. Schousboe, and M. T. Larsen (eds) *Literacy and Society*: 91-119. Copenhagen: Akademisk Forlag.

Fassone, A. 2015. Egypt and the outside world, in *Museo Egizio*: 212-219. Turin: Museo Egizio.

Faulkner, R. O. 1962. *A Concise Dictionary of Middle Egyptian*. Oxford: Griffith Institute.

Faulkner, R. O. 1969. *The Ancient Egyptian Pyramid Texts*. Oxford: Oxford University Press.

Faulkner, R. O. 1977. *The Egyptian Coffin Texts I*. Warminster: Aris and Phillips Ltd.

Faulkner, R. O. 1985. *The Ancient Egyptian Book of the Dead*, Revised Edition. London: Book Club Associates.

Firth, C. M. 1927. *The Archaeological Survey of Nubia: Report for 1910-1911*. Cairo: Government Press.

Firth, R. 1973. *Symbols Public and Private*. London: Allen and Unwin.

The Fitzwilliam Museum 2016, Collector: Gayer-Anderson, (Major) Robert Grenville 'John' (1881-1945) [Online]. Cambridge: The Fitzwilliam Museum. Available from: http://www.fitzmuseum.cam.ac.uk/collections/egypt/collectionhistory/gayeranderson (Accessed 26 March 2016)

Fletcher, J. 1995. Ancient Egyptian Hair: A Study in Style, Format and Function. Unpublished PhD dissertation, University of Manchester.

Fox, M. V. 1980. The Cairo Love Songs. *Journal of the American Oriental Society* 100 (2): 101-109.

Fox, M. V. 1985. *The Song of Songs and the Ancient Egyptian Love Songs.* Madison: University of Wisconsin Press.

Frankfort, H. and J. D. S. Pendlebury 1933. *City of Akhenaten: Part II.* London: Egypt Exploration Society.

Freed, R. E. 1981. *Egypt's Golden Age: The Art of Living in the New Kingdom 1558-1085 B.C – A Picture Book.* Boston: Museum of Fine Arts Boston.

Freed, R. E. 1982. Cosmetic arts, in R. E. Freed (ed.) *Egypt's Golden Age: The Art of Living in the New Kingdom 1558-1085 B.C.: Catalogue of the Exhibition*: 199-200. Boston: Museum of Fine Arts.

Friedman, F. D. (ed.) 1998. *Gifts of the Nile: Ancient Egyptian Faience.* London: Thames and Hudson.

Friedman, F. D. 2004. Archaeology's Interactive Dig: Nubians at Hierakonpolis, week 5, Part 2. [Online] Archaeological Institute of America: Archaeology Magazine: Available from: http://interactive.archaeology.org/hierakonpolis/field/2004f.html (Accessed 23 March 2012).

Gahlin, L. 2007. Creation myths, in T. Wilkinson (ed.) *The Egyptian World*: 296-309. London: Routledge.

Gardiner, A. H. 1935. *Chester Beatty Gift.* London: British Museum.

Gardiner, A. H. 1955. *The Ramesseum Papyri.* Oxford: Oxford University Press.

Garstang, J. 1901. *El Arábah.* London: Quaritch.

Garstang, J. 1909. Excavation at Abydos, 1909: Preliminary description of the principle finds. Liverpool Institute of Archaeology. *Liverpool Annals* ii: 125-129.

Gasse, A. 2005. *Catalogue des ostraca littéraires des Deir al-Medîna.* Cairo: Institut Français d'Archéologie Orientale.

Gauthier-Laurent, M. 1935-38. Les scénes de coiffure feminine dans l'ancienne Égypte, in G. C. C. Maspero (ed.) *Mélanges Maspero*, Volume 1: 675-695. Cairo: Institut Français d'Archéologie Orientale.

Germond, P. 2008. En marge du décor des tombes thébaines du nouvel empire, in L. Gabolde (ed.) *Hommages à Jean-Claude Goyon*: 215-224. Cairo: Institut Français d'Archéologie Orientale.

Giddy, L. 1999. *The Survey of Memphis II: Kom Rabi'a: The New Kingdom and Post-New Kingdom Objects.* London: Egypt Exploration Society.

Glanville, S. R. K. 1934. Two head-rests and other Egyptian antiquities. *British Museum Quarterly* 8 (3): 105-108.

Gobeil. C. Oxford Handbooks Online, 2015. The IFAO Excavations at Deir el-Medina Available from http://www.oxfordhandbooks.com/view/10.1093/oxfordhb/9780199935413.001.0001/oxfordhb-9780199935413-e-32 (Accessed 10 January 2019)

Goedicke, H. 1970. The story of the herdsman. *Chronique d'Égypte* 89: 244-267.

Goedicke, H. and E. F. Wente 1962. *Ostraka Michaelides.* Wiesbaden: Otto Harrassowitz.

Grandet, P. 2003. *Catalogue des ostraca hiératique non littéraires de Deîr el-Médînéh.* Volume 9. Cairo: Institut Français d'Archéologie Orientale.

Grandet, P. 2008. Cinq ostraca hiératiques documentaries du musée du Louvre, in C. Gallois, P. Grandet and L. Pantalacci (eds) *Mélanges offerts à François Neveu*: 161-178. Cairo: Institut Français d'Archéologie Orientale.

Grandet, P. 2011. *Catalogue des ostraca hiératique non littéraires de Deîr el-Médînéh.* Volume 11. Cairo: Institut Français d'Archéologie Orientale.

Greenlees, T. H. 1923. An unusual tomb scene from Dirâ 'Abu'l-Negâ. *Journal of Egyptian Archaeology* 9: 131.

Harer, W. 1985. Pharmacological and biological properties of the Egyptian lotus. *Journal of the American Research Center in Egypt* 12: 49-54.

Harrington, N. 2005. From the cradle to the grave: Anthropoid busts and ancestor cults at Deir el-Medina, in K. Piquette and S. Love (eds) *Current Research in Egyptology 2003*: 71-88 Oxford: Oxbow Books.

Hartwig, M. K. 2004. *Tomb Painting and Identity in Thebes, 1419 - 1372 BC/ by Melinda K. Hartwig.* Turnout: Foundation Egyptologique Reine Elisabeth.

Hartwig, M. K. 2013. *The Tomb Chapel of Menna (TT 69): The Art, Culture and Science of Painting in an Egyptian Tomb.* Cairo: American University in Cairo Press.

Hayes, W. C. 1959. *The Scepter of Egypt: A Background for the Study of Egyptian Antiquities in the Metropolitan Museum of Art. Part 2: The Hyksos Period to the New Kingdom (1675 - 1080 B.C.).* New York: Harper and Brothers.

Haynes, J. 1977. The development of women's hairstyles in Dynasty Eighteen. *Journal of the Society for the Study of Egyptian Antiquities* 8: 18-24.

Helck, W. 1963. *Materialien zur Wirtschaftsgeschichte des Neuen Riches (Teil IV).* Mainz: Akademie der Wissenschaften und der Literature.

Hellinckx, B. R. 2001. The symbolic assimilation of head and sun as expressed by headrests. *Studien zur Altägyptischen Kultur* 29: 61-95.

Hepper, F. N. 1990. *Pharaoh's Flowers: Botanical Treasures of Tutankhamun.* London: Her Majesty's Stationery Office.

Hickmann, H. 1954-55. La danse aux miroirs. *Bulletin de l'Institut d'Égypte* 37: 151-190.

Hugonot, J. C. 1994. Le liseron et le lierre dans l'Égypte ancienne. *Göttinger Miszellen: Beiträge zur ägyptologischen discussion* 142: 73-81.

Husson, C. 1977. *L'offrande du miroir dans les temples égyptiens de l'époque gréco-romaine.* Lyons: Audin Imprimeurs.

Janssen, J. J. 1975. *Commodity Prices from the Ramessid Period: An Economic Study of the Village of the Necropolis Workmen at Thebes.* Leiden: Brill.

Janssen, J. J. 1980. Absence from work by the necropolis workmen of Thebes. *Studien zur Altägyptischen Kultur* 8: 127-152.

Janssen, J. J. 1982. Gift giving in ancient Egypt as an economic feature. *Journal of Egyptian Archaeology* 68: 253-258.

Janssen, J. J. 1997. *Village Varia: Ten Studies on the History and Administration of Deir el-Medina.* Leiden: Brill.

Janssen, R. M. H. 1995. Costume in New Kingdom Egypt, in J. M. Sasson (ed.) *Civilizations of the Ancient Near East*, Volume I: 383-394. New York: Scriber.

Jauhiainen, H. 2009. 'Do Not Celebrate your Feast Without your Neighbours' A Study of References to Feasts and Festivals in Non-Literary Documents from Ramesside Period Deir el-Medina. Unpublished PhD dissertation, University of Helsinki.

Keimer, L. 1940-45. *Études d'égyptologie* 1. Cairo: Institut Français d'Archéologie Orientale.

Keimer, L. 1948. *Remarques sur le tatouage dans l'Egypte ancienne.* Cairo: Institut Français d'Archéologie Orientale.

Kemp, B. J. 1979. Wall paintings from the workmen's village at El'Amarna. *Journal of Egyptian Archaeology* 65: 47-53.

Kemp, B. J. 1987. The Amarna workmen's village in retrospect. *Journal of Egyptian Archaeology* 73: 21-50.

Kemp, B. J. 2013. Tell El-Amarna, 2012-13. *Journal of Egyptian Archaeology* 99: 1-34.

Killen, G. 1980. *Ancient Egyptian Furniture: Volume I 4000-1300 BC.* Warminster: Aries and Phillips.

Kitchen. K. A. 1999. *Poetry of Ancient Egypt.* Jonsered: Paul Aströms.

Klasen, J. 1952. *A Magical Statue Base (Soule Behague) in the Museum of Antiquities at Leiden.* Leiden: Brill.

Koltsida, N. 2006. Birth-bed, sitting place, erotic corner or domestic altar? A study of the so-called elevated bed in Deir el-Medina houses. *Studien zur Altägyptischen Kultur* 35: 165-17.

Koltsida, N. 2007. *Social Aspects of Ancient Egyptian Architecture.* Oxford: Archaeopress.

Kozloff, A. P. 1992. *Egypt's Dazzling Sun: Amenhotep III and His World.* Cleveland: Indiana University Press.

Lacovara, P. 1997. *The New Kingdom Royal City.* London: Kegan Paul International.

Landgráfová, R. 2008. Breaches of cooperative rules, metaphors and parody in ancient Egyptian love songs, in C. Graves-Brown (ed.) *Sex and Gender in Ancient Egypt: 'Don your Wig for a Joyful Hour'*: 71-83. Swansea: University of Wales.

Landgráfová, R. and H. Navrátilová 2009. *Sex and the Golden Goddess I: Ancient Egyptian Love Songs in Context.* Prague: Czech Institute of Egyptology.

Lansing, A. 1940. A faience broad collar of the Eighteenth Dynasty. *Bulletin of the Metropolitan Museum of Art* 35 (3) March: 65-68.

Leach, E. R. 1958. Magical hair. *Journal of the Royal Anthropological Institute of Great Britain and Ireland* 88 (2): 147-164.

Leclant, J. 1961. Sur un contrepoids de menat au nom de Taharqa: allaitement et 'apparition' royale. *Mélanges Mariette, bibliothéque d'études* 32: 263-7.

Leclant, J. 1966. Fouilles et travaux en Egypte et au Soudan 1964-1965. *Orientalia* 35: 127-178.

Lefebvre, M. G. 1923. *Le tombeau de Petosiris. Vocabulaire et planches.* Volume 3. Cairo: Institut Français d'Archéologie Orientale.

Lichtheim, M. 1973. *Ancient Egyptian Literature: The Old and Middle Kingdom.* Berkeley: University of California Press.

Lichtheim, M. 1976. *Ancient Egyptian Literature: The New Kingdom.* Berkeley: University of California Press.

Lilyquist, C. 1979. *Ancient Egyptian Mirrors from the Earliest Times through the Middle Kingdom.* Munchen: Deutscher Kunstverlag.

Lilyquist, C. 1982. Mirrors, in R. E. Freed (ed.) *Egypt's Golden Age: The Art of Living in the New Kingdom 1558-1085 B.C: Catalogue of the Exhibition:* 184-188. Boston: Museum of Fine Arts.

Lilyquist, C. 2003. *The Tomb of the Three Foreign Wives of Tuthmosis III.* New York: Metropolitan Museum of Art.

Lilyquist, C. 2005. Egypt and the Near East: Evidence of contact in the material record, in C. H. Roehrig, D. Dreyfus and C. A. Keller, (eds) *Hatshepsut, from Queen to Pharaoh:* 60-67. New York: Metropolitan Museum of Art.

Lilyquist, C. 2007. Reflections on mirrors, in Z. Hawass and J. Richards (eds) *The Archaeology and Art of Ancient Egypt: Essays in Honour of David B. O'Connor:* Volume II, 95-109. Cairo: Supreme Council of Antiquities.

Loose, J. 1993. Laborious 'Rites de Passage': Birth crisis in this world and the beyond, in *International Congress of Egyptology, 1-8 September 1991, Turin. Sesto Congresso Internazionale di Egittologia*: Volume II: 285-290. Turin: International Association of Egyptologists.

López. J. 1978. *Ostraca Hieratici, n.57001-57092.* Milano: Instituto Editoriale Cisalpino – La Goliardica.

Loret, V. 1892. *La flore pharaonique: d'après les documents hiéroglyphiques et les spécimens découverts dans les tombes.* 2nd Edition. Paris: Ernest Leroux.

Lucas, A. 1930. Cosmetics, perfumes and incense in ancient Egypt. *Journal of Egyptian Archaeology* 16 1/2: 41-53.

Manniche. L. 1989 *An Egyptian Herbal.* London: British Museum Publications.

Manniche, L. 1999. *Sacred Luxuries: Fragrance, Aromatherapy and Cosmetics in Ancient Egypt.* London: Opus Publishing.

Marciniak, M. 1974. *Deir el-Bahri: I Inscriptions hiératiques du temple de Thoutmosis III. Varsovie:* PWN-Editions Scientifiques de Pologne.

Martin, G. T. 1974. *The Royal Tomb at El-Amarna, Volume 2: The Reliefs, Inscriptions and Architecture.* London: Egypt Exploration Society.

Maspero, G. 1912. *Guide du visiteur au Musée du Caire.* Cairo. Institut Français d'Archéologie Orientale.

Mathieu, B. 2003. La litterature égyptienne sous les Ramsès d'apres les ostraca littéraires au Deir el-Médineh', in G. Andreu (ed.) *Deir el-Mèdineh et la Vallée des Rois: la vie en Égypte au temps des pharaons du nouvel empire. Actes du colloque, les 3 et 4 mai 2002*: 119-137. Paris: Louvre Éditions.

Maystre, C. 1936. *Tombes de Deir el-Médineh: La tombe de Nebenmât (no. 219).* Cairo: Institut Français d'Archéologie Orientale.

Meeks, D. 1992. Le nom du dieu Bès et ses implications mythologiques, in U. Luft (ed.) *The Intellectual Heritage of Egypt: Studies Presented to Lászlo Kákosy:* 423-436. Budapest: Studia Aegyptiaca XIV.

Meskell, L. 1998. Archaeology of social relations in an Egyptian village. *Journal of Archaeological Method and Theory* 5/3: 209-243.

Metropolitan Museum of Art: (2000-2005). Collection Online: Building a Catafalque, Tomb of Ipuy (MM.30.4.116). [Online] New York: The Metropolitan Museum of Art. Available from: http://images.metmuseum.org/collections-online/search/548572 (Accessed 3 August 2015).

Metropolitan Museum of Art: (2000-2005). Collection Online: Jar from the Tomb of Sennedjem (MM.86.1.10). [Online] New York: The Metropolitan Museum of Art. Available from: http://www.metmuseum.org/collection/the-collection-online/search/544702 (Accessed 17 May 2015).

Metropolitan Museum of Art: (2000-2005). Collection Online; Ipuy and Wife Receive Offerings from their Children (Restored) (MM.30.4.114). [Online] New York: The Metropolitan Museum of Art. Available from: http://www.metmuseum.org/collection/the-collection-online/search/548567 (Accessed 17 May 2015).

Metropolitan Museum of Art (2000-2005). Collection Online; Blue Painted Jar from Malqata. (MM 11.215.462) [Online] New York: The Metropolitan Museum of Art. Available from: https://www.metmuseum.org/art/collection/search/544507 (Accessed 20 July 2019).

Michailidis, G. 1963. Bès aux divers aspects. *Bulletin de l'Institut d'Égypte* 45: 53-93.

Michalowski, K., C. Desroches-Noblecourt, J. de Linage, J. Manteuffel and M. Żejmo-Żejmis 1939. *Fouilles franco-polonaises rapports: Tell Edfou 1939 III.* Cairo: Institut Français d'Archéologie Orientale / l'Université de Varsovie.

Miller, R. L. 2009. 'Was convolvulus erotic?', in S. Ikram and A. Dodson (eds) *Beyond the Horizon: Studies in Egyptian Art, Archaeology and History in Honour of Barry J. Kemp*, Volume I: 247-261. Cairo: Supreme Council of Antiquities.

Millward, E. 2012. Children of sorrow: Infants and juvenailes in ancient Egyptian funeral processions during the New Kingdom, in C. Graves, G. Hefferman, L. McGarrity, M. Millward and M. S. Bealby, *Current Research in Egyptology 2012*: 117-12. Oxford: Oxbow Books.

Minault-Gout, A. 2002. *Carnets de pierre: l'art des ostraca dans l'Égypte ancienne.* Paris: Hazen.

Moret, A. 1902. *Le rituel du culte divin journalier en Égypte.* Paris: Leroux.

Naguib, S. A. 1990. Hair in ancient Egypt. *Acta Orientalia* 51: 7-26.

Naville, E. H. 1896. *The Temple of Deir el Bahari, Part II Plates XXV-LV: The Ebony Shrine, Northern Half of the Middle Platform.* London: Egypt Exploration Society.

Naville, E. H. 1907. *The XIth Dynasty Temple at Deir el-Bahari.* Part I. London: Egypt Exploration Fund.

Newberry, P. E. 1890. The ancient botany, in W. M. F. Petrie, *Kahun, Gurob and Hawara:* 46-50. London: Kegan Paul.

Newberry, P. E. 1927. Report on the floral wreaths found in the coffins of Tutankhamen, in H. Carter *The Tomb of Tut-ankh-Amen, Volume 2: The Burial Chamber:* 189-196. London: Cassell.

O'Connor, D. 2011. Satire or parody? The interaction of the pictorial and the literary in Turin Papyrus 5501, in M. Collier and S. Snape (eds) *Ramesside Studies in Honour of K. A. Kitchen:* 361-380. Bolton: Rutherford Press.

Omlin, J. A. 1973. *Der Papyrus 55001 und seine satirisch-erotischen Zeichnungen und Inschriften.* Turin: Edizioni d'Arte Fratelli Pozzo.

Ossian, C. 1999. The most beautiful of flowers, water lilies and lotuses in ancient Egypt. *KMT: A Modern Journal of Ancient Egypt* 10 (1): 48-59.

Padgham, J. 2012. *A New Interpretation of the Cone on the Head in New Kingdom Egyptian Tomb Scenes.* Oxford: Archaeopress.

Parkinson, R. 1997. *The Tale of Sinuhe and Other Ancient Egyptian Poems 1940-1640 BC.* Oxford: Oxford University Press.

Parkinson, R. 2008. *The Painted Tomb-Chapel of Nebamun.* London: British Museum Publications.

Peck, W. H. and J. G. Ross 1978. *Drawings from Ancient Egypt.* London: Thames and Hudson.

Peet, E. T. and L. C. Woolley 1923. *The City of Akhenaten, Part I: Excavations of 1921 and 1922 at El'Amarneh.* London: Egypt Exploration Society.

Perdrizet, P. 1921. *Les terres cuites grecques d' Égypte de la collection Fouquet*: Volume I – Text, Volume II – Plates. Nancy: Berger Levault.

Peterson, B. E. J. 1973. *Zeichnungen aus einer Totenstadt: Bildostraka aus Theben-West, ihre Fundplätze, Themata und Zweckbereiche mitsamt einem Katalog der Gayer-Anderson-Sammlung in Stockholm.* Stockholm: Medelhavsmuseet.

Petrie, W. M. F. 1890. *Kahun, Gurob and Hawara.* London: Kegan Paul.

Petrie, W. M. F. 1891. *Illahun, Kahun and Gurob.* London: David Nutt.

Petrie, W. M. F. 1894. *Tell el Amarna.* London: Methuen.

Piankoff, A. 1937-1938. Sur une statuette de Bès. *Bulletin de l'Institut Français d'Archéologie Orientale* 37: 29-33.

Piankoff, A. 1954. *The Tomb of Ramesses VI: Egyptian Religious Texts and Representations,* Volumn I. New York: Bollington Foundation.

Pinch, G. 1983. Childbirth and female figurines at Deir el-Medina and el-Amarna. *Orientalia* 52: 405-414.

Pinch, G. 1993. *Votive Offerings to Hathor*. Oxford: Griffith Institute.

Pinch, G. 2002. *Egyptian Mythology.* Oxford: University Press.

Posener, G. 1938. *Catalogue des ostraca hiératiques littéraires de Deir el Médineh*. Cairo: Institut Français d'Archéologie Orientale.

Quibell, J. E. 1908. *Catalogue général des antiquités égyptiennes du Musée du Caire. Nos. 5100 - 51191 Tomb of Yuaa and Thuiu*. Cairo: Institut Français d'Archéologie Orientale.

Quirke, S. 1992. *Ancient Egyptian Religion*. London: British Museum Press.

Randall-MacIver, D. and L. C. Woolley 1911. *Buhen*. Volume I - Text, Volume II - Plates. Philadelphia: University of Pennsylvania.

Raven, M. J. 2014. Women's beds from Deir el-Medina, in B. J. J. Haring, O. E. Kaper and R. van Walsem (eds) *The Workman's Progress: Studies in the Village of Deir el-Medina and Other Documents from Western Thebes in Honour of Rob Demarée*: 191-204. Leiden: Nederlands Instituut voor Nabije Oosten.

Ritner, R. K. 2008. Household religion in ancient Egypt, in J. Bodel and S. M. Olyan (eds) *Household and Family Religion in Antiquity*: 171-196. Oxford: Blackwell Publishing.

Robins, G. 1993. *Women in Ancient Egypt*. London: British Museum Publications.

Robins, G. 1994. Some principles of compositional dominance and gender hierarchy in Egyptian art. *Journal of the American Research Center in Egypt* 31: 33-40.

Robins, G. 1996. Dress, undress, and the representation of fertility and potency in New Kingdom Egyptian art, in N. B. Kampen (ed.) *Sexuality in Ancient Art: Near East, Egypt, Greece and Italy*: 27-40. New York: Cambridge University Press.

Robins, G. 1997. *The Art of Ancient Egypt*. London: British Museum Publications.

Robins, G. 1998. Some images of women in New Kingdom art and literature, in B. S. Lesko (ed.) *Women's Earliest Records: From Ancient Egypt and Western Asia*:105-116. Atlanta: Scholars Press.

Robins, G. 1999. Hair and the construction of identity in ancient Egypt c.1480 - 1350 B.C. *Journal of the American Research Center in Egypt* 36: 55-70.

Robins, G. 2001. Colour Symbolism, in D. B. Redford (ed.) *Oxford Encyclopaedia of Ancient Egypt,* Volume I: 291-293. Oxford: Oxford University Press.

Roehrig, C. H. 2005. Figure vases, in C. H. Roehrig, D. Dreyfus and C. A. Keller (eds) *Hatshepsut, from Queen to Pharaoh*: 233-241. New York: Metropolitan Museum of Art.

Romano, J. F. 1980. The origin of the Bes image. *Bulletin of the Egyptological Seminar* 2: 39-56.

Russman, E. R. (ed.) 2001. *Eternal Egypt: Masterworks of Ancient Art from the British Museum.* London: British Museum Publications.

Schäfer, H. 1916. Ägyptische Zeichnungen auf Scherben. *Jahrbuch der Königlich Preussischen Kunstsammlungen* 37: 23-51.

Schäfer, H. 1986. *Principles of Egyptian Art.* Edited, with an Epilogue by Emma Brunner-Traut. Translated and Edited with an Introduction by John Baines. Foreword by E. H. Gombrich. Reprinted with Revisions. Oxford: Griffith Institute.

Schneider, T. 2007. Contextualising the tale of the herdsman, in T Schneider and K. Szpakowska (eds) *Egyptian Stories: A British Egyptological Tribute to Alan. B. Lloyd on the Occasion of his Retirement:* 309-318. Münster: Ugarit-Verlag.

Schott, S. 1953. *Das schöne Fest vom Wüstentale: Festbräuche einer Totenstadt*. Steiner: Wiesbaden.

Smith, S. W. 1998. *Art and Architecture of Ancient Egypt.* Revised with additions by William Kelly Simpson. Revised Edition. Haven: Vale University Press.

Spieser, C. 2012. Les nourrices égyptiennes, in V. Dasen and M. Gérard-Zai (eds) *Art de manger, art de vivre, nourriture et société de l'antiquité*: 19-39. Gollion: Infolio.

Stevens, A. 2006. *Private Religion at Amarna: The Material Evidence*. Oxford: Archaeopress.

Steindorff, G. (1937) *Aniba*, Volume I - Text, Volume II - Plates. Hamburg: Gluckstadt.

Sugi, A. 2000. Semantics of New Kingdom Iconography: A Case Study of the '*nḫ* Symbol as a Paradigm of Understanding the Interaction between Pictoral Metaphor and Literary Expression. Unpublished PhD dissertation, University of Liverpool.

Szpakowska, K. 2003a. The open portal: Dreams and divine power in pharaonic Egypt, in S. Noegel, J. Walker and B. Wheeler (eds) *Prayer, Magic and the Stars in the Ancient and Late Antique World:* 111-124. University Park Pa: Pennsylvania State University Press.

Szpakowska, K. 2003b. Playing with fire: Initial observations on the religious uses of clay cobras from Amarna. *Journal of the American Research Center in Egypt* 40: 113-122.

Szpakowska. K. 2007. Flesh for fantasy: Reflections of women in two ancient Egyptian dream manuals, in T. Schneider and K. Szpakowska (eds) *Egyptian Stories: A British Egyptological Tribute to Alan B. Lloyd on the Occasion of his Retirement*: 393-404. Műnster: Ugarit-Verlag.

Szpakowska, K. 2012. Striking cobra spitting fire. *Archiv für Religionsgeschichte* 14: 27-45.

Szpakowska, K. (2015) Snake cults and Egyptian military bases, in T. P. Harrison, E. B. Banning and S. Klassen (eds) *Walls of the Prince: Egyptian Interactions with Southwest Asia in Antiquity: Essays in Honour of John S. Holladay Jr*: 275-291. Leiden: Brill.

Täckholm, V. 1974. *Students' Flora of Egypt*. 2nd Edition. Cairo: Cairo University Press.

Taylor, J. H. (ed.) 2010. *Journey through the Afterlife: Ancient Egyptian Book of the Dead*. London: British Museum Publications.

Teeter, E. 2010. *Baked Clay Figurines and Votive Beds from Medinet Habu*. Chicago: Oriental Institute Publications.

Temkin, O. 1991. *Soranus' Gynecology*. Baltimore: Johns Hopkins Press.

Thomas, A. P. 1981. *Gurob: A New Kingdom Town: Introduction and Catalogue of Objects in the Petrie Collection*, Volume I – Text, Volume II – Plates. Warminster: Aris and Phillips.

Thompson, S. E. 1998. The significance of anointing in ancient Egyptian funerary beliefs, in L. H. Lesko (ed.) *Ancient Egyptian and Mediterranean Studies in Memory of William A. Ward*: 229-243. Rhode Island: Providence.

Tobin, V. A. 2003. The Love Songs and the Song of the Harper, in W. K. Simpson (ed.) *The Literature of Ancient Egypt: An Anthology of Stories, Instructions and Poetry*: 307-333, 3rd Edition. New Haven: Yale University Press.

Toivari-Viitala, J. 2001. *Women at Deir el-Medina: A Study of the Status and Roles of the Female Inhabitants in the Workmen's Community during the Ramesside Period by Jaana Toivari-Viitala*. Leiden: Nederland Instituut Voor Het Nabije Oosten.

Toivari-Viitala, J., T. Alsheimer, A. Eklund and V. Perunka (2010) Academy of Finland and University of Helsinki, Workmen's Huts in the Theban Mountains Project: Preliminary Report on the Work Performed during Season in 2010. [Online] Helsinki: Academy of Finland and University of Helsinki. Available from: http://www.egyptologinenseura.fi/fieldwork/Preliminary%20Report_Toivari-Viitala_Academy%20of%20Finland_Season2010_for%20ASAE.pdf (Accessed 10 October 2012).

Toivari-Viitala, J., P. Paulin-Grothe, T. Alsheimer, V. Perunka and A. Eklund (2012) Academy of Finland and University of Helsinki, Workmen's Huts in the Theban Mountains Project: Preliminary Report on the Work Performed during the Fourth Season in 2011-2012. [Online] Helsinki: Academy of Finland and University of Helsinki. Available from: http://www.egyptologinenseura.fi/fieldwork/Preliminary%20report_WHTM%20Project_fourth%20field%20season%202011-2012.pdf (Accessed 10 September 2012).

Toivari-Viitala, J. 2014. A lady of the hut in the Theban mountains in B. J. J. Haring, O, E. Kaper, and R van Walsem (eds) *The Workman's Progress: Studies in the Village of Deir el-Medina and Other Documents from Western Thebes in Honour of Rob Demarée*: 233-236. Leiden: Nederlands Instituut voor Nabije Oosten.

Trapani, M. 2012. Statutte femminili al mae di Torino. *Rivista Degli Studi Orientali* 85 1/4: 533-552.

Tyldesley, J. 1998. *Nefertiti*. London: Penguin.

Fondazione museo de le antichità Egizie di Torino. Le Collezione:S.06305RCGE10736.[Online]Turin:Museo Egizie di Torino. Available from: http://collezioni.museoegizio.it/eMuseumPlus?service=direct/1/ResultLightboxView/result.t1.collection_lightbox.$TspTitleImageLink.linkand sp=10and sp=Scollectionand sp=SfieldValueand sp=0and sp=1and sp=3and sp=Slightbox_3x4and sp=0and sp=Sdetailand sp=0and sp=Fand sp=Tand sp=0 (Accessed 12 Oct. 2014).

Fondazione museo de le antichità Egizie di Torino. Le Collezione:S.07403RCGE10739.[Online]Turin:Museo Egizie di Torino. Available from: http://collezioni.museoegizio.it/eMuseumPlus?service=direct/1/ResultLightboxView/result.t1.collection_lightbox.$TspTitleImageLink.linkand sp=10and sp=Scollectionand sp=SfieldValueand sp=0and sp=2and sp=3and sp=Slightbox_3x4and sp=0and sp=Sdetailand sp=0and sp=Fand sp=Tand sp=0 (Accessed 12 Oct. 2014).

Fondazione museo de le antichità Egizie di Torino. Le Collezione: S.06289 RCGE 9741. [Online] Turin: Museo Egizie di Toirno. Available from: http://collezioni.museoegizio.it/eMuseumPlus?service=direct/1/ResultLightboxView/result.t1.collection_lightbox.$TspTitleImageLink.linkand sp=10and sp=Scollectionand sp=SfieldValueand sp=0and sp=3and sp=3and sp=Slightbox_3x4and sp=0and sp=Sdetailand sp=0and sp=Fand sp=Tand sp=0 (Accessed 12 Oct. 2014).

Tylor, J. J. 1896. *Wall Drawings and Monuments of el-Kab: The Tomb of Sebeknekht*. London: Quaritch.

UCL Petrie Collection Online Catalogue. (2015) Ostraca UC33251. [Online] London: The Petrie Museum, University College London. Available from: http://petriecat.museums.ucl.ac.uk/detail.aspx (Accessed 2 May 2014).

UCL Petrie Collection Online Catalogue. (2015) Ostraca UC45679. [Online] London: The Petrie Museum, University College London. Available from: http://petriecat.museums.ucl.ac.uk/detail.aspx (Accessed 2 May 2014).

University of Leiden, R. J. Demarée, B. J. J. Haring, W. Hovestreydt and L. M. J. Zonhoven 2018. A Systematic Bibliography on Deir el-Medîna. [Online] Available from https://dmd.wepwawet.nl/bibliography.htm (Accessed 20 July 2019).

Valbelle, D. 1985. *Les ouvriers de la tombe: Deir el-Médineh à l'époque ramesside*. Cairo: Institut Français d'Archéologie Orientale.

Van Dijk, J. 2009. The death of Meketaten, in P. J. Brand and L. Cooper (eds) *Causing his Name to Live; Studies in*

Egyptian Epigraphy and History in Memory of William J. Murnane: 83-86. Leiden: Brill.

Vandier d'Abbadie, J. 1937. *Catalogue des ostraca figurés de Deir el Médineh*, Volume I-III, numbers 2001-2733. Cairo: Institut Français d'Archéologie Orientale.

Vandier d'Abbadie, J. 1938. Une fresque civile de Deir el Médineh. *Revue d'Égyptologie* 3: 27-35.

Vandier d'Abbadie, J. 1954. *Deux tombes ramessides à Gournet-Mourrai*. Cairo: Institut Français d'Archéologie Orientale.

Vandier d'Abbadie, J. 1957. Deux ostraca figurés. *Bulletin de l'Institut Français d'Archéologie Orientale* 56: 21-34.

Vandier d'Abbadie, J. 1959. *Catalogue des ostraca figurés de Deir el Mèdineh*, Volume IV, numbers 2734-3053. Cairo: Institut Français d'Archéologie Orientale.

Vandier d'Abbadie, J. 1972. *Catologue des objets de toilette égyptiens*. Paris: Editions des Musées Nationaux.

Vandier d'Abbadie, J. and G. Jourdain 1939. *Deux tombes de Deir el- Médineh: I La chapelle de Khâ. II La tombe du scribe royal Amenemopet*. Cairo: Institut Français d'Archéologie Orientale.

Vassilika, E. 2010. *The Tomb of Kha: The Architect*. Torino: Founazione Museo dell Antichità Egizie di Torino.

Vogelsang-Eastwood, G. 1993. *Pharaonic Egyptian Clothing*. Leiden: Brill.

Volokhine, V. 2000. *La frontalité dans l'iconographie de l'Égypte ancienne*. Genève: Société d'Égyptologie.

Walter, P., P. Martinetto, G. Tsoucari, R. Brniaux, M. A. Lefebvre, G. Richard, J. Talabot and E. Dooryhee (1999). Making make-up in ancient Egypt. *Nature* 397: 11th February 1999, 483-484.

Waraksa, E. 2009. *Female Figurines from the Mut Precinct: Context and Ritual Function*. Fribourg: Academic Press.

Watson, T. 2016. Sacred tattoos found on Egyptian mummy. *Nature* 533:155.

Wegner, J. 2009. A decorated birth-brick from south Abydos: New evidence on childbirth and birth magic in the Middle Kingdom, in D. P. Silverman, W. K. Simpson and J. Wegner (eds) *Archasim and Innovation: Studies in the Culture of Middle Kingdom Egypt*: 447-496. New Haven: Yale University.

Weiss, L. 2009. Personal religious practice: House altars at Deir el-Medina. *Journal of Egyptian Archaeology* 95: 193-208.

Weiss, L. 2015. *Religious Practice at Deir el-Medina*. Leuven: Peeters.

Wente, E. F. 2003. The contending of Horus and Seth, in W. K. Simpson (ed.) *The Literature of Ancient Egypt: An Anthology of Stories, Instructions and Poetry*: 91-103. 3rd Edition. New Haven: Yale University Press.

Werbrouck, M. 1953. Ostraca à figures. *Bulletin des Musées Royaux d'Art et d'Histoire* 25: 93-111.

Wilfong, T. G. 1999. Menstrual synchrony and the 'Place of the Women' in ancient Egypt (OIM 13512), in E. Teeter and J. A. Larson (eds) *Gold of Praise: Studies on Ancient Egypt in Honour of Edward F. Wente*: 419-434. Chicago: Oriental Institute Publications.

Williams, B. B. 1992. *New Kingdom Remains at Cemeteries R, V, S, and W at Qustal and Cemetery K at Adindan*. Chicago: Oriental Institute Publications.

Winlock, H. E. 1942. *Excavations at Deir el-Bahri 1911-1931*. New York: Macmillan.

Winlock, H. E. 1948. *The Treasure of Three Egyptian Princesses*. New York: Metropolitan Museum of Art.

Wimmer, S. J. 2000. Ancient egyptian love songs: Papyrus Harris 500, in M. Krysztof (ed.) *The Art of the Love Lyrics*: 25-33. Paris: J. Gabalda et Compagnie.

Wreszinski, W. 1927. *Bericht über die photographische Expedition von Kairo bis Wadi Halfa*. Halle: Niemeyer.

Yoyotte, J. 2003. À propos de quelques idées reçues: Méresger, la Butte et les cobras, in G. Andreu (ed.) *Deir el- Médineh et la Vallée des Rois: la vie en Égypte au temps des pharaons du nouvel empire. Actes du colloque, les 3 et 4 mai 2002*: 283-307. Paris: Louvre Éditions.

Index